SHIFTING THE KALEIDOSCOPE

This book belongs to Lance Phillips

Complicated Conversation

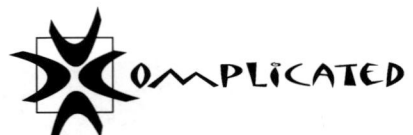

A Book Series of Curriculum Studies

William F. Pinar
General Editor

Volume 46

The Complicated Conversation series is part of the Peter Lang Education list.
Every volume is peer reviewed and meets
the highest quality standards for content and production.

PETER LANG
New York • Bern • Frankfurt • Berlin
Brussels • Vienna • Oxford • Warsaw

JON L. SMYTHE

SHIFTING THE KALEIDOSCOPE

Returned Peace Corps Volunteer Educators'
Insights on Culture Shock,
Identity & Pedagogy

PETER LANG
New York • Bern • Frankfurt • Berlin
Brussels • Vienna • Oxford • Warsaw

Library of Congress Cataloging-in-Publication Data
Smythe, Jon L.
Shifting the kaleidoscope: returned Peace Corps volunteer educators' insights
on culture shock, identity & pedagogy / Jon L. Smythe.
pages cm. — (Complicated conversation; Vol. 46)
Includes bibliographical references and index.
1. Educational anthropology.
2. Volunteer workers in education—Developing countries—Attitudes.
3. Volunteer workers in education—United States—Attitudes.
4. Peace Corps (U.S.) 5. Culture shock. 6. Reverse culture shock. I. Title.
LB45.S594   306.43—dc23   2014033102
ISBN 978-1-4331-2684-0 (hardcover)
ISBN 978-1-4331-2683-3 (paperback)
ISBN 978-1-4539-1437-3 (e-book)
ISSN 1534-2816

Bibliographic information published by **Die Deutsche Nationalbibliothek**.
Die Deutsche Nationalbibliothek lists this publication in the "Deutsche
Nationalbibliografie"; detailed bibliographic data are available
on the Internet at http://dnb.d-nb.de/.

The paper in this book meets the guidelines for permanence and durability
of the Committee on Production Guidelines for Book Longevity
of the Council of Library Resources.

© 2015 Peter Lang Publishing, Inc., New York
29 Broadway, 18th floor, New York, NY 10006
www.peterlang.com

All rights reserved.
Reprint or reproduction, even partially, in all forms such as microfilm,
xerography, microfiche, microcard, and offset strictly prohibited.

Printed in the United States of America

For Mal Harouna

CONTENTS

Acknowledgments   xi

Introduction: Insights Into Otherness   1
   Study Overview   7
   The Participants   8
      Joe, Peace Corps Moldova 2006–2008   9
      Harley, Peace Corps Kazakhstan 1999–2001   10
      Ryder, Peace Corps Kenya 1987–1990   11
      Hyacinth, Peace Corps Kenya 1984–1986   12
   Looking Through a Post-Structural Hermeneutic Lens   14

Chapter 1: Back Stories   21
   The Internationalization of Curriculum Studies   21
   The Peace Corps and Returned Peace Corps
      Volunteer Educators   27
   Culture Shock   34
   Reverse Culture Shock   39

Chapter 2: Toward a Pedagogy of Creativity and Caring   43
  Introduction   43
  Culture Shock I: Intercultural Experience
    as Vulnerability and Danger   45
  Re-reading Culture Shock I: Vulnerability as
    Strength and Danger as Useful   48
  Identity Shift I: Acceptance as Healing and a Lack of Resistance   51
  Re-reading Identity Shift I: Acceptance as
    Resistance and Not Healing   53
  Reverse Culture Shock I: Materialism and Not Playing the Game   55
  Re-reading Reverse Culture Shock I:
    Postmaterialism and Playing the Game Differently   58
  Identity Shift II: Taking on a New Identity
    and Caring as Self-Sacrifice   60
  Re-reading Identity Shift II: Adding New Layers
    of Identity and Caring as Self-Gain   62
  Pedagogy I: Rote Learning and the Need to Teach Creativity   64
  Re-reading Pedagogy I: Rote Learning as Meaningful
    Learning and Creativity as Cultural Reproduction   66

Interplay 1: A "Subject" in Motion   69

Chapter 3: Toward a Pedagogy of Non-Prejudice   77
  Introduction   77
  Culture Shock I: Philippines = Collectivism,
    America = Individualism   80
  Re-reading Culture Shock I: Individualism (?), Collectivism (?)   82
  Culture Shock II: Corruption in Kazakhstan
    as Survival and a Lack of Development   86
  Re-reading Culture Shock II: Corruption
    in the U.S. as Hidden Amidst Development   89
  Reverse Culture Shock I: Clock Time Versus Event Time   92
  Re-reading Reverse Culture Shock I: Intermixing Clock
    Time and Event Time Through the Use of Media   95
  Pedagogy I: Identity Shock and Being Treated
    as an "Extra Foreigner" and "International Student"   97

Re-reading Pedagogy I: The (Potential)
Benefits of Bi-Culturality 102
Pedagogy II: Cultural Adjustment as "Context" or "Consistency" 103
Re-reading Pedagogy II: Cultural Adjustment
as an Ability to "Flex" 107

Interplay 2: Who Am I (Becoming)? 109

Chapter 4: Toward a Pedagogy of Social Justice 119
Introduction 119
Culture Shock I: Western Time as Linear/Control,
Kenyan Time as Cyclic/Fatalistic 122
Re-reading Culture Shock I: Fatalism as
Self-Management and Humility 123
Culture Shock II: Generosity as Measurable 125
Re-reading Culture Shock II: Generosity as
Self-Interest and Impossible 128
Identity Shift I: Sexuality as Moral
Hypocrisy and Social Control 130
Re-reading Identity Shift I: Social Control (?)
and the Problem With Labels 132
Reverse Culture Shock I: Reality vs. Non-reality 134
Re-reading Reverse Culture Shock I: Reality as Multiple 137
Pedagogy I: Teaching an Appreciation for
"Dialect Diversity" as Social Justice 140
Re-reading Pedagogy I: Questioning the
Notions of Standard and Non-Standard Dialects 143

Interplay 3: Chez nous c'est ne pas comme chez vous! 147

Chapter 5: Toward a Pedagogy of Interconnectedness 155
Introduction 155
Culture Shock I: Male Privilege in Kenya 157
Re-reading Culture Shock I: Male Privilege in America 159
Identity Shift I: The Self as Cultural Product 162
Re-reading Identity Shift I: The Self
as Cultural Process 165

Identity Shift II: "Interweaving" as Cultural Practice ... 167
Re-reading Identity Shift II: "Interweaving"
   as Gendered Practice ... 170
Reverse Culture Shock I: Sameness as
   Competition and the U.S. as Un/Real ... 171
Re-reading Reverse Culture Shock I: A Different
   Kind of Sameness and Reality as Floating ... 174
Pedagogy I: Teacher as "Ambassador" and "Bridge" ... 175
Re-reading Pedagogy I: The Ambassador as
   Distance and the Bridge as Separation ... 180

Interplay 4: And a Good Time Was Had by All ... 183

Chapter 6: Similarities, Contrasts, and Shades ... 191
   Drawing Gender Lines ... 191
   Resistance, Negotiation, and Shift ... 194
   Making Time to Get Real ... 196
   Metaphorically Speaking ... 197
   Home Is Where the Hurt Is ... 199
   Looking for Traces and Signs ... 202

Interplay 5: Returning Home to Fantasyland ... 205

Chapter 7: Envisioning a Kaleidoscopic Curriculum ... 213
   Multiplicity ... 214
   Movement ... 217
   Juxtaposition ... 219
   Ambiguity ... 221
   Surprise ... 224

References ... 229

Index ... 247

ACKNOWLEDGMENTS

Although my name appears front and center on this book, many people behind the scenes helped to bring it to fruition. Foremost among these was Dr. Hongyu Wang, who acted as a light along the pathway. Through her gentle yet determined guidance as well as her unwavering support and belief in my stories, she has opened up innumerable possibilities for reimagining my research and my relationship with the world in general. Without her, this book would not be possible. For that I am both grateful and humbled. I also want to express my deep gratitude to my professors at Oklahoma State University: Dr. Kathryn Castle, Dr. Denise Blum, Dr. Ravi Sheorey, Dr. Pam Brown, Dr. Gretchen Schwartz, and Dr. Gene Halleck. Each of these professors' teaching and insights have helped get me moving in the right direction, and their caring support of both me and my work has taught me the invaluable role of an educator in a student's life. Special thanks also go to William F. Pinar for his support of this book. His critical and imaginative work continues to inspire new generations of educators and curriculum theorists. Thanks, too, to Chris Myers and all the staff at Peter Lang Publishing for helping bring this book to life.

    I also want to thank the Returned Peace Corps Volunteers who participated in this study for sharing their provocative and insightful stories. The stories

I have included in this book, including my own, represent our individual views and not those of the U.S. government or the Peace Corps.

I am also greatly indebted to Eileen Kenney, who was instrumental in helping recruit participants for this study; to Charica Daugherty and fellow Returned Peace Corps Volunteer Charlotte Germundson, for reading and commenting on my initial manuscript; to Pam Chew, whose intercultural experiences and insights have continually nourished my thinking; and to my close friends and colleagues at Tulsa Community College, who have supported me throughout the writing process. I especially need to acknowledge my "at-work wife" Lennette Lawless for making up songs with me on a daily basis; the other two-thirds of the "Soundpony trio," Lindsay Fields and Chad Goodwin, for their comradery; Denise Baldwin, for encouraging me to complete my PhD; Sam Reeves for taking care of me and making me laugh; Amy Hawley for sharing my sense of irony; Traci Heck for her gentle leadership (and fondness for Johnny Depp); Dr. Jan Clayton for engaging me in stimulating conversations that often lasted after the close of business; Melody Simmons, Diana Allen, and Keilah Deatherage for their thought-provoking input and my immediate staff at TCC—Ruby Kimmons, Debbie Salmon, Jerri Clark, Minerva Castaneda, Amber Coburn, and John Brown for keeping our office running so smoothly.

I also need to thank a few folks outside of TCC whose friendship and guidance helped sustain me, specifically, Tim Van Meter for believing in me; Mattias Reiff for his generosity; John Ayers and Chad Stephens for their thoughtfulness; Roy Daniels for his artistry; Renny Berry for introducing me to Lorna Hansen Forbes; Richard Fox, who can build and fix anything; and Dr. Lawrence Lieberman for keeping all the working parts moving.

Additionally, I want to express my love and gratitude to my father, Austin, for being the best story-teller I know, and to my mom, Sharon, for wisely teaching me not to believe all my Dad's stories. Their hard work and sacrifice have gotten me where I am today. I also wish to convey my love to my wonderful African son, Mal Harouna Bello. Without him, my Peace Corps experience would not have been as rich and fulfilling as it was.

Thank you all for sharing in my journey and for shouldering a piece of the burden. Simply put, WE did it!

INTRODUCTION

Insights Into Otherness

In the realm of culture, outsideness is a most powerful factor in understanding....A meaning only reveals its depths once it has encountered and come into contact with another, foreign meaning: they engage in a kind of dialog, which surmounts the closedness and onesidedness of these particular meanings, these cultures....Each retains its own unity and open totality, but they are mutually enriched. (Bakhtin, 1986, p. 7)

"What words come to mind when you think about Africa?" I ask students at the various local schools and other institutions where I speak about my experiences in the Peace Corps. The answers are remarkably similar—"violence," "AIDS," "malaria," "wild animals," "poverty," "corruption," and "starvation." Probing a bit further, I ask if Africa could be a place of health, love, happiness, and good-tasting food. The response: a resounding "No!" "Have you ever been to Africa?" I continue. "Uh, well, no." When I ask students where they learn about Africa, they tell me TV programs such as "Animal Planet," "Save the Children," and the nightly news. They also tell me they learn about Africa through their teachers and their textbooks. When I ask why it might be important to experience a place directly for themselves, they light up: "Because it helps you learn more about a place when you go there yourself," and because "other people can lie." They also point out, though, that not everyone can go to Africa and that they have to rely on the media and their teachers for information about the world in general.

How closely the students' mediated perceptions of Africa matched my own before I joined the Peace Corps as a volunteer English teacher in 1996. When my acceptance letter came, I was informed I was to be sent to a country called Cameroon. Although I had taken Oklahoma and U.S. history, I had not taken one world history or geography course at any point during my high school or university education, and therefore I was left to guess exactly where Cameroon was located. To be perfectly honest, I thought it was a tropical island where they made brightly colored shirts. And then somehow I got the name confused and thought it had something to do with a cookie, which I realized later was a macaroon, not a Cameroon. To the Internet!

What I discovered on the Internet was that Cameroon is a country in Africa that has this lake that belched up a big gas bubble that smothered—actually smothered—thousands of people in the surrounding area. I could just picture myself up at the chalkboard, teaching the alphabet when there would be another gas bubble. Something like, "a, b, c, d…the gas…the gas…it's choking me, arrrrrrrrgh!" Then I would see all this stuff on TV about Africa—tribal warring, corruption, poverty, Ebola virus, and white people getting killed by an angry mob. After seeing all these things, I wasn't so sure that Africa was the right place for me to go. I certainly hadn't requested to be sent to Africa on my Peace Corps application.

So when I called the Peace Corps people, I was naturally subdued. I asked, "What if I don't want to go to Cameroon?" and followed with "I haven't heard of anything good coming out of Africa lately." To which the Peace Corps man politely replied, "If you don't accept this position, you really won't get another chance to go." He pointed out that my Bachelor's degree in Journalism/Advertising wasn't exactly a Master's in Teaching English. "Besides," he said, "Cameroon is very safe and the Peace Corps wouldn't send you there if it wasn't." I wondered how the Peace Corps people in Washington, D.C., would know if I got my head chopped off in the jungle and thrown in a ditch by a mob of angry Cameroonians—but I didn't feel like arguing, so I hesitantly accepted. And now, with head still firmly intact, I am certainly glad that I did!

After working as an English teacher in a small, rural, largely Muslim, agricultural village in Cameroon, I realized that my carefully constructed image of Africa was only partially accurate. Was there poverty? Yes. Disease? Certainly.

Corruption? Well, yeah. But those things didn't offer a complete picture of my daily existence in Cameroon. There was also beauty, intelligence, humor, abundance, creativity, an awareness of global politics, an attunement to interpersonal and social relationships, and a spirit of hospitality I have not experienced anywhere else.

In turn, my experiences in Cameroon have opened my eyes to other ways of seeing and experiencing the United States. For instance, I have learned that many of the generalizations that position the U.S. as a country of freedom, justice, equality, and a world leader, for example, fail to express the ways in which it is not. Not to mention that even in the richest nation in the world (or one of the richest) there is also still poverty, disease, and corruption. It seems clear to me now that the labels that are applied to any country and any cultural group often serve purposes other than that of expressing a uniform reality. Moreover, these labels appear to be more indicative of the power relations between groups than anything else.

So, how do I explain to students that the words and labels used to build up one country and denigrate another work to mask the diversity and differences that lie beneath the labels applied to both countries? How do I urge them to break open these labels in order to see the multiplicity and the differences underneath? How do I inspire them to accept their own multiplicity and respect the multiplicity of those who are culturally different in ways that are both ethical and nonviolent? Or perhaps, given that teachers often act in place of lived experience, as some students suggest, how do I encourage other educators (and myself) to do these same things?

In thinking about the value of appreciating cultural differences as a curriculum practice, I return to Bakhtin's (1986) opening quote for a moment. I appreciate Bakhtin's suggestion that cultures and meanings gain greater depth, and are mutually enriched, through the engagement of cultural differences. Further, that it is the "outsideness" of the Other that creates the condition for deeper understanding of the self and one's own culture. Moreover, that a certain sense of "unity" and "totality" is retained by both cultures so that personal and cultural enrichment does not come at the cost of completely abandoning one's identity. From an educational perspective, Todd (2003) also argued that preserving rather than eliminating differences makes teaching and learning possible by creating new opportunities and new challenges for both educators and learners. She also believed that resisting the desire to eliminate personal and cultural differences creates a pathway for the development of ethical, non-violent relationships. Both authors pointed to the unique and interdependent relationship between the self and the Other for purposes of learning.

In my view, the need to recognize the important role that cultural and individual differences can play in the development of curriculum is necessary and urgent, as globalization, which may be described as the "intensification and rapidity of movement and migration of people, ideas, and economic and cultural capital across national boundaries" (Matus & McCarthy, 2003, p. 73), brings greater cultural diversity to otherwise homogenous environments. By several accounts, American high school and university classrooms are becoming increasingly culturally, linguistically, and religiously diverse (Planty et al., 2009; Institute of International Education, 2012; Gorski, 2013, pp. xi–xii). For educators, working with increasingly culturally diverse student populations can be especially anxiety-provoking, as they are tasked with creating spaces within curricula that are open to the diverse thoughts and experiences of all students, even when those perspectives challenge their own personal and cultural expectations. This can lead to "various new kinds of identity crises" and "difficult questions…about how knowledge is produced, represented, and circulated" (Smith, 2003, p. 36).

For example, in a survey of 641 first-year school teachers, when asked to consider a list of 14 proposals and indicate which ones would be "very effective" for teacher development, "preparing teachers to adapt or vary their instruction to meet the needs of a diverse classroom" was second only to "reducing class size" (Rochkind, Ott, Immerwahr, Doble, & Johnson, 2008, p. 15). The survey analysis further suggested that the "anxiety about dealing with diverse classrooms" is felt more strongly in communities with little experience in dealing with cultural diversity (p. 12). Along these lines, the report cited a teacher who found himself teaching students from 20 different "linguistic backgrounds" in a "historically white" neighborhood (p. 12).

Similarly, in a faculty guide for "Teaching in an Increasingly Multi-cultural Setting" produced by Carnegie Mellon University (n.d.), a faculty member noted,

> In the past, I could assume that all or most of my students shared certain kinds of understandings or experiences. With classrooms increasingly made up of students from other countries, or from ethnically identified subgroups within the U.S., I can no longer make any assumptions at all. This is a disconcerting realization for an instructor. (Contents)

Clearly, for educators who come from mainstream backgrounds, who have little experience with teaching diverse populations, who may not have ever been a cultural outsider themselves or who teach in a culture that espouses a curriculum of sameness, universality, and standardization, the task of educating students from diverse backgrounds can be, as research indicates, anxiety-provoking.

I would argue that the anxiety that teachers experience when encountering cultural differences in the classroom can be considered a form of culture shock. According to Furnham (2004), the term "culture shock" was popularized by the anthropologist Kalervo Oberg in 1960 to denote, among other things, "surprise, anxiety, even disgust and indignation after becoming aware of cultural differences," as well as "confusion in role, role expectations, values" (p. 17). Although "culture shock" is generally applied to those who travel to a foreign country, the anthropologist Fuchs (1969) and educators Kron (1972) and Kron and Faber (1973) made the connection between teaching and the culture shock teachers experienced when "placed in a new subculture (e.g., the middle-class teacher placed in an inner city school, the black teacher placed in an all-white suburban school)" (Kron & Faber, 1973, p. 506). Kron and Faber also noted in 1973 that "Few social scientists have written about [culture shock] and still fewer have applied the culture shock concept to education" (p. 506).

Since the 1970s, despite the widespread globalization that is changing the cultural makeup of the American classroom, there have been few articles that have focused on educator culture shock at the public primary, secondary, or university level. In the last decade, for example, the majority of articles explicitly related to culture shock and education have focused on college students—specifically, international students studying in the U.S. (Gilton, 2005; Godwin, 2009; Zhou, Jindal-Snape, Topping, & Todman, 2008); black students (Torres, 2009); first-generation students (Cushman, 2007); "Third Culture Kids" who grew up in a culture different than their American parents now coming to the U.S. to attend college (Hervey, 2009; Huff, 2001); and Adult ESL students (Buttaro, 2004). Only one article dealt with the culture shock experienced by the teacher, and it had to do with the acculturation necessary for teaching in the prison system (Wright, 2005). Considering that globalization has paved the way for rapidly increasing cultural diversity in schools, that such rapid changes can produce anxiety, and that it is the teacher, instructor, or professor who is "faced with the challenge of making instruction 'culturally responsive' for all students" ("How Important Is," n.d.,

p. 1), I think it is important to understand how educators navigate both the positive and negative aspects of culture shock.

One type of educator with particular experience in dealing with issues related to culture shock, both abroad and at home, is the Returned Peace Corps Volunteer (RPCV) educator. Peace Corps Volunteer educators typically teach English, math, science, health, or another subject in schools and/or universities for two years in a foreign country. As cultural outsiders in those foreign countries, they often experience culture shock. In addition, many RPCV educators return home to continue teaching or working in a variety of education-related jobs, only to find that their overseas teaching experiences have made them cultural outsiders in their home country, leading to what has been termed "reverse culture shock" (Gullahorn & Gullahorn, 1963).

The insights of RPCV educators have been captured in newspaper/magazine articles across the country. These insights provide snapshots into the perspectives RPCV educators have developed through intercultural contact, culture shock, and reverse culture shock. For example, in one article, an RPCV art teacher reconsidered the practice of using food in art and other class projects (potatoes for potato stamp prints, macaroni to make designs, Cheerios for counting, etc.) as "wasteful" after confronting the poverty and starvation that her African students and colleagues faced on a daily basis (Brown, 2005). A second teacher spoke about wastefulness after a trip home to the U.S., noting, "My shock came when I returned for a visit in the Christmas holidays. So much waste! The buying of gifts that people didn't need" (Armstrong, 1986). Another talked about the differences in student behavior, stating that "It was kind of a culture shock....Coming from a place where kids are very respectful to coming here [the U.S.], where kids are disruptive and don't respect authority" (Fernandez, 1999). One RPCV educator developed empathy for internationals coming to the U.S. after she began to "understand a little bit about what it is like to be a minority" in her host country (Nacelewicz, 2002). Another RPCV educator gained insight into American race relations after he reflected on how easy it was for him, a white male teacher in Africa, to lie about one of his African students in order to have the student expelled from the school (Meyers, 1999). Certainly, these brief remarks are only a small sample and cannot be generalized as representative of all RPCV educators' experiences or points of view. They do, however, offer various kinds of insights that bridge issues of power, identity, culture, and experience that I hope to expand upon in the current study.

The purpose of this study is to gain insight into issues related to teaching and learning in intercultural contexts by examining RPCV educators' experiences with culture shock and reverse culture shock. An examination of the ways in which RPCV educators respond to the experience of culture shock and reverse culture shock provides openings for other educators to reflect on their own experiences with cultural differences inside and outside the classroom. As an RPCV educator myself, I have found my intercultural experiences to be both shocking and enlightening with regard to what they reveal about intercultural and pedagogical relationships. My hope is not to somehow alleviate the anxiety that educators may experience in the face of cultural differences, but rather to recognize the different ways in which culture shock and reverse culture shock may influence teaching in an age of globalization. In this sense, I also suggest that culture shock and reverse culture shock can be valuable tools for learning, both about oneself and others.

Study Overview

For this study, I gathered the culture shock and reverse culture shock stories of four RPCV educators who had taught with the Peace Corps overseas and who were currently working in an educational institution in the United States. Specifically, I travelled to each participant's town for one weekend where I conducted open-ended, face-to-face interviews. Participants also responded to two writing prompts, one before we met for our interviews and one after all of the interviews were completed. Additionally, participants were invited to share artifacts from their teaching or personal life that they felt were meaningful. For the participants in the study, these included photographs, a video biography, gifts from students, a motorcycle, an earring, and various souvenirs. All of the participants, their friends, and the villages and cities in which they have lived have been given pseudonyms.

The focus of this study is the intercultural meaning created through participants' experiences and then shared through their stories. A number of authors have stressed the important role that story-telling plays in expressing lived experience, in representing a sense of identity, and in connecting to issues with broader social significance (Clandinin & Connelly, 2000; Rosenwald & Ochberg, 1992; Fox & Kloppenburg, 1998). As RPCV educators and their shifting intercultural teaching contexts are the topic under study, I note especially Clandinin and Connelly's (2000) claim that narrative inquiry within the education field is concerned with "broad questions of how individuals teach and learn, of how temporality (placing things in the context of time) connects with change and learning, and of how institutions frame our lives" (p. 1). They also saw "teaching and teacher knowledge as expressions of embodied individual and social stories" (p. 4). In this sense, teachers do not simply tell stories, they live them through "epiphanies, rituals, routines, metaphors, and everyday actions" (p. xxiv), in specific moments in time, and in relation to other people.

Interviewing each participant in their home contexts, accompanying them through their daily routines, and reading their reflective writings proved invaluable for giving me a sense of how participants constructed and negotiated their perceptions of self and their social relationships. Their stories also highlighted their changing theories about what is pedagogically relevant to teaching in intercultural and multicultural contexts. After reading through the interview transcripts and participant writings, four broad story categories emerged: culture shock stories, reverse culture shock stories, identity shift stories, and pedagogical stories. For this study, I have included five stories for each participant: one for each of the above categories plus an additional story in any of these categories that I found especially interesting.

Additionally, as an RPCV educator myself in Cameroon, Africa, from 1996–1998, I have included some of my own stories between the other chapters, which I have labelled "interplay" stories. Thematically, these stories intersect, converge with, and at times diverge from participants' stories. My goal is not to suggest that my experiences and insights have more value than those of my participants. My hope in including these "interplay" stories is to add layers of complexity and multiplicity to the other chapters as I struggled to develop my own self- and intercultural awareness.

The Participants

The participants for the study were four RPCVs who were educators both overseas as part of their Peace Corps assignments and in the United States at the time of participation in the study. In addition, two of the participants taught secondary school classes before joining the Peace Corps, and the other two participants worked as educators in other countries following their Peace Corps service. All of the participants were recruited through purposeful "snowball sampling," which involved the use of social networks to locate participants

(Warren & Karner, 2010, p. 143). I did not know any of the participants prior to this study. A brief biography of each participant is presented below.

Joe, Peace Corps Moldova 2006–2008

"Joe" was a 58-year-old Hispanic male. He was divorced with three children. Prior to joining the Peace Corps, Joe had worked as an oil field hand for 20 years, competed in karate tournaments as well as managed and taught in karate schools for 15 years, and worked as a private investigator and a bail bondsman in addition to many other short-term jobs. He had also taught at two different high schools after earning a bachelor's degree in English/Journalism in 2000 (he went on to earn a teaching certificate in 2004). First, he taught speech at an inner city high school for 1 year and then he taught speech and journalism for 5 years at a different high school.

When I met with Joe, he was teaching sophomore English at the same high school where he had taught for 5 years prior to joining the Peace Corps. Joe also noted that the town where he was currently living revolved largely around a "huge" and "powerful" local ranch. The majority of students at Joe's school were the children of the Hispanic ranch workers and the children of newly arrived Hispanic immigrants who lived in a neighboring farming town. Joe also had a few international students, from a nearby university that attracted some international families, and he also taught some of the children of the white ranch owners. For his Peace Corps service, Joe taught English as a foreign language at a university in an urban city in Moldova, a country in Eastern Europe, for two years from 2006 to 2008. His students at the university were older professional adults, most of whom were women and many of whom had some knowledge of English.

When I asked Joe why he joined the Peace Corps, he said that he "had always had a really restless spirit," that he was "never happy" wherever he was, and that he always felt that he should "be somewhere else because it might be better over there." He also said that after 6 years of teaching, which he described as "sitting and worrying about these kids," teaching felt "kind of trivial," which I understood as meaning "lacking excitement," since he contrasted it with his exciting life as an investigator and bail bondsman, during which time he tracked down fugitives. In short, Joe believed the Peace Corps would give him the chance to see if teaching in another setting would be "better," or rather, more stimulating.

Harley, Peace Corps Kazakhstan 1999–2001

"Harley" was a 33-year-old Filipino American woman who was working as an associate director of International Programs and Services at a Midwestern university at the time of our interviews. Her job entailed welcoming international students, providing orientations for them, and ensuring they followed the Department of Homeland Security's regulations regarding study in the United States. She also taught a class called "Transitions," which she described as a freshman experience course to help international students adjust to American culture. The topics she covered ranged from U.S. classroom culture, academic dishonesty, local history, and finding ways to interact socially with Americans, among other topics. In addition, as an educator and a world traveler, she also offered intercultural communication presentations, not only for international students, but also for local students and community members.

For her Peace Corps service, Harley had hoped to be posted in the Philippines, since she was familiar with the language and culture, but due to the timing of the next group of volunteers leaving for the Philippines, she decided to accept a post in Kazakhstan, which she happily discovered was considered a part of Central Asia. Harley taught English at the primary and secondary levels and held conversation classes for local teachers for 2 years from 1999–2001. Additionally, she was the first volunteer to serve in the small rural village where she taught. After completing her Peace Corps service, Harley began teaching English for a private company, and taught in Japan (2001–2002), Thailand (2002–2004), Poland (2004–2006), and Kyrgyzstan (2006–2007). Altogether, she lived outside the U.S. for 8 years and returned in the fall of 2007 to begin a PhD program in education and human resource studies. Although she said she would have felt comfortable getting her doctorate overseas, she also believed that a degree from another country would not have been perceived as carrying the same weight as a degree from the United States.

In discussing her personal background, she noted that her parents were born and raised in the Philippines and therefore she grew up with many Filipino values and customs in addition to her American ones. She herself was born in the U.S. on the East coast but raised since the age of 4 on the West coast. I couldn't help but think of the symbolism of East meeting West as Harley talked about her experiences living between Filipino and American cultures and her considerable travels in both Asian and European countries as well. When we talked about why she wanted to join the Peace Corps, two significant experiences stood out for her: travelling to the Philippines, and taking care of her younger brother who was in a coma due to a near fatal drowning accident, both of which had occurred since she was 10 years old. She said that travelling to the Philippines made her realize that "people don't live the same way as we live in the United States." By travelling to the Philippines, she also began to recognize that although she was American, she was different than other Americans, and likewise, that although she was Filipino she was different from other Filipinos as well. She said this sparked her interest in learning about different cultures and their customs.

With regard to her brother, she noted that, "all my time from when I was 10, the rest of primary school and the rest of high school, everything was about my brother; taking care of him." She also said that she attended a university within a short driving distance of home so she could help take care of him on the weekends. She mentioned that she struggled with the desire to leave her brother to go and help other people, but ultimately, she felt that she had a "need" and a "calling" to join the Peace Corps. She also felt spiritually connected to her brother and that she had his blessing to pursue her calling. Her parents were another story. She said they were "pissed" about her joining the Peace Corps because they "worked so hard to get out of that" so that she would not have to grow up "poor and would have all these opportunities." She explained to them it was because she had "opportunities" that others didn't that she felt the need to "give back to the people" who didn't have those opportunities. She added that her parents finally began to accept her decision but only about six or seven months after she had left for the Peace Corps.

Ryder, Peace Corps Kenya 1987–1990

"Ryder" was a 46-year-old white male who was an assistant professor of English at a Midwestern university at the time of the study. For his Peace Corps service Ryder taught English in forms 1–4 (basically ninth–12th grade) at a rural boarding secondary school in Kenya from 1987 to 1990. His students were the children of subsistence farmers who grew crops mainly for survival. Ryder taught with the Peace Corps for 3 years and then stayed in Kenya on his own for a fourth year during which time he home-schooled adult non-Kenyan students in English. While Ryder was in Kenya, he also married a Kenyan woman who returned with him to the United States in December of 1991. They subsequently had one child together and a few years later they divorced. Following his return from Kenya, Ryder also began work on a master's degree in English, which he completed in 1994. After completing his degree, he took a job as a curriculum writer in Saudi Arabia, but switched to teaching English in a college preparatory program for a large oil company there. He stayed in Saudi Arabia 6 years and returned to the U.S. in 2000. He ultimately received his PhD in linguistics in the fall of 2008 and began teaching in his current position that same semester.

As Ryder described his life prior to joining the Peace Corps and his reasons for joining it, he began,

> Maybe I should preface this by telling you I grew up in a four-room house with no inside toilet...there was no water heater...[the bathtub] hung on a pinning nail from the backside of the house...that's the level of poverty I'm talking about. I'm not talking about working class.

He also explained that his mother left their home when he was very young so that his father, with the assistance of social services, raised him, his three brothers, and one sister. Additionally, Ryder felt that due to his poor upbringing, others had little expectation that he would be successful. In turn, this gave him the desire to "prove people wrong" and to be successful.

Ryder had originally intended to join the Air Force until he discovered that his weak eyesight would prevent him from being a pilot. He offered, "I wanted to get out...I wanted to go somewhere I had never been before and where I'd never known anyone who had been." The thought of travelling was appealing but he couldn't afford it on his own. He said he had always thought the Peace Corps "looked cool." He remembered a specific Peace Corps commercial with a "guy in a t-shirt and a pair of shorts walking up a muddy, slippery hill" carrying a bucket of water on his shoulders while drums were playing in the background. But, it wasn't until his college roommate received a letter from the Peace Corps that it brought the idea of joining the Peace Corps closer and gave him "another possibility...to see the world."

Hyacinth, Peace Corps Kenya 1984–1986

"Hyacinth" was a 52-year-old white female who had been teaching English as a second language (ESL) at the middle school level for 11 years when we met. Before joining the Peace Corps, she had taught 2 years of seventh- and eighth-grade language arts, 12th-grade remedial English, and ninth-grade Spanish at an inner-city school. After returning from the Peace Corps, she taught ESL for 13 years at a high school in an American city on the Mexican border.

When I asked how she arrived at the pseudonym "Hyacinth," she explained that she and her husband enjoyed watching the British comedy *Keeping Up Appearances* and Hyacinth was the main character. Having watched and enjoyed the show myself, I knew that Hyacinth was a snobbish middle-class housewife who failed miserably and humorously at her attempts at social climbing—often because neither her richer nor her poorer siblings (or anyone else for that matter) behaved in exactly the way that she believed they should according to their social status. Having spent a good deal of time getting to know Hyacinth (the teacher), I found her to be quite the opposite of her television namesake. Because, Hyacinth's husband played an important role in her Peace Corps experience, I have given him the pseudonym Richard, which was Hyacinth's husband's name on the TV show.

For her Peace Corps service, Hyacinth spent 2 years teaching English in a secondary school in a small town in the central highlands of Kenya. She, like Ryder, taught the children of subsistence farmers, and although there was some overlap in the Kenyan cultural practices they pointed out, their experiences and the insights they drew from them were largely different. When I asked why Hyacinth joined the Peace Corps she explained that her brothers were "hippies in the 1960s" and the ideals related to the Peace Corps were "floating around" in the "general consciousness" of the 1970s when she was in high school. She had also been a Rotary exchange student in Australia the year after she graduated high school, which she counted as a "really, really positive experience," so she felt "eager" for "another international experience," especially one that was "helpful to others," "adventurous," and "a real learning experience."

Hyacinth also said that joining the Peace Corps would offer the opportunity to meet "like-minded," "adventurous," "fun," people with "similar values" who were "trying to make a positive difference in the world." She added that in the back of her mind, she thought it "would be a great place to meet a life partner," which turned out to be true in her case. Richard was also a Peace Corps volunteer leaving for Kenya at the same time as Hyacinth. While he recalled meeting her during their Peace Corps training in the U.S., she remembered meeting him on the flight to Kenya. She explained that they were seated alphabetically and that due to the spelling of their last names there was another volunteer in the seat between them. She said, "My last name started with an A, I was sitting next to Cindy [A] who got up and went to the rest room. He was a B, he moved over, it was a 27-hour flight." Even though Hyacinth noted it "was not a done deal," by the time their plane landed they felt a "real connection" to each other and they ultimately married in Kenya 3 months before their Peace Corps service ended. At the time of my interviews with Hyacinth, she and Richard had just celebrated their 25th anniversary.

Looking Through a Post-Structural Hermeneutic Lens

At the heart of the current study is the question of how the self/Other relationship is perceived and acted out personally, culturally, and pedagogically through RPCV educators' experiences. For this study, I chose to examine RPCV educators' experiences through a post-structural hermeneutic lens. A post-structural hermeneutic lens seemed especially suited to this study as post-structuralism works to elucidate not only how the Other is created, but also how the encounter with the Other can stimulate learning, a sense of ethics, and the claiming of human agency. It does this in different ways. First, post-structural hermeneutics calls for openness of, and play with, the structure through a process of "decentering," which challenges the hierarchy of self over Other. Second, it suggests that meaning is not fixed, objective, and singular, but rather changing, subjective, and multiple, implying the need for the negotiation of meaning between self and Other. Third, it examines the ways in which social institutions engage in the process of othering, that is, using differences to create and exclude the Other. And lastly, it takes the stance that recognizing the differences between self and Other rather than making the Other over in the image of the self or silencing the Other has both ethical and educational implications. Each of these topics is discussed below.

To appreciate how post-structural hermeneutics seeks openness of, and play with, the structure it is important to understand how Western cultures such as the United States are shaped by a structuralist view of reality. Stam (2008) wrote that "According to the 'binary opposition' theory of the structuralists, reality is formed by certain theoretical and cultural opposites, often arranged in a hierarchy, which structure reality" (p. 12). Some examples of binary pairs include male/female, logic/emotion, light/dark, clarity/ambiguity, and so on. Within each of these pairings is a hierarchical center whose purpose is to "orient, balance, and organize the structure" (Derrida, 1978, p. 278). In order to achieve a sense of stability, all movement within the structure is directed toward supporting and maintaining the hierarchical center. As such, playing with the structure or shifting the focus of the structure is strongly discouraged and often punished.

In order to open up the structure and allow for play, Derrida (1978) proposed "decentering" (p. 280)—a move that rejects the center's primacy and destabilizes the structure. While this destabilization can produce anxiety, clinging to an inflexible structure based on binary oppositions creates as much anxiety as it seeks to avoid by attempting to fix people into simple dualistic categories that fail to acknowledge the multiplicity of self and Other. Post-structural hermeneutics rejects a dualistic view of reality by recognizing the "multi-memberships, the mutations, the individualizations and the personalization of behavior and conduct, the contraventions, the crossings, the stripes, the alternate routes, and the cultural margins" (Abdallah-Pretceille, 2006, pp. 481–482) that challenge dualistic structures. For the intercultural relationship, this involves resisting the hierarchical privilege of self over Other. It also implies the need to tolerate the anxiety and perceived loss of control in rejecting this structure while simultaneously locating the "secret place" (Derrida, 1978, p. 6) within the structure that is open to change.

In a related way, Derrida also demonstrated that meaning, like structure, is not fixed, but is open to multiple interpretations. He did this by exposing and subverting the dualistic oppositions in texts, by going below the surface of the text to find "hidden alternative meanings," and by pointing out the "undecidables" or "aporias" within a text that do not "conform to either side of a dichotomy or opposition" (Reynolds, 2010, Introduction). In the poststructural sense, then, meaning is "never fully present" in words or the concepts they signify; rather, meaning is "contextual," relational, and infinite, making any final definitive meaning impossible (Quigley, 2009, p. 6).

This view underscores the slipperiness of meaning and points to the difficulty in assigning meaning to the words and actions of others. For the intercultural self/Other relationship, this signals a need to suspend judgment and assume a position of "not knowing" the Other. In not knowing the Other, meaning is developed through the questioning of the self and through the negotiation of meaning along with the Other within a specific context. Even then, such meaning is not fixed but subject to (re-)interpretation at a later time.

Understanding the ways in which social institutions work to structure the self/Other relationship within society and the self is another poststructural theme relevant to the current study. In *Civilization and Madness*, Foucault (1965) demonstrated how social institutions such as churches, hospitals, and government agencies work in concert to create the Other through the "exclusion" of difference. Foucault related this exclusion to the rise of leprosy in Europe, and explained that exclusion was a means of keeping leprosy "at a sacred" (p. 6) distance from polite society. But even after leprosy began to disappear, both the physical and theoretical structures for excluding difference remained, creating a cultural demand for the exclusion of other differences that could be labeled as "madness."

On a more personal level, Wang (2004) showed how the social structuring of the self/Other relationship becomes inculcated both *in* and *as* the self. Through her historical deconstruction of Western Greco-Roman philosophy and Eastern Confucian philosophy, Wang revealed how a masculine hierarchical structuring of both philosophies creates the feminine Other. She argued that "Due to the cultural demand for feminine invisibility, woman does not really have a self" (p. 46) and therefore anything feminine is seen as Other. In highlighting the ways in which the feminine Other is created socially, Wang urged the fluid claiming of one's own subjectivity and human agency in response to culturally prescriptive narratives, while recognizing that notions of subjectivity are culturally embedded in their own right. This suggests that while the reach of social structures may be inescapable, one can shift one's response to it and find other meanings within it. It also implies the need to reclaim that which has been excluded, including the feminine Other.

For the intercultural teaching/learning relationship, I think it is important to be aware of how social institutions, including schools, may be engaged in this process of Othering. Likewise, it is equally important to recognize the ways in which the post-structural subject—in this case the RPCV educator—negotiates their culturally nominated social positions in order to create freer, more complex inter/subjective relationships within the curriculum. I would also argue that recognizing the subjectivity of both self and Other has ethical implications, as both self and Other reject their object positions, and differences between self/Other become valued.

A post-structural hermeneutic view of the ethical self/Other relationship is expressed in Todd's (2003) *Learning From the Other*. Drawing on the work of Levinas, she wrote that it is the "break between self and Other where… both the conditions for ethics and the possibility of teaching and learning" (p. 29) are located. Maintaining the "break" between self and other involves resisting attempts to change, fix, or make the Other over in the image of the self. Preserving difference also provides the self with opportunities for learning and growth in that difference creates the need for the (re-)negotiation and (re-)consideration of unshared meanings. Without the difference to self, the self has the potential to stagnate in a pool of sameness.

This understanding of learning and ethics as connected to the rupture between self and Other has profound implications for curriculum development in a globalized world. Certainly it shifts the role of the teacher and the focus of curriculum that have been primarily concerned with standardization, unification, and the elimination of difference, toward a curriculum that also allows for the non-violent cultivation of, and learning from, difference. But while the ethical relationship with the Other can help foster this shift, Todd (2003) also recognized that it is the "very anxiety over encountering difference that...provides learning with its fiercest form of resistance" (p. 11). For the current study, however, I believe that the anxiety and resistance over encountering difference in the form of RPCV educator culture shock and reverse culture shock can also promote learning and ethical understanding in the intercultural relationship for purposes of curriculum development.

Using a poststructural hermeneutic framework to guide my analysis, the data (the interview transcripts, the writing samples, and the personal artifacts) were treated as texts and were analyzed in two separate "readings." The first reading of each text was more hermeneutic and interpretive in nature. This reading focused more on the "significance" and "meaning" that certain aspects of intercultural experience held for the participants for the purpose of creating a shared understanding (Wong, 2005). The second reading was more deconstructive and destabilizing in nature. For this reading, I looked at the beliefs that were "privileged" by the participants in their stories as well as those that were "deemphasized, overlooked, or suppressed" (Balkin, 1995–1996). For both readings, I used a variety of techniques in conjunction with various theoretical positions, empirical research findings, popular media views, and my own experiences, in order to analyze the texts. By offering a doubled reading of participant texts, I hoped to both demonstrate the value in participants' perspectives and then decenter those perspectives as a way of making a space for other potential meanings.

Operationalizing post-structural hermeneutic theory as a method of analysis proved no easy task, however. Without any specific guidelines, I used a number of strategies to aid me in my analysis. One strategy I used was to offer two different readings of the metaphors that participants generated in their stories, similar to Koro-Ljungberg's (2004) post-structural metaphorical analysis. One example of this can be found in Joe's metaphor of intercultural experience as "walking on ice," which I analyzed in terms of danger and vulnerability in the first reading and then as part of the process of "learning to ice skate," in which feelings of danger and vulnerability were part of the process of navigating intercultural contexts for the re-reading. Another technique was to shift the focus of the story from one country to another in order to destabilize the internal meanings of certain themes. For instance, Hyacinth focused on male privilege in Kenya and then I switched the focus to male privilege in the U.S. for the second reading by adapting McIntosh's (1989) process for revealing "white privilege" as a way of making "male privilege" more visible in the United States. I also sometimes analyzed a story in terms of its positive and negative aspects, such as in Harley's story about her bicultural identity, which offered both challenges and benefits in different ways. In addition, I looked at different cultural and personal meanings for the same words used by participants as in the case of "caring" and "acceptance" for Joe, "fatalism" and "generosity" for Ryder, "individualism" for Harley, and "sameness" and "difference" for Hyacinth. I also sometimes used two different "lenses" to read and re-read a story. In Hyacinth's story about learning to "weave" people into the fabric of her life, I used a cultural lens in the first reading and a gendered lens for the second.

Additionally, for both layers of analysis, I used available empirical research, theoretical perspectives, popular media reports, and my own experiences as an RPCV educator to guide my analysis. My goal, as previously stated, was to offer alternative readings of the same experience in order to demonstrate the elusiveness of a single, unified meaning. It was not to inadvertently create a dualistic hierarchy between the two readings or to minimize the participants' views or beliefs by suggesting that other perspectives were more "correct," but to offer various viewpoints that may be more reflective of the range of diverse perspectives of RPCV educators overall.

Further, by using a post-structural hermeneutic perspective to analyze data I hope to bring theoretical depth to narrative inquiry as well as to enrich theoretical understandings of the experience of culture shock and reverse culture shock. In considering the place and balance of theory in narrative inquiry, Clandinin & Connelly (2000) noted that others have criticized narrative inquiry as "not theoretical enough" (p. 42). Although they did not reject theory out of hand, they suggested that the starting point of narrative inquiry is "experience as expressed in lived and told stories" (p. 40) rather than the study's theoretical implications. Their concern seems to be related to the ways in which theory may work to structure or overshadow experience through theory's privilege over experience within formalistic traditions.

Recalling Derrida's (1978) insistence that the relationship between self and Other be understood "from within a *recourse to experience itself*" (p. 83), I believe that the close relationship between theory and experience within a post-structural hermeneutic paradigm can work to allay this concern, in that it privileges neither theory nor experience but accepts both as parts of a whole that cannot exist completely separately. In fact, I argue that individuals act with certain theoretical intentions in mind. The actions they ultimately take in relation to others and the ways in which they perceive the outcomes, in turn, add support for their perspectives. Englehart (2001) asserted that attempts to dichotomize theory and practice create a "confusing enigma" (p. 371). She explained, "Practice is theory-in-place. Theory is practice-to-be, waiting to be enacted. Theory, then, is one's understanding of the world. Practice is the enactment of that understanding" (p. 372).

She also noted that despite the perhaps uncomfortable "marriage" between practitioners and theorists, "neither divorce nor separation is possible" (p. 372). To that extent, I attempt to demonstrate the strong connection between post-structural hermeneutic theory and lived experience and to show that the two are not necessarily mutually exclusive, even if there is the tendency to think of theory and practice in this way.

· 1 ·

BACK STORIES

Before getting to the participants' stories there are other "stories" that need to be told in order to create the context from which this study springs. These stories include a discussion about the current movement toward the internationalization of curriculum studies, some of the important questions being asked in this ongoing dialogue, how this internationalization shapes educators' identities, and some of the ways in which educational institutions are promoting this internationalization. A second section offers a brief look at the Peace Corps—its beginnings, its proposed functions, the critiques levelled against it, and the storied perceptions of Returned Peace Corps Volunteer (RPCV) educators. A third section outlines the ways in which culture shock has been defined and conceptualized psychologically and metaphorically, with particular attention paid to aspects related to self-awareness, identity, learning, and growth. A fourth section similarly considers the ways in which reverse culture shock has been defined as well as some of the reasons why it remains relatively less explored than culture shock.

The Internationalization of Curriculum Studies

Since 2001, the International Association for the Advancement of Curriculum Studies (IAACS) has envisioned the internationalization of curriculum studies as both a "worldwide" dialogue regarding curriculum practices and a critique of the uniformity and standardization of curriculum encouraged by marketplace globalization (Pinar, n.d.). Gough (2003) further defined the internationalization of curriculum studies as "a process of creating transnational spaces in which scholars from different localities collaborate in reframing and decentering their own knowledge traditions and negotiate trust in each other's contributions to their collective work" (p. 68). Others added that it is geared toward "the promotion of global peace and well-being" (Lee, 2007) and pointed out that such work is "never over, always on-going" (Smith, 2003, p. 46).

Pinar (2000) visualized the internationalization of curriculum studies not as an attempt to create a unified or standardized global curriculum but rather as a "conversation" (p. 5) that transcends national boundaries. He also argued that the internationalization of curriculum studies can work to counteract the "naïve," narcissistic, and "imperialistic" inward focus of the American curriculum (pp. 4–5) by seeking to share with and learn from the practices of other educators working on both the local and global stages. I particularly appreciate this notion of curriculum as conversation, in that it suggests that through the sharing of thoughts, beliefs, and feelings from differing perspectives, something unique may be created in the interplay. I also note that such interplay requires the ability to reframe one's way of knowing not as *the* way, but as one of many ways, to trust others and to be trusted, and to recognize that any conclusions about curriculum are never final, making such conversation both ongoing and multi-directional.

Within this transnational curriculum conversation, educators and curriculum researchers are voicing their concerns about the ways in which the neo-liberalist market practices that drive globalization are affecting the nature of public education and curriculum. Smith (2003) argued that these practices work to "delegitimize public education," "commercialize the school environment" and pressure governments and schools into "adopting a human capital model of education" (p. 38). Sahlberg (2004) added that a key focus of the neo-liberalist agenda is standardization (especially through testing), which pits students, teachers, and schools in competition against one another, de-professionalizes teaching, and "narrows curriculum and learning to basic skills in core academic subjects" (p. 76). While responding to these challenges, curriculum scholars are also asking broad questions particularly relevant to teaching in a globalized world: "How can we think globally *without* entering some form of epistemological imperialism" (Gough, 2003, p. 63)? How do teach "ethics and a sense of global responsibility that go beyond the b of the knowledge economy" (Sahlberg, 2004, p. 66)? And, "How should we address the topics of culture and identity in the organization of school knowledge" (Matus & McCarthy, 2003, p. 76)? Certainly, there are no easy answers to these questions, but in their asking and in contemplating issues related to the globalization of public education, one gets an idea of the tenuous contexts within which educators operate. While it seems that economic globalization works to standardize the curriculum without regard for local contexts or individual experiences and reduces both teachers and students to economic tools of the marketplace, the internationalization of curriculum studies, as a critique of globalization, works to engage educators in local, national, and international contexts in a dialogic exploration of differences, ethics, culture, and identity through curriculum in pursuit of self-understanding and mutual respect.

Another thread within this conversation on the internationalization of curriculum studies attends to the identity and position of teachers. Speaking at the LSU conference on the internationalization of curriculum, Pinar (2000) offered the following point of view:

> we teachers are conceived by others, by the expectations and fantasies of our students and by the demands of parents, administrators, policymakers, and politicians, to all of whom we are sometimes the "other." We are formed as well by their and our own internalized life histories. These various spheres or levels of self-constitution require investigation. Locating the process of knowing in the politics of identity suggests escaping the swirling waters created by the demands and pressure of others. The capacity to stand calmly in a maelstrom can come only with the knowledge of other worlds, with living in other realities, not split off or dissociated from the world of work. "Separate but connected" permits us to enter the work world in larger, more complex roles than those prescribed for us, making it less likely that we will collapse upon the social surface, reduced to what others make of us. (p. 10)

This perspective underscores some of the basic assumptions of my study, specifically that teachers are made "other" through the "expectations," "fantasies," and "demands" of others as well as through their own "internalized life histories." This offers a fertile ground for curriculum inquiry in the spaces between and among the fantasies and the lived realities. Also, that the "process of knowing" is linked to the "politics of identity" underlies the belief that what one experiences of the world shapes both one's identity and what one knows of the world, including teacher beliefs about the nature and the delivery of curriculum. Additionally, that "knowledge of other worlds" and "living in other realities" enables one to move beyond the teaching roles created by others and implies that the experience of otherness holds the potential for learning and growth. And lastly, that embodying an identity that is separate from, but connected to, the insular world of the school prevents one from becoming immersed in institutionalized definitions of one's role. It also permits drawing insights and developing one's identity in spaces beyond the school walls.

Pinar's (2000) assertion that knowing is connected to identity, that teachers are formed (in part) by their own life histories, and that knowledge of, and experiences living in, other realities are important for teacher self-understanding, begs the question: What life experiences do teachers draw upon in order to teach inter- or transnationally? This theme is explored by Merryfield (2000), who examined the lived experiences of 80 teacher educators who were recognized for preparing teachers to "teach for diversity, equity, and interconnectedness in the local community, nation, and world" (p. 430). An important goal of her study was to examine the relationship between the lived experiences of these teachers and how they conceptualize their work as educators. In reviewing the life histories of these teacher educators she identified a number of experiences that guide them in their teaching. These include experiences of being seen as "different" (p. 432) or as "the Other" (p. 434), experiences that enable them to recognize "contradictions between beliefs, expectations or knowledge and the multiple realities of experience" (p. 439), developing a "double consciousness" in response to experiences of racism (p. 433), experiences with teachers and parents (as children) (p. 434), experiences with students and parents (as teachers) (pp. 437–438), travel (p. 434), and living in another country (pp. 435–436). Merryfield also noted that many of the teacher educators in her study experienced "culture shock" at various transition points in their lives and that living abroad was often cited as being the most influential experience for middle-class white teacher educators in their work as multicultural and global educators (p. 439). That the experience of "otherness" led to a "double consciousness" and that culture shock and living abroad were key experiences in developing their intercultural understanding (especially for middle class white teachers) helps provide direction for the current study. It also leaves me wondering what the experiences of living and teaching abroad may hold for teachers who do not represent the majority. Additionally, this leads me to explore the relationship between the internationalization of curriculum studies and research on educator study/teach abroad programs more in depth.

In a poll conducted by the International Association of Universities (IAU) that asked 176 higher education institutions in 66 different countries about their "practices and priorities of internationalization," two of the key findings are that "Faculty are seen as the drivers for internationalization" and that the "Mobility of students and teachers is considered to be the most important reason for making internationalization a priority" (Knight, 2003, p. 3). Along these lines, Schneider (2003) found that study abroad is the top strategy for internationalizing secondary teacher education employed by many colleges and universities across the United States. More recently, Fischer (2008) argued that study abroad programs aimed at college/university faculty members themselves have been posited as a means to "create more-global campuses by cultivating a faculty of internationalists," and such programs are recognized as a "bright spot" in higher education institutions' "otherwise uneven efforts at internationalization" (p. 1). These findings underscore the important role that faculty and educators in general play in the area of internationalization. They also suggest that study abroad programs are a key factor in the development of educators' international and intercultural awareness. It should be pointed out that study abroad is perhaps a misnomer in that such programs for teachers often involve not only studying but also teaching abroad. My subsequent use of the term "teacher study abroad" is used to denote the case in which educators not only travel abroad, but also teach abroad. In that the Peace Corps offers the opportunity to live and teach abroad, I would argue that it too is a special type of teach-abroad program, although there are considerable differences in structure, mission, and time spent in the host country. In spite of these differences, many of the experiences and the challenges faced by teachers in foreign environments are similar. Therefore, I think a brief review of the research on teacher study abroad, specifically those with a teaching component, can offer insights into the experiences, opportunities, and tensions that RPCV educators face in teaching in foreign environments, as well as what it may mean for the internationalization of curriculum studies.

Sandgren, Elig, Hovde, Krejci, and Rice (1999) theorized that educator experiences abroad lead to both self-awareness, defined as a "new or keener recognition of one's thoughts, emotions, traits or behaviors," and social awareness, described as a "new or keener recognition of social reality," and that these changes in awareness foster changes in course content, teaching techniques, philosophy of teaching, and/or interactions with students (pp. 48–49). Many of the studies reviewed here seem to draw upon this same understanding, that experience is the key to unlocking other ways of viewing and interacting in the world. In general, the experiences that pre- and early service primary and secondary teachers in teacher study abroad programs engage in are related to dealing with differences in culture, both outside the school (adjusting to housing, shopping, and travelling) and within the school, through differences in curriculum, teacher roles, classroom management styles, school facilities, and teaching materials. They also sometimes deal with language differences. According to the research, navigating these differences provides opportunities for teachers to challenge mis/perceptions of the host culture, to shift their worldviews, and to develop self-awareness, self-confidence, intercultural awareness, personal and professional efficacy, and empathy for, or trust in, those seen as culturally different (Brindley, Quinn, & Morton, 2009; Cushner & Mahon, 2002; Escamilla, Aragon, & Fránquiz, 2009; Malewski & Phillion, 2009b; Pence & Macgillivray, 2008; Schlein, 2009; Tang & Choi, 2004; Willard-Holt, 2001; Zhao, Meyers, & Meyers, 2009). Other teachers, reflecting several years later how early teaching experiences abroad affected them in the long-term, also noted that teaching abroad gave them a greater self-confidence as well as a "more flexible sense of themselves and their own teaching" and an "increased comfort and ability to work with ambiguity and uncertainty" in foreign contexts (Garii, 2009, pp. 96–97). But, Garii (2009) wondered too how this "increased flexibility" translates to their teaching practices back home (p. 99), a theme I explore in the current study.

Although these studies point to the positive and transformative effects of teacher study abroad, some argue that neither placing people from different cultures in close proximity (Leask, 2004) nor experience by itself (Merryfield, 2000) is enough to foster the ability to teach from an intercultural or transnational perspective. Others contend that educator study abroad can be linked to "neo-imperialism, empire building, and the advance of global economic, cultural, and political systems" (Malewski & Phillion, 2009a). These assertions point to tensions within the study abroad literature. Willard-Holt (2001), for example, found that after teaching abroad for one week in Mexico, one teacher exhibited not just self-confidence, but "overconfidence," saying that they could now "do anything," and two others appeared to consider themselves "experts on multicultural teaching and the Mexican culture" (p. 514). Other research suggests that some teachers have difficulty making a connection between their experiences teaching abroad and teaching in the contexts of their classrooms at home (Schlein, 2009; Tang & Choi, 2004; Willard-Holt, 2001). And while teacher study abroad is touted as providing white middle-class teachers—who represent the majority of the primary and secondary teacher population in the U.S.—the opportunity to experience life as an Other (Garii, 2009; Merryfield, 2000; Schlein, 2009), Phillion and her colleagues observed that for some white teachers, the study abroad experience actually "reinforced—rather than challenged—feelings of blessedness and engendered…a 'revival' of White privilege" (Malewski & Phillion, 2009b, p. 53). In the case of minority educators, however, some reported greater acceptance, even popularity in some cases, or experienced less overt racism while teaching abroad than they did in the U.S. (Cushner & Mahon, 2002; Garii, 2009; Malewski & Phillion, 2009b; Zhao, Meyers, & Meyers, 2009).

In various ways, these tensions enable both educators and curriculum researchers to examine more closely the "interrelationships across identity, power, and experience that lead to a consciousness of other perspectives and a recognition of multiple realities" (Merryfield, 2000, p. 440). For example, Escamilla, Aragon, and Fránquiz (2009) utilized the tension between U.S. teachers' "unconscious internalized beliefs about the inferiority of Mexican schools" (p. 275) and the reality they experienced in Mexican classrooms during a study abroad trip, to enable a shift in the U.S. teachers' thinking about Mexican schools' ability to provide a good education. Additionally, Malewski and Phillion (2009b) investigated how race, class, and gender shaped the study abroad experience and the worldview of two pre-service teachers—one a socioeconomically disadvantaged white female, the other a Hispanic male. In both of these studies, the tensions related to identity, power, and experience were generative sources for understanding relationships in "embodied and shifting" (Schlein, 2009, p. 28) intercultural contexts. Therefore, I argue that the tensions between differing perspectives are beneficial and should be incorporated into, rather than eliminated from, the learning process. In that these tensions develop contextually and relationally, the implication is that they cannot be "taught" through a curriculum of standardization, but rather are "experienced" and can be analyzed in an internationalized curriculum of conversation for both the challenges and the opportunities they may reveal.

The Peace Corps and Returned Peace Corps Volunteer Educators

In this section I offer information about the Peace Corps past and present in order to provide a historical context for the current study. I also present some of the critiques of the Peace Corps, followed by research related to RPCV educators and their insights. According to the Peace Corps (2010b) website, as of this writing there are 8,655 volunteers and trainees working in 77 countries. Of those that are serving, 60% are women, 40% are men, and 19% are minorities. The average age of a volunteer is 28, although there is no age limit. The largest numbers of volunteers work in the Education sector (37%) and the largest percentage of volunteers serve in Africa (37%), followed by Latin America (24%), and Eastern Europe/Central Asia (21%). The website also indicates that the task of the Education volunteer is to "introduce innovative teaching methodologies, encourage critical thinking in the classroom, and integrate issues like health education and environmental awareness into English, math, science, and other subjects" (Peace Corps, 2010a). To me, it seems that the goal of introducing "innovative teaching methodologies" implies the superiority of PCVs' teaching methodology, even though the majority of volunteer teachers are not education majors, lack teaching experience, and have little to no knowledge of the local teaching context (myself included). Likewise, "encouraging critical thinking" suggests a lack of critical thinking in the countries being served. Nowhere is it suggested that the education volunteer should be the learner, but rather a leader and an expert.

According to government documents (in Schur, 2000), the Peace Corps was created through Executive Order 10924, signed by President John F. Kennedy on March 1, 1961. It was later established as an independent agency through Public Law 87-293, approved by Congress on September 22, 1961 (pp. 10–14). The Peace Corps' three-point mission, which hasn't changed since its creation in 1961, is "To help the people of interested countries in meeting their need for trained men and women," "To help promote a better understanding of Americans on the part of the peoples served," and "To help promote a better understanding of other peoples on the part of Americans" (Peace Corps, 2008, "The Peace Corps' Mission"). While, on the surface, this mission points to the somewhat altruistic goals of providing assistance in the form of trained workers to countries in need and promoting cross-cultural understanding in those countries, another more political motive seems to underlie this mission: the use of American idealism to stamp out the spread of communism in developing countries. President Kennedy noted that unlike the U.S., the Soviet Union "had hundreds of men and women, scientists, physicists, teachers, engineers, doctors, and nurses…prepared to spend their lives abroad in the service of world communism" and he was looking for a way to actively involve Americans in what he saw as the fight for democracy (Peace Corps, n.d.). Additionally, Schur (2000) believed that Kennedy hoped to "counter negative images of the 'Ugly American' and Yankee imperialism" by sending idealistic young Americans to spread goodwill in Third World countries and "help stem the growth of communism there" (p. 5). This means that the Peace Corps would be used, not only to supply other countries with trained workers or to promote cross-cultural learning, but also to create a positive image of America while spreading a decidedly American vision of democracy and freedom. And while Fischer (1998) agreed that the early Peace Corps administration promoted a form of cultural imperialism, he also argued that it is the experiences and the stories of Peace Corps volunteers that challenge that mission as well as the negative stereotypes of people in the non-Western world. Perhaps this is what may be called the "Peace Corps paradox"—that in some ways the Peace Corps, even today, functions to both support and counteract its own neo-colonialist assumptions.

Critiques of the Peace Corps, both at home and abroad, seemed to spring up almost immediately after its inception. At home, in August 1961, the Daughters of the American Revolution (DAR) were worried that volunteers would be "living under abnormal conditions and encouraged to take part in the life of the nation, tribe, or community…as individuals.…Separated from the moral and disciplinary influences of their homeland" and that "serious consequences" would result (in Longsworth, 1971, p. 84)—the implication being that the American way of life is "normal" and that volunteers need constant reminding of this normalcy or they may be led astray. Abroad, on the other hand, the Austrian philosopher/Roman Catholic priest Ivan Illich (1968) was concerned about U.S. volunteers' effects on his adopted country of Mexico. In a speech he gave at the Conference on InterAmerican Student Projects (CIASP), he referred to all U.S. volunteers as "salesmen for the middle-class American Way of Life" and "vacationing do-gooders" who turn up in every corner of the world to "pretentiously" impose themselves and "create disorder" in other cultures, without considering the people in those cultures. He also noted that

> The Peace Corps spends around $10,000 a year on each corps member to help him adapt to his new environment and to guard him against culture shock. How odd nobody ever thought about spending money to educate poor Mexicans in order to prevent them from the culture shock of meeting you? (p. 3)

He has a point. While Peace Corps volunteers (myself included) are often heralded as martyrs for a cause, it seems that little thought is given to the damage we may do—inadvertently or otherwise—in the countries we are intended to "serve."

Another critique from the early days of the Peace Corps is that media portrayals of the Peace Corps experience are "too glowing, too glamorous, and too pat" in that they offer an "unvarying image of hardship, of sacrifice," overstate the PCV's potential as change agents, and that the difficulties some volunteers face are often "depressingly ordinary" ("Congress Told of Volunteer Problems, Too," 1963, p. 4). This is not to say that volunteers do not face challenges or make sacrifices in joining the Peace Corps, simply that media images that present a uniform picture of Peace Corps life fail to capture the multiple facets of the actual experience. These media portrayals may also lead to unrealistic expectations on behalf of volunteers and affect the ways in which they envision their role.

More recent critiques include Strauss' (2008) contention that the Peace Corps too often recruits young, inexperienced volunteers for jobs overseas for which they are ill-prepared, and as such they fail to offer the kind of assistance that host countries need. He also argued that the Peace Corps fails to properly assess its development efforts. A former Peace Corps Country Director in Cameroon from 2002–2007, Strauss wrote:

> This lack of organizational introspection allows the agency to continue sending, for example, unqualified volunteers to teach English when nearly every developing country could easily find high-caliber English teachers among its own population. Even after Cameroonian teachers and education officials ranked English instruction as their lowest priority (after help with computer literacy, math and science, for example), headquarters in Washington continued to send trainees with little or no classroom experience to teach English in Cameroonian schools. One volunteer told me that the only possible reason he could think of for having been selected was that he was a native English speaker.

In response, some argued that "The Peace Corps is really more of a cultural-exchange program than an international development organization" (Clark, 2008) whose success "should be measured by how many cultural barriers and misconceptions have been cast aside and been replaced with a deeper and more meaningful understanding of the world around us" (Phillips, 2010).

In my own experience as an RPCV English teacher in Cameroon, each of the critiques above, as well as their counter-arguments, hold some merit and none alone present a complete picture of life in the Peace Corps. They do however provide certain tensions that RPCV educators *must* and *do* negotiate in various ways. A recurring tension seems to exist between the way RPCV educators' roles are envisioned and portrayed by others and the actual lived reality of the RPCV educators' experience. The ways in which RPCV educators negotiate this and other tensions are a prime concern of the current study.

Turning more specifically to the literature on RPCV educators, their experiences and insights have been catalogued in three main venues: through research on inner city/urban schools, through doctoral dissertations, and through newspaper and magazine articles (which were presented in the introduction). I begin with the research on inner city/urban schools. Immediately after the first groups of RPCV educators returned to the United States, they were assumed to possess certain attributes that made them especially qualified to teach in the inner city, namely, a "sense of commitment, desire to serve, flexibility, understanding and energy" (Daly, 1975, p. 385), as well as "knowledge of developing lands and peoples, their experience with different cultures, their adaptability to new and unfamiliar conditions, their skill in applying knowledge to practical problems" and the willingness to work in "undesirable" conditions (Ashabranner, 1968, p. 40). A more recent article makes a similar claim, suggesting RPCV educators' suitability for teaching in inner-city schools because they "have learned how to deal with the economics of scarcity" ("Peace Corp is Good Preparation for Teaching," 1993, p. 20). Ashabranner also saw similarities between teaching in Third World countries and teaching in inner cities. He wrote:

> The volunteer usually must function in classrooms plagued by overcrowding, insufficient and irrelevant textbooks, bad discipline, and negative attitudes stemming from his students' poor preparation, low physical stamina, and weak motivation. He encounters, in short, conditions strikingly similar to those in our own blighted inner-city schools: the nation's number one problem in education today. (p. 39)

In his research, Longsworth (1971) found, however, that there are differences in the teaching contexts, namely that the respect shown teachers in other countries is not necessarily the case in the American classroom (p. 87). And RPCV educators respond to the classroom management issues they face in U.S. schools in a number of ways, including scaling down their expectations of students, finding ways to remain flexible and innovative—even more so than in their Peace Corps classrooms—and quitting teaching altogether (Ashabranner, 1968, p. 41).

In spite of these challenges, RPCV educators have been recruited for at least two notable projects that focus on inner-city and urban education: The Cardozo Project in Urban Teaching and the Peace Corps Fellows/USA program. In 1963, the Cardozo Project sought to recruit 10 RPCVs to labor alongside social workers in developing curriculum at Cardozo High School in Washington, D.C. Their task was to develop "teaching techniques and teaching materials which are meaningful for culturally deprived children" as well as to "determine the kind of teacher-training best suited to urban high schools" ("Congress Told of Volunteer Problems, Too," 1963, p. 5). In a letter sent to potential RPCV candidates, the principal of the school wrote that the project would determine:

> whether two ingredients—a mostly Negro mid-city school in the center of a disadvantaged area of Washington, and the enthusiasm, creativity, and sense of social dedication which Peace Corps Volunteers have shown abroad—can be put together in a way which will light an intellectual fire and thereby perhaps begin a revolution in American urban education. (p. 5)

Later, the Cardozo Project began recruiting other types of teachers besides Peace Corps volunteers and the program eventually closed in 1968 (Daly, 1975, p. 385). Almost two decades later, the Peace Corps Fellows/USA program was started by former Peace Corps volunteer, Dr. Beryl Levinger, to recruit RPCV educators to work in the New York City school system in recognition of their "Innovative and practical ideas about education," their "Sensitivity to cultural differences" and their "Tenaciousness in adverse conditions" (Peace Corps, 2010c). Today, Peace Corps Fellows complete internships in "underserved American communities" in a variety of areas including: Education, Community/Economic development, Business Administration, Public Policy, Leadership, Environmental Affairs, and International Political Economy and Development (Peace Corps, 2010c).

While much of the research, as noted above, is focused on the RPCV educator as especially, if not magically, qualified for teaching in the inner-city or urban school, I think it is also important to understand how the RPCV educator might function in public schools in general. The need to work, perhaps more diligently, with suburban and rural teachers in exploring the curriculum from an intercultural perspective is also suggested by a report from the National Comprehensive Center for Teacher Quality and Public Agenda (Rochkind, Ott, Immerwahr, Doble, & Johnson, 2008). Through their phone interviews with 641 1st-year teachers, they found that in contrast to those teachers who plan to work in "high-needs schools," the teachers "headed for more suburban and working-class schools are just not prepared for the diversity they will find" (p. 12).

Scholarly dissertations have also provided insights into RPCV experiences with teaching and living abroad. A Peace Corps Wiki chronicling the "Dissertations Relating to Peace Corps" (2010) provides an index of 51 master's theses and/or doctoral dissertations written between 1964 and 2008. Nine of these dissertations relate to RPCV educators. Three of these dissertations are particularly relevant to the current study (Cross, 1998; Hammerschlag, 1996; Myers, 2001). In general, these dissertations examine RPCV educator's experiences teaching abroad and their effects on teaching at home, albeit in slightly different ways. While Cross (1998) looked at how the Peace Corps experience affected RPCV's personal and professional efficacy, Hammerschlag (1996) and Myers (2001) wanted to learn how RPCV educators incorporated their overseas experience in their teaching. While all of the studies found that the Peace Corps experience increases RPCV educators' intercultural awareness, Myers and Cross discovered that the effects of the Peace Corps experience were more profound on the teacher as an individual rather than on their teaching. At the same time, Hammerschlag noted that RPCV educators perceive a more direct connection between their experience and "how and what they teach" (p. 147). Cross, who was the only researcher to perform classroom observations, however, indicated that the increased intercultural awareness that RPCV educators spoke about during their interviews was not necessarily observable in their teaching. Additionally, the RPCVs in these studies are framed in uniformly positive and glowing terms as "gentle idealists, supporting forms of activism for human rights, and helping people help themselves to build a better future for themselves, their children, and families" (Myers, 2001, p. 21); as having "spirit," a "can-do attitude," and "the ability to triumph in the face of difficult school situations" (Cross, 1998, p. ii.); and as possessing the "traits of altruism, dedication, selflessness" and a willingness to "offer more time than they are paid," engendering jealousy and resentment among some of their host country counterparts (Hammerschlag, 1996, p. 51). Further, despite being labeled altruists, Myers discovered that the main reason the RPCV educators in her study joined the Peace Corps was "personal achievement and self-gain" (p. 201). In some ways this suggests that RPCV educators are shaped a great deal by the media images indicated in the critiques presented earlier in this section. Some might say that the uniformly positive portrayals of RPCVs, despite what their experiences reveal, point to a gap in intercultural awareness by providing a one-sided perspective and concealing the complicated nature of Peace Corps experiences. I suggest that exploring all facets of Peace Corps experience, both the seemingly "positive" and "negative" aspects, does not detract, but rather adds to that experience.

Culture Shock

In this section, I offer some of the ways in which culture shock has been conceptualized and defined, the causes of culture shock, the stages of, and emotional reactions to, culture shock, the limited research on teacher culture shock, and potential uses of culture shock in the curriculum. According to the literature, the term "culture shock" was initially used by Cora Du Bois in 1951 to describe the experiences of anthropologists working in the field, but it was another anthropologist, Kalervo Oberg, who later popularized the term and extended its use to include other groups working in foreign countries (La Brack, n.d.; Hart, 2005). In 1954, Oberg referred to culture shock as "a malady...an occupational disease of people who have been suddenly transplanted abroad" with its own "etiology, symptoms, and cure" (p. 1). Along these lines, some have suggested that culture shock is similar to some forms of mental illness (Kron & Faber, 1973; Weaver in Hart, 2005). This categorization seems to focus on the "negative" emotional reactions associated with culture shock. Others, however, tend to emphasize the positive outcomes of culture shock as a "learning experience" (Sitton, 1976) leading to "a state of high self- and cultural awareness" (Adler, 1976). Still, others point out that self- and cultural awareness are not necessarily givens, that "emotional...stagnation" (Garza-Guerrero, 1974), or the development of negative stereotypes of other cultures may result (David, 1971). Taking these perspectives together, perhaps it is safe to say that there are both negative and positive aspects of culture shock, the experience of which holds at least the *potential* for learning and growth.

The most common causes of culture shock for the sojourner in the foreign culture are a loss of familiar cues such as words, gestures, customs, and beliefs (David, 1971; Kron & Faber, 1973; Oberg, 1954); the enormous loss of "love objects" such as family, friends, language, music, and food (Garza-Guerrero, 1974, p. 410); a lack of understanding of other cultures as well as a means to fully communicate within those cultures (Oberg, 1954); and ethnocentrism (Oberg, 1954; Sitton, 1976), which Oberg defined as the "belief that not only the culture but the race and the nation are the center of the world" (p. 6). The literature also suggests additional causes that compound the experience of culture shock for Americans, such as the middle-class focus on "practical and utilitarian values" and "work as a means to personal success" (Oberg, 1954, p. 7) rather than relating success to the interrelationships of race, power, and social status, leading to the belief that Americans are "culture-free" (Adler, 1976; Stillar, 2007) products of their own individuality, and therefore able to "adjust to anything" (Adler, 1976, p. 21). In reviewing these causes, it seems that culture shock involves the realization that one's own meaning and value systems are not shared universally. They also suggest that the experience may be especially difficult for sojourners who do not consider their values and beliefs as culturally derived.

A good deal of the literature also focuses on the stages of, and emotional reactions to, culture shock. Zapf (1991) identified 19 examples of stage models from 1954 to 1985 (p. 108) and his is not an exhaustive list. Although each model uses different terms for each stage, they tend to follow a similar four-stage model expressed by Oberg (1954), with an initial Honeymoon stage characterized by a superficial fascination with the new culture (p. 2); a second Crisis stage when the newness wears off and physical and/or emotional discomfort sets in (p. 3); a third Recovery stage in which the sojourner begins to adapt linguistically and culturally to the new environment (pp. 3–4); and a final Adjustment stage in which the sojourner accepts and enjoys the new culture as "just another way of living" (p. 4). And within these stages, the research lists a number of variable emotional reactions to culture shock, including some that are considered "negative," such as frustration, anxiety, depression, anger, helplessness, fears of being cheated, contaminated, or disregarded, and a strong desire to return to the home culture (Adler, 1976; David, 1971; Oberg, 1954), and some that are "positive," such as excitement, fascination, creativity, a sense of challenge, stimulation, enthusiasm, and confidence (Zapf, 1991).

While it is important to be aware of the stages of, and responses to, culture shock as points of reference, Garza-Guerrero (1974) and La Brack (n.d.) suggested that the models may be too simplistic and too linear in their focus. For example, La Brack wrote that these models

> did not capture either the apparent "messiness" and unpredictability of the process, nor did they account for cases where it appeared that the stages did not occur in order, were frequently repeated, seemed compressed or blended, or were absent altogether. In that culture shock may or may not occur in stages with or without accompanying emotional responses, the research suggests the need to approach culture shock as perhaps a predictable occurrence, yet one that has contextual and individual implications which cannot be predicted in advance.

One might conceivably ask at this point how the study of culture shock relates to teaching and how it may be utilized for educational purposes. Kron and Faber (1973) believed that the "great increase in student and teacher mobility" (p. 507) is cause for examining student/teacher relationships in terms of culture shock. They further argued that teacher performance is "adversely affected by culture shock" and that students also "suffer if the teacher's reaction to culture shock is highlighted by anxiety, frustration, self-doubt, shouting, fear, and other disabling symptoms common to the phenomenon" (p. 507). In the time following Kron and Faber's article, little (if any) research has dealt explicitly with teacher culture shock within public education, even though the statistics presented in the opening of that paper indicate heightened student mobility leading to teacher anxiety over cultural differences. For teachers in teach-abroad programs, culture shock was alternately mentioned in negative terms by Cushner and Mahon (2002), in positive terms as a form of "dissonance" by Tang and Choi (2004), while a third study found the interplay of both "consonance" and "dissonance" equally meaningful in shaping teachers' experiences (Brindley, Quinn, & Morton, 2009). I expected to read more detailed accounts of culture shock in the Peace Corps dissertations I reviewed earlier, however, culture shock was offered almost in passing, and there was no real attempt to link culture shock to the myriad experiences and perspective shifts their participants recounted. It is possible that the label "culture shock" may have negative or painful connotations that conflict with the positive image of the Peace Corps, but while I agree that the experience of culture shock may be a painful one, it need not be disabling. I share Adler's (1976) assertion that culture shock is at once a "form of alienation" as well as symbolic of the "attempt to comprehend, survive in, and grow through immersion in a second culture" (p. 14). In short, the so-called disabling aspects of culture shock listed above appear to be an integral part of the process of developing a sense of self and intercultural awareness. The trick is in utilizing the "negative" aspects of culture shock to stimulate learning and growth.

In considering how a notion of culture shock may be invited into curriculum in a broad sense, I draw on the literature that brings together the theoretical (Adler, 1976), practical (Sitton, 1976; David, 1971), analytical (Archer, 1986), and metaphorical/spiritual (Hart, 2005) aspects of culture shock. From a theoretical perspective, Adler considered culture shock as a transitional experience indicative of a shift from low to high personal and cultural awareness. Unlike the models that view culture shock as a sickness to be cured, Adler believed that the final stage of culture shock "is a state of dynamic tension in which self and cultural discoveries have opened up the possibility of other depth experiences" (p. 18). In order to understand culture shock as a transitional experience, Adler made the following four assumptions: Each person experiences the world through culturally prescribed values, assumptions, and beliefs; most people are unaware of their values, beliefs, and attitudes, and movement into new environments and new experiences "tend to bring cultural perceptions and predispositions into perception and conflict"; through the resulting "psychological, social, or cultural tension, each person is forced into redefinition of some level of his/her existence"; and "The reorientation of personality at higher levels of consciousness and psychic integration is based upon the disintegrative aspects of personality" (pp. 14–15). For the teacher, this implies developing an awareness of, and ability to separate, one's culturally nominated and personally modified values, assumptions, and beliefs with regard to cultural differences. It also suggests tolerating and exploring the tensions that such a realization may produce, recognizing all the while that before growth, a certain sense of disintegration and disorientation must be experienced. These are certainly no easy tasks, especially since there is what I perceive to be an American cultural value on avoiding and/or escaping the state of dynamic tension that is key to Adler's theory.

Focusing more specifically on classroom practice, Sitton (1976) argued that culture shock has largely been ignored in schools. He suggested taking an interdisciplinary anthropological approach to curriculum that focuses on cultural differences despite his notion that a "melting pot dogma, along with the fear of controversy and lack of teacher preparation, has worked to keep curriculum and methods designed to teach about cultural difference out of the classroom" (p. 207). According to Sitton, a foreign culture (or subculture) may act as a "necessary other" providing the "supreme pedagogic strategy for studying one's own culture and oneself" (p. 209). Within his intercultural curriculum, the primary role of the teacher becomes that of cultural "learner" and only secondarily that of change agent (p. 209). While Sitton urged the study of "whole cultures" through ethnographic accounts, especially in the Social Studies classroom, he did not indicate clearly how the *experience* of culture shock may be brought into the classroom. In that culture shock may be considered a form of experiential learning, David (1971) believed that the "extremeness of the experience seems to be important in developing self-awareness" because it "takes a severe jolt for many of us to overcome our complacent acceptance of culturally determined behaviors" (p. 47). While I appreciate Sitton's emphasis on cultural differences, the role of the teacher as cultural explorer, and the self-awareness that culture shock may inspire, I am also concerned that cultures may be presented as simplistic, static, unchanging and that their study at such a level may not advance the learner beyond the Honeymoon stage. I also wonder if the RPCV educator can take on the role of "necessary other" in order to create the culture shock needed to inspire self and cultural awareness, not only abroad where they are necessarily the Other, but also at home, where they may be expected to support the status quo.

From an analytical perspective, Archer (1986) discussed a self-reflective process for teachers to use in analyzing what she called "culture bumps" in the classroom. She said that "A culture bump occurs when an individual from one culture finds himself or herself in a different, strange or uncomfortable situation when interacting with persons of a different culture" (pp. 170–171). She believed that in recognizing and depersonalizing the uncomfortable encounter with cultural differences in the classroom, the teacher may use the discomfort to open dialogue with the self and with students in order to explore differences at an emotionally safer cultural level. Archer's (1986) process asks teachers to:

1. Pinpoint some time when they felt "different" or noticed something different when they were with someone from another culture.
2. Define the situation.
3. List the behaviors of the other person.
4. List their own behavior.
5. List their feelings in the situation.
6. List the behaviors they expect from people in their own culture in that same situation.
7. Reflect on the underlying value in their culture that prompts the behavior expectation. (pp. 171–172)

From my perspective, Archer's reflective process is a non-threatening and non-violent method for exploring cultural differences in the self, the classroom, and the curriculum. It also points to the role of underlying cultural expectations as a factor leading to culture shock. The questions she posed may also be useful for analyzing my own participants' experiences with culture shock in their classrooms.

And, lastly, I note a metaphorical/spiritual approach to culture shock in Hart's (2005) linking of the stages of culture shock and reverse culture shock to Campbell's study of the "hero's journey" in ancient mythology. In using the metaphor of the hero's journey, Hart opened a pathway for understanding culture shock and reverse culture shock in a way that resonates, at least in Jungian terms, deep within the psyche. The myth of the hero's journey spans many cultures and is readily accessible in popular literature and media. It involves an otherwise ordinary person leaving home, facing seemingly insurmountable challenges, completing some type of heroic task, and returning home with new-found wisdom. Some examples of the hero's journey in American film culture can be found in the *Star Wars* series, the *Alien(s)* series, the movie *Avatar*, and certainly all of the comic book hero film series. The myth of the hero's journey also appears in the ancient stories of spiritual teachers—Jesus, Buddha, Lao Tzu, and many others. These spiritual stories seem to form the basis from which current hero's journey myths are drawn. I would also argue that it is the myth of the hero's journey that underscores the Peace Corps ideology and experience.

With regard to culture shock, I note that in Hart's (2005) schematic the "Ultimate Ordeal" in the hero's journey is related to the "Crisis" stage in culture shock. According to Hart it is through this stage that the hero "gains enlightenment through her actions" and is thus transformed. I think it is also interesting that through this process, the hero learns to walk in "both worlds," which may complicate her life once she returns home. In fact, as Hart noted, "Sometimes the hero returns and her world does not want what she brings" (2005). I feel the significance of this work is to point out the spiritual aspects of culture shock in a way that is easily accessible to teachers and students due to the proliferation of hero's journey myths in the popular media of many cultures. I wonder too if the participants in my study drew upon their own myths and metaphors in order to understand their Peace Corps teaching experience.

Reverse Culture Shock

Unlike culture shock, reverse culture shock (also called reentry shock) appears to be somewhat ignored and under-theorized in the literature even though many consider it to be more challenging than the experience of culture shock (Anjarwalla, 2010; La Brack, 1985; Miller, 1988; Sussman, 1986; Szkudlarek, 2009; Weaver, n.d.). For example, La Brack (1985) believed that reverse culture shock is under-theorized because it is not seen as a problem, and in some "conservative and hierarchical societies" reverse culture shock is a sign of "disloyalty, subversion, or even mental incompetence" (p. 16).

I think it is also possible that some consider reverse culture shock simply a mirror image or extension of culture shock and therefore it needs no further theoretical underpinning. However, the research suggests that while the emotional reactions to culture shock and reverse culture shock may be similar, the causes are somewhat different. Therefore, I begin by reviewing some of the causes and emotional responses to reverse culture shock, followed by a review of the scant literature on teacher reverse culture shock.

One of the most frequently cited causes of reverse culture shock appears to be its unexpectedness and consequently the sojourner's lack of preparedness for the experience (Anjarwalla, 2010; La Brack, 1985; Miller, 1988; Sussman, 1986; Szkudlarek, 2009; Weaver, n.d.). That returnees do not expect to experience reverse culture shock is due to a number of reasons. One reason is the way in which the notion of "home" has been idealized. La Brack (1985) said thoughts of "going home" seem to "conjure up images of warmth, acceptance, familiarity, scenes of reuniting, and leave no room for negativity or ambiguity" (p. 4). Returnees may also be unaware of the changes in themselves and their home culture that occurred while they were abroad (Sussman, 1986) and fail to consider that their "self-system and the former social system" have been progressing along "divergent paths" (Jansson, 1975, p. 136). Returnees also expect the people in the home culture to be understanding and supportive, yet may find that friends, family, and colleagues lack interest in their experiences abroad and may expect the returnee to act "normal" (Sussman, 1986). Family and friends may also show little empathy for the difficulties returnees face upon their return (Weaver, n.d.) or view the returnee's problems as being due to a willful "refusal to act 'normal' and 'fit in'" (La Brack, 1985). The returnee may be labeled as a "deviant" (Jansson, 1975; La Brack, 1985) and as a "minority" as "defined by those who remained in the group" (Jansson, 1975, p. 137). Adler (1981) added that xenophobia, or the lack of understanding of and appreciation of foreigners and foreign experience, also plays a negative role in the way returnee's workplace effectiveness is rated.

In addition, Weaver (n.d.) believed the underlying cause for the difficulties related to reverse culture shock appears to be a breakdown in interpersonal communication. He wrote:

> When people communicate, they send messages not meanings. The meanings are in their heads, and the messages merely express them...what would be a message to one person may have no meaning whatsoever to another. Of course, most people assume everyone else pays attention to the same messages they do and that everyone gives the messages the same meaning. (p. 3)

This research points to the seemingly overwhelming mismatch in expectations on behalf of both the returnee and those in the home culture as a major cause of reverse culture shock. Chief among these expectations appears to be the belief that meanings are shared, perhaps due to the illusion that neither the sojourner nor the home culture has changed. The research also points to the home culture's considerable attempts to divest the returnee of their hard-won, newly acquired "deviant" identity. It is the RPCV educator's struggle with the home culture's attempts to redefine them and the ways in which they communicate and obfuscate their deviant identity in their teaching that helps shape the current study.

Some of the emotional responses to reverse culture shock include: euphoria, anger, a sense of powerlessness, a fear of rejection, guilt, pain, a sense of being out of control, frustration, aggression, hopelessness, helplessness, disillusionment, increased sleep, avoidance of others, and a denial of the impact of reverse culture shock (Jansson, 1975; Weaver, n.d.). Weaver (n.d.) also offered that "The increased global-mindedness of returnees is sometimes accompanied by increased intolerance of parochialism on the part of those at home" (p. 8). But, as with culture shock, it is difficult to predict how the returnee will respond or make meaning in any specific context. While the research here paints a somewhat negative experience of reverse culture shock, the opposite is also possible, and more likely there is a mix of both positive and negative experiences that accompany reverse culture shock.

Despite La Brack's (1985) contention that as a stressful transitional experience, reverse culture shock can, like culture shock, be a valuable learning experience (p. 11), I could find no explicit attempt to explore its utility in the public school curriculum. Perhaps this is due to the stigma surrounding reverse culture shock that La Brack hinted at in the opening of this section, or perhaps it's because of the lack of teachers who experience reverse culture shock. For this review, I located only one autobiographical example of teacher reentry (Miller, 1988), but the teacher apparently did not go back to classroom teaching upon her return, so it is not clear how her experience of reverse culture shock may have affected her teaching at home. Still, her experiences and insights are valuable in preparation for the current study.

Miller's (1988) experiences of reverse culture shock tend to confirm the research presented above. She was unprepared for the force of the reverse culture shock she experienced and felt unable to adequately communicate her experiences teaching abroad, especially to friends, who seemed to lack interest in her experiences and simply wanted her to be the same person that she was before.

Issues surrounding food and shopping seem to be especially shocking. She spoke of the shock she felt regarding overinflated prices, waste, and excess, and the occurrence of obesity among so many young people. These perceptions are similar to those of RPCVs who indicated in U.S. Peace Corps & Graul (in Szkudlarek, 2009) that some of the most challenging aspects of reverse culture shock were "materialism, waste of goods, indifference of home country citizens, and the fast pace of living" (p. 11). Additionally, Miller felt "paralyzed" by having so many choices in her market and "immoral" after eating a meal in a restaurant equal to six weeks' salary for a teacher in her host country (p. 15). She also indicated that as a woman who left her 51-year-old husband and two children (who live away from home) to teach for a year abroad, she was criticized particularly harshly. Although painful, Miller's experiences with reverse culture shock also enable her to challenge some of her cultural beliefs:

> Many basic American cultural assumptions make no sense to me. I do not believe that more is better, that it is wise to borrow now and pay later (or never), or that history has no place in current affairs. I believe that it is socially destructive to pursue policies geared to short-sighted monthly balance and to brazen competitiveness. (p. 21)

Despite the overwhelming cultural force to negate her overseas experience, she refused to reject her experience as "non-transferable" (p. 22). To overcome her feelings of helplessness, she seeks out the company of others who have taught in her host country, keeps contact with friends in her host country, continues to study and practice the art form that she learned in her host country and helps prepare other teachers to teach abroad. Spending time with others who share both experiences teaching abroad and reverse culture shock at home has enabled her to laugh at other "peoples' insensitivity and superficial questions" (p. 23) and led her to characterize American life as focused on "Emotionalism," "Expense," and "Ego" (p. 24).

Miller's (1988) narrative evokes her struggle to maintain her double consciousness while her home culture seems indifferent to this heightened awareness and in some ways seems intent on negating it. I think it is important to note, however, that her initial feelings of shock and paralysis caused her to reflect on her intercultural beliefs and challenged her to develop a creative synthesis of both her foreign and home cultures in her personal life. Yet, missing from her story are the ways in which her experience of reverse culture shock and the resulting insights affected her classroom teaching, a gap I hope to address in the current study.

· 2 ·

TOWARD A PEDAGOGY OF CREATIVITY AND CARING

Introduction

Joe was a 58-year-old Hispanic male teaching sophomore English at the time of my interviews with him. Joe had also taught speech at an inner-city high school for 1 year and then speech and journalism at another high school for 5 years prior to joining the Peace Corps. During his Peace Corps service, Joe taught English as a foreign language at a university in an urban city in the Eastern European country of Moldova from 2006 to 2008. I met Joe at his home on a hot and dry sunny summer morning. Outside, cotton-candy clouds filled the wide blue sky. Inside, we sat face to face with a small table between us in front of two large open windows at the front of his house. As we talked, the curtains floated up from time to time thanks to a gentle breeze, and as they moved back and forth, they sounded like soft ocean waves lapping the seashore. During the interview there were also birds chirping, a mourning dove cooing, and cicadas intermittently stopping and starting their engines. It was as if nature were providing both an audience and background music for our interview. Later we also took a short tour of the town where Joe lived and continued our interview at the high school where he taught.

One of the first things I noticed about Joe was that he wore a small golden cross earring. During the interview, Joe referred to the earring as being part of his Christian identity. He noted, "I wear this earring because I'm a Christian....I'm letting people know this is who I believe in." When I asked him what the Moldovans he encountered thought about his earring, he said they "hated it" because they saw it as "sacrilegious." Our brief discussion about the meaning of Joe's earring reminded me of a time when I bought a large wooden carved statue of Ganesha, a Hindu god in the form of an elephant, while I was in India to attend a friend's wedding. Upon my return to the U.S., I moved the statue around my house trying to find the perfect spot for it, ultimately deciding it looked best in my guest bathroom. When my Indian friends saw the statue in the bathroom, they were, well, horrified. A god in the bathroom with a toilet!? I ultimately gave the statue to them as a belated wedding present because I realized that while for me the statue was a beautiful work of art, for them, it was a living deity. That these religious objects—the golden cross earring and the Ganesha statue—held different meanings from different cultural perspectives, raises issues of negotiating meaning across cultural boundaries. Who "owns" the meaning of an object? How does one show dis/respect for such objects? Can different meanings co-exist? To what extent am I willing to hold fast to my meaning? As borders open and boundaries shift, these questions become more relevant. Perhaps an important first step in contemplating these questions lies in realizing that other perspectives exist to begin with.

Although Joe addressed a number of themes in his stories, he seemed to continually return to the notion of care—especially how his Peace Corps experiences made him a more caring person and educator. He also emphasized the need to teach students how to be creative, so I have titled his chapter *Toward a Pedagogy of Creativity and Caring*. For Joe's chapter, I have included one culture shock story, two identity shift stories, one reverse culture shock story, and a final story about his pedagogy. The first story deals with the culture shock Joe experienced while attempting to learn the languages of Moldova. In the first reading of the story, Joe shared his feelings of vulnerability and sense of danger involved in learning a new language and negotiating a different culture. In re-reading the story I look at the ways in which vulnerability may be considered a strength and how danger might be useful. In the Identity Shift I story, Joe shares an experience in which he discovers a woman who had committed suicide outside his apartment building in Moldova and how uncaring the other Moldovans were with regard to the woman's death. He also talks about the Moldovan's acceptance of their domination by others and how healing this acceptance was for him. I read this story in terms of acceptance as a lack of resistance and as a form of healing. In re-reading the story, I find that acceptance can actually be a form of resistance but that it is not necessarily healing. In the Reverse Culture Shock story, Joe talks about how his return to the U.S. made him realize how uncaring and materialistic Americans are. Through his Peace Corps experiences, Joe explains how he became less materialistic and more caring and how he refused to "play the game." In re-reading this story I look at the concept of "postmaterialism" and how one may "play the game differently." In the fourth story, Identity Shift II, Joe discusses how he took on a new Moldovan identity and became more caring, which he related to self-sacrifice. In re-reading the story, I question the notion of taking on a completely new identity and look at caring in terms of self-gain. In the fifth and final story related to Joe's pedagogy, he explains how teaching in Moldova, where rote learning was the standard pedagogy, highlighted the need to teach his students (both in Moldova and the U.S.) how to be creative. Through my re-reading, I find that rote learning can be a form of so-called "meaningful" learning and that creativity is not necessarily a positive value.

Culture Shock I: Intercultural Experience as Vulnerability and Danger

Despite his craving for adventure and excitement, Joe thought it was "strange" that he was sent to teach English in Moldova, given that he was fluent in Spanish. He had assumed that he would be posted in a Spanish-speaking country and would not need to learn a new language. He also felt he could have "done so much more" as a teacher in a Spanish-speaking country because he understood the language and the culture. Nonetheless, he accepted his Peace Corps assignment, but his difficulty in learning the languages in Moldova (Romanian and Russian) was an ongoing source of culture shock for Joe.

Ironically, it was because he was often surrounded by so many people that spoke English (his Moldovan English teaching counterparts, his language tutor that followed him everywhere and translated for him, his homestay mother and sister who had studied in the U.S., etc.) that it was "so horrible" to be "alone" when attempting to communicate with Moldovans who did not speak English. Joe said that "Language is such an indicator of who you are" that he felt "extremely vulnerable" because he couldn't learn Romanian as quickly as he wanted to. He said that in the beginning he was only able to use the "most basic of words," like a "small child," and that he talked "like a baby," which was a "very humiliating experience."

When I asked him to describe a time when this difficulty with language made him uncomfortable, he stated emphatically, "if you're asking me was I uncomfortable, my God, I was uncomfortable all the time, unless I was in the classroom teaching." He said that in the classroom, if one of the students was having difficulty understanding him, the other students would happily assist by translating in Romanian. He also elaborated that he felt "inadequate" in his ability to learn the language and said that "the whole experience there was sort of like walking on ice…you didn't know when you were going to give way because…you weren't prepared." He added that "not knowing how to communicate is the worst damn thing you can have…it stopped me from doing a lot of things that I would've liked to do because I didn't know…how to speak to people."

Joe also shared a story about a time in which his difficulty with language added to his sense of culture shock. It was during his first commute to the capital city where, as part of his training, he was to participate in a practice school at a prestigious university. He explained that his language skills at the time were very basic, and that although he was "honored" and "excited" to teach at the university, he simultaneously felt "nervous to break away from the group [of other Peace Corps volunteers] and the comfort they gave in familiarity." As he waited for the "rutiera" (a 16-passenger van used for public transport) to arrive, he noted that the villagers were "staring" at him. Once inside the van, people filled both the seats and the aisles to the point that he "was pressed by people on all sides," which made him "uncomfortable" due to the lack of "personal space."

Joe only had a large bill to pay for the trip and he passed it forward with the assistance of the other passengers, but he didn't receive any change back and didn't know how to ask for it. During their first stop, Joe decided to confront the driver in his "best broken Romanian" but to no avail. He felt angry that the driver was ignoring him and trying to cheat him by pretending he didn't know what Joe was saying. He recalled, "I was at a loss. I kept thinking, 'Why in the hell did I come here?' The people seemed so rude and uncaring. I was fuming and I felt so helpless. It was the helplessness that made it so unbearable."

Fortunately for Joe, several of the women from his village began to yell excitedly at the driver, and the driver, giving a sheepish grin, finally returned Joe's change. Joe felt "overwhelmed with gratitude" to the women, especially since they really didn't know him, or anything about him, except that perhaps he lived in their village. He felt equally "helpless" in trying to express the depth of his gratitude so he simply said "thank you" in Romanian. Satisfied that he had finally gotten his change, he waited quietly for the van to depart. But a few minutes later, the van driver announced that he would not be driving them on into the capital. Joe watched as the other passengers quietly left the vehicle and began looking for an alternative van. He said he was "blown away with the fact that [the van driver] just quit driving us. The people there just accepted his decision without even a grumble."

Once Joe finally arrived at the university, he used his experience as a discussion topic with his students. He wrote, "We had a great time getting to know each other based on the hardships of travel in a developing nation." He also thought about the women in the van. He reflected that "in the hustle and bustle of getting [to the university], I suddenly realized the women of my village and how much it meant to me. It was heroic efforts like theirs that helped me to decide to stay there."

In this narrative, Joe experienced some of the classic symptoms of culture shock (Oberg, 1954; David, 1971; Adler, 1976) including feeling "nervous" about leaving the comfort and familiarity of the other American Peace Corps volunteers, feeling "helpless" and angry about being cheated and not being able to communicate well, feeling "uncomfortable" due to being stared at as well as the lack of personal space, feeling "surprise" at the other passengers' response to the driver's decision to quit driving them in the middle of their trip, and, ultimately, questioning why he chose to be in Moldova in the first place. I was also struck by Joe's feelings of vulnerability. According to Straub (2009), vulnerability is a part of the intercultural experience and is linked to the threat to one's identity. He wrote,

> Those who open up towards the Other and the Strange in certain ways compromise the Self...allowing the appearance of "weakness," of vulnerability and mutability to encourage fellow humans in a way scarcely controllable to intrude upon, and interfere with the Self. (p. 220)

In "opening up towards" Moldovan culture through language learning and social interaction, Joe expressed both his vulnerability and the threat to his identity when he described feeling like a "small child," "talking like a baby," and feelings of unbearable "helplessness." Small children and babies are especially vulnerable and dependent on others. Thinking of himself as both helpless and dependent challenged Joe's notion of himself as an independent adult, which in turn made him feel "humiliated."

Joe's simile/metaphor of his intercultural experience as "like walking on ice" also spoke to his vulnerability. When someone is "vulnerable," they are "capable of being physically or emotionally wounded" ("Vulnerable," 2012). Similarly, in "walking on ice," there is always the threat of slipping, falling down, and getting hurt. Joe's metaphor seems to express Joe's underlying belief that intercultural experience can be dangerous. In describing his "whole experience" as "like walking on ice" because "you didn't know when you were going to give way," Joe also implied that the danger was ever present and could occur in ways that were "scarcely controllable" as alluded to in the quote above.

Re-reading Culture Shock I: Vulnerability as Strength and Danger as Useful

Joe's intercultural experience seemed to draw out his feelings of vulnerability that he perceived in a negative light. However, some research has linked vulnerability to the development of emotional growth through the experience of stressful or traumatic experiences (Murphy & Moriarity, 1976; Updegraff & Taylor, 2000). Jordan (2008) shared the view that vulnerability holds the potential for "real growth" (p. 198), and she challenged dominant views of vulnerability as weakness. She wrote,

> Models of strength, both in our psychological theories and in culture at large, emphasize strength in separation, supremacy of thought over feeling, objectification, and instrumentality....While this is supposedly a model of strength, it basically rests on a fear-based model that denies vulnerability. (p. 193)

Instead, she argued that in recognizing, "respecting," and "supporting" (p. 198) our own and others' vulnerability (but not over-valorizing it) one moves "toward empathy, true connection, and toward a model of deep human caring" (p. 190), an approach that she calls "*strength in vulnerability*" or "*supported vulnerability*" (p. 194). I agree with Jordan's suggestion that acknowledging one's vulnerability enables relating to both self and others in a different way. For example, in their study of vulnerability in the medical profession, Malterud and Hollnagel (2005) found that when doctors, who were often viewed as "omnipotent, detached, and impersonal," shared their own feelings and experiences of vulnerability with their patients, their patients "appreciated" this sharing and found it to be "beneficial" to their own treatment (p. 348). In re-examining Joe's story through the lenses of relation and connection, I found that while Joe's vulnerability drew out a manipulative response from the bus driver, it also enabled the other passengers to demonstrate their caring and sympathy for Joe. This shifted Joe's perception of Moldovans (at least some) from "uncaring" to "heroic," which in turn encouraged him to stay in the country. Likewise, in sharing his vulnerability with his students after he arrived at the university, he was able to make a connection with them.

Jordan (2008) also argued that there is a gendered element to Western beliefs on vulnerability and strength that shapes and distorts gender differences. She quoted Miller, who stated that "In Western society men are encouraged to dread, abhor or deny feeling weak or helpless, whereas women are encouraged to cultivate this state of being" (p. 193). It is possible that Joe's perception of his own vulnerability was cultured and gendered and heightened his experience of culture shock. I especially noted the way that Joe said it was his "helplessness that made it so unbearable." I would also point out that it was specifically the *women* in the van who, despite not sharing a common language or cultural ties with Joe, appeared to acknowledge and respond to Joe's vulnerable position.

Part of Joe's experience of vulnerability was also expressed in his metaphor "walking on ice." With regard to this metaphor, I note the underlying belief that intercultural experience is dangerous. While I had the distinct impression that, for Joe, the feelings of danger were negative, I consider the ways in which the notion of danger may be useful or helpful in intercultural experience. Foucault once argued that "everything is dangerous, which is not exactly the same as bad. If everything is dangerous, then we always have something to do" (In Butin, 2001, p. 173). In viewing everything as dangerous, Foucault suggested that there are no definite solutions or final conclusions in the social world and that social relationships are unstable and shifting. This makes labeling the behaviors, the meanings, and the motives of others problematic. Through Joe's experience (in this and in other stories), Joe's labeling of Moldovan culture shifted a number of times between caring and uncaring, making any final conclusion about the culture as being one or the other impossible. Viewing everything as dangerous, in a sense, calls for staying attentive and attuned to these shifts and being careful in relationships with intercultural others not to confine them within stereotypical labels.

In re-reading Joe's metaphor "walking on ice," I also used Koro-Ljunberg's (2004) post-structural metaphor analysis technique to locate alternative meanings within the metaphor. Two alternate meanings within Joe's metaphor that come to mind are "Intercultural Experience as Learning to Ice Skate" and "Intercultural Experience as Un/Preparedness." While for Joe, falling was seen as hurtful and as a failure to be "prepared," in "Learning to Ice Skate," falling down and feeling pain are parts of the learning process. Getting back up and moving past the fear of falling are parts of the process as well. For me, it seemed that it was Joe's fear of falling that shaped his intercultural experience, especially in learning and using a new language. He noted feelings of inadequacy and helplessness when attempting to communicate with Moldovans in general, which in turn "stopped" him from interacting with them at times.

Additionally, when learning a new skill, such as learning how to navigate a new culture, it seems unlikely that one could be prepared in all circumstances. In a way, it was Joe's expectation that he could or should have been prepared that created his feelings of failure. He also implied that if he had prepared for the culture shock, he would not have felt the negative emotions so strongly. In considering "Intercultural Experience as Un/Preparedness," I argue that while it may not be possible to escape the tension, the discomfort, and the surprise of the culture shock, one can learn to accept that one cannot entirely prepare for or know the other culture. One can also learn to recognize and tolerate the discomfort inherent in the shock and find ways to negotiate unshared meaning with intercultural "others." While Joe was unable to communicate well in Romanian, the context, and Joe's verbal and non-verbal responses in the situation, apparently spoke volumes to the other passengers who came to his aid.

In brief, "walking on ice" in an intercultural sense almost certainly involves slowing down at times and taking small steps toward understanding. It also involves taking risks and perhaps falling down. While the thought of failure may heighten the sense of anxiety and feelings of danger, it may also lead to mutual understanding through a shared sense of vulnerability for which few words are needed.

Identity Shift I: Acceptance as Healing and a Lack of Resistance

In this story, Joe makes a cultural and historical leap back to his roots in the United States during the Civil Rights Movement, when both he and his family fought for recognition of Hispanic American culture and history. According to Joe, by witnessing the way in which Moldovans responded to Russian domination he was able to view his own struggles with Anglo American culture from a different perspective. The story began in Moldova just as Joe left his apartment building on his way to work. He was startled to see a dead woman lying on the pavement in front of him. Apparently, the woman had committed suicide a few moments earlier by jumping from an upper floor of his building. From the policemen that showed up on the scene who were very "rough" with her body, to the Moldovan friends who implied she was just some lady "who liked to drink," once again, he was left with the feeling that Moldovans were "uncaring." He clarified that

> it wasn't as though they were mean I think that they kind of expected that people would do this. That's the cultural part that got to me. I think they expected it was natural for people to take their life because it was kind of meaningless.

He explained further that when Moldova was under Russian rule, everything was provided for them—housing, education, jobs—but that since the Iron Curtain fell, the Moldovans were suddenly left to fend for themselves.

According to Joe, this put quite a bit of power into the hands of shopkeepers, apartment managers, and administrators, who would do things like shut the heat off for an entire apartment building if one person didn't pay their bill, refuse to pay people their salaries (teachers included), or kick people out of their apartments at will. What Joe found odd was the Moldovans' response in the face of this power. He says, "They were very accepting you know...they'd say, 'Oh, you know, they told us we just lost our apartment. Why? Cause they said so!' [Chuckles], just like that you know...it was that kind of attitude that left me feeling uncomfortable about the people."

As Joe reflected how unfairly the Moldovans were treated he began to make the connection to how he was treated in the United States during his youth. He explained that just as the Russians dominated the Moldovans, the "Anglos" likewise dominated the "Hispanics" in the United States. He talked about both his and his family's struggles during the Civil Rights Movement and afterward to have Hispanic history and rights recognized by his home state. He said that his life had been threatened and that his family received flack, not only from whites but also from Hispanics who did not want them to "stir it up because it causes more problems." He also recalled that he was often told to go back to Mexico, which seemed insulting because his family could trace its roots within the United States back to the 15th–16th century. Joe said he was making this connection "to two places" (Moldova and the U.S.),

> to give you the idea that being in Moldova made me realize that the anger that I have for having lived that was not specific to me, that it happens all over the world. And I think that was very good for me, because it was very healing that to know that it isn't that Anglos were mean or anything it's just that whoever wins controls the game. And, so even at my older age, it was very healing to understand that I shouldn't take it so personally—isn't that weird? [Laughs]

Joe's narrative reminded me of a Buddhist story about a girl named Kisagotami. While many versions of the story exist, I first came across it in Aoki's (2005) *Curriculum in a New Key*. It is the story of a young mother named Kisagotami who became mentally distraught over the death of her child. After frantically searching for someone who could revive her dead child, Kisagotami was referred to the Buddha, who agreed to heal the child if she could bring him some mustard seeds from a house in which death had not visited. After travelling from door to door she slowly began to realize that there was no house where death had not arrived in some form or fashion. Upon this realization, "her mind cleared" (p. 409). In a similar vein, Joe said it was "healing" to realize that his suffering was not personal, but rather a product of power relations in general that affected many people around the world, not just him. I should point out that while death is a natural part of life and social injustice is not, the Buddhist story seemed to capture Joe's sentiment of healing through the recognition of the suffering of others in similar circumstances.

Through his experiences in Moldova, Joe also seemed to come to the realization that another response to domination was possible. While Joe and his family fought for their rights and endured both insults and death threats, the Moldovans accepted their situation rather than confront or try to change the system. It was this acceptance that made Joe "uncomfortable" about the Moldovans because Joe had not previously seen acceptance as a viable option in the United States. Yet, by observing a different response to domination—acceptance rather than conflict—a space for re-thinking his own response over what had happened to him in the past was opened up. Joe's story also suggested that learning new responses to strong emotions also makes it possible to shift one's identity and/or worldview.

Re-reading Identity Shift I: Acceptance as Resistance and Not Healing

One of the tensions that emerged through Joe's experience with culture shock was the tension between his and the Moldovans' response to what Joe referred to as "domination." In the stories that Joe told, he had been more confrontational in the United States, whereas he felt that the Moldovans were more accepting. While Joe did not offer a clear definition of what he meant by the Moldovans' acceptance, the examples he used implied their lack of confrontation, resistance, or emotional response to being dominated by others. Essentially, what Joe described was the Moldovans' "passive acceptance," in the sense that they decided to "go with the flow" because "nothing can be done about the situation" (Morgan, 2009). For Joe, the tension between the two responses was at first disconcerting, but later he found that the Moldovans' style of acceptance was "healing." In re-reading Joe's story I question the implication that acceptance implies a lack of resistance. I also explore the ways in which acceptance is not universally healing.

In questioning Joe's view that Moldovans were unilaterally accepting, I drew on Barbalet's (1985) claim that acceptance does not imply a lack of resistance—rather, acceptance and resistance can co-exist simultaneously. Barbalet argued,

> an acceptance of power does not preclude resistance. Pragmatic or expedient acceptance of power includes a significant resistive element, either because of an absence of interest in the realization of the goals of power, or because of an overt hindrance of its proper operations....Resistance can take different forms, but none are necessarily associated with conflict. (p. 531)

Some key points in this statement are that acceptance can be based on "pragmatic" or "expedient" needs. In other words, one may accept (or resist) based on the context and one's needs in the moment. One may also resist at a later time and in a fashion that may not be obvious to others. Additionally, the goals of domination may be ignored as a resistive counter-measure in that confronting those goals outright may actually give them more force. And because there is no outward conflict or violent act, what may seem like acceptance on the surface may actually be resistance from another perspective.

Building on this view, it seemed that because Joe's style of resistance involved direct confrontation and the Moldovans' style did not, he labeled Moldovans as accepting when it was possible and even likely that they weren't entirely accepting. For example, the women in Joe's first culture shock story directly confronted the van driver by yelling at him when he failed to return Joe's change, even though later they did not confront the driver when he decided not to continue driving them into the city. One might ask why the Moldovans were resistant in one instance but not another. Joe resolved that seeming contradiction by concluding that Moldovans were accepting, but it stands to reason that if they could be resistant in some circumstances, they could be resistant in other situations as well. Additionally, in their study on behavioral responses to discrimination, Louis and Taylor (1999) suggested that it is difficult to judge another person's response to injustice because one cannot see the "wide variety of potential behaviours [that] are available to the individual" (p. 20). As a cultural outsider, it was therefore likely that Joe wasn't aware of all the subtle forms of resistance available to the Moldovans.

In addition, while Joe seemed to find healing in Moldovan acceptance, acceptance did not appear to be healing for the Moldovans. According to Joe, Moldova has the "worst alcoholic problem in Europe." He even showed me a photo of a young man passed out in the park during the daytime and noted Moldovans "wouldn't live very long" because "They would drink themselves to death." He also used the story of the woman's suicide to develop his concept that Moldovans were accepting and that acceptance was healing for him. For me, the fact that alcoholism and suicide were prominent subjects in Joe's experiences in Moldova suggested that Moldovans neither simply accepted domination, nor found it healing. Rather, their response denoted (at least in part) a painful struggle against domination. This seems to lend support to Tuan's (1998) belief that accepting one's domination could be both "burdensome" and freeing—burdensome in the sense that one must live with the knowledge and effects of being dominated, freeing in the sense that one can be free from choosing how to respond to one's dominator(s) (p. 131). That Joe had carried the burden of his own "domination" at the hands of "Anglos" for so long perhaps made acceptance seem more appealing or freeing and allowed Joe to ignore the ways in which Moldovans struggled against their domination.

Reverse Culture Shock I: Materialism and Not Playing the Game

For Joe, returning to the U.S. "was a lot harder...than going over there." Even though he had read about reverse culture shock, he thought it was "the biggest bunch of bullshit" until he realized it was happening to him. Several times, Joe reiterated that it was difficult to pinpoint why readjustment was so "painful" and "awful." As we talked, though, he kept returning to issues related to the American mentality toward work and money and the ways in which his Peace Corps teaching experiences in Moldova changed his perspective.

He began by relating that prior to the Peace Corps he had always been an "hourly guy" who was focused on making money. As a bail bondsman, he said he played on his clients' ignorance of the legal system in order to make a lot of money. However, when he returned to the U.S., Joe recalled "I didn't belong in the U.S. anymore because I didn't have that same kind of 'Let's all go make money, let's see how much money we can make, see who gets the most toys' [mentality]." In addition, Joe felt that life here in the U.S. was "competitive as hell" and that the mindset was that "it's all about the rat race" and making money. He argued that people here are "working just so that they can satisfy their little comforts—their television, their computer, their air conditioning," which seemed wasteful to Joe. He also felt that in turn he was expected, not to save, but rather to be wasteful as well. For Joe, readjustment meant "selling" and "sharpening" himself in order to get a job and "play the game."

In contrast, Joe explained that in Moldova he felt appreciated even though he was being paid very little money. He also saw that Moldovans were able to live without certain material comforts, which made Joe realize, "it's not bad being poor." Since earning money to procure material goods was not a focus in Moldova, Joe says the "pressure...was kinda lifted as far as...what you expected of yourself or, or what was expected of you as a...person."

Joe's first response to the discomfort he felt upon his return to the U.S. was to go back overseas. But he said he was tired of running and then returning to face the same problems at home. Instead, he decided that if he didn't want to play the game, he wouldn't "play the game then." So, he began to give up the creature comforts that other Americans seemed to value such as television, the Internet, and air conditioning. He suggested that even without these things he was "very comfortable," and noted that when he told other people that he didn't use air conditioning, "they freak out!" and when he explained that he doesn't have a "television, they wanna go through the roof!" He also felt that if he sat and watched television he would be "wasting" his life and that he would "die an old man there watching TV re-runs." For these reasons, he decided to focus on ways to gratify himself such as doing leatherwork, engaging in physical exercise, developing his spirituality through Bible study, and learning to accept both his self and his life circumstances.

That Joe did not expect to experience reverse culture shock upon his return home was a common response, as was his assertion that returning home was "harder" than going to a foreign country (La Brack, 1985; Sussman, 1986; Miller, 1988; Szkudlarek, 2009; Anjarwalla, 2010; Weaver, n.d.). Joe seemed to find happiness in the simplicity of life in Moldova, where the pressure was off to make money and the emphasis was on his job (albeit not in the money-making sense), where maintaining personal relationships was valued, and conserving resources was necessary. Upon his return to the U.S., he found that Americans were concerned only about making money to satisfy "their little comforts," being competitive, and being wasteful. These cultural differences in approaches to work, personal relationships, and materialism caused Joe to feel conflicted. Because of this conflict, Joe decided "not to play the game" in the U.S. and instead, he focused on other spiritual and personal pursuits.

In this vein, Joe indicated that focusing on money and material gain (materialism) was antithetical to maintaining active and positive social relationships. There was considerable support for this perspective in the research literature. Before touching on this literature, I begin by offering Belk's (1984) definition and historical overview of materialism, followed by a review of Moeller's (2012) report on how extrinsic and intrinsic value orientations relate to the notion of materialism. Belk (1984) defined materialism as "the importance a consumer attaches to worldly possessions. At the highest levels of materialism, such possessions assume a central place in a person's life and are believed to provide the greatest sources of satisfaction and dissatisfaction (p. 291).

In tracing the history of materialism Belk (1985) noted that research has placed its origins in Western cultures, variously in 15th- and 16th-century Europe, 18th-century England, 19th-century France, and/or 19th- and 20th-century America. He also pointed out, however, that many ancient civilizations have dealt with issues related to materialism down through the centuries. Despite these differences regarding the date and location of the emergence of materialism, Belk (1985) indicated that seeking "psychological well-being via discretionary consumption" has become more attainable by greater numbers of people within the past few hundred years, most notably perhaps in the United States, given "Americans' high incomes and relatively low taxes" (p. 265).

Likewise, Moeller (2012) believed that the American drive for "greater material rewards" has steadily increased over the past several decades, so much so that the "pursuit of money and materialism" currently "plays a central role" in American culture (on-line). He argued that this shift toward materialism is the result of a greater emphasis in the U.S. on "extrinsic" rather than "intrinsic" values. In making his case, he drew on the work of three university professors (among others). Kennon Sheldon, a professor of psychology at the University of Missouri, explained that "intrinsic factors are about personal growth and self-knowledge, connections and social intimacy with other people, and wanting to help the human community for altruistic reasons....Extrinsic goals...are related to money, luxury, appearance, attractiveness, status, popularity, looks, and power" (In Moeller, 2012).

In addition, Jean Twenge, professor of psychology at San Diego State University, suggested that "Extrinsic values tend to be correlated with narcissism and a high sense of self," self-gain, and competition. She said that most people mistakenly believe,

> We have to be this way because the world is so competitive....They have become convinced that the way to succeed is to become very self-focused, and to get money, fame, and image. However, narcissistic people don't do better....That's a myth. (In Moeller, 2012)

Certainly, there has been a proliferation of reality shows that reinforce the image that competition and self-interest equal success by turning everything from cooking, dancing, selling real estate, designing clothes, decorating houses, surviving on tropical islands, and simply being roommates into a contest.

And finally, Tim Kasser, professor of psychology at Knox College in Galesburg, Illinois, argued that American capitalism is inimical to the development of intrinsic values in that it requires consumption for its operation and promotes materialism by bombarding people with "commercial messages" (In Moeller, 2012). Along these lines, Muncy and Eastman (1998) argued that marketers (and business owners, by implication) have a "self-interest in encouraging materialism," and, to the extent that materialism "has a negative overall effect on the quality of life," they suggested that the promotion of materialism may be considered "socially irresponsible" (p. 137).

Indeed, many have noted the negative influences of materialism on both the individual and society. For example, focusing on money and materialistic pursuits "makes people less likely to help acquaintances, to donate to charity, or to choose to spend time with others" (Dunn, Aknin, & Norton, 2008, p. 1687); can lead to "possessiveness," "non-generosity," and "envy" (Belk, 1985, p. 268); may "become addictive, compulsive, or mindless" (Belk, 2001, Effects Section); creates conflicts between "material values and more collective-oriented values such as family cohesion, community ties, and religious fulfillment" (Burroughs & Rindfleisch, 2002, p. 248); generates considerable debt (Stone, Wier, & Bryant, 2008); and among married couples, increases perceptions of financial difficulties, which alternately has a negative influence on marital satisfaction (Dean, Carroll, & Yang, 2007). For Diener and Oishi (2000), materialism also leads to "sacrifices in self-growth, leisure time, and intimate relationships" as well as "happiness" in that it creates feelings of dissatisfaction when materialistic desires are not fulfilled (p. 186). It also holds the potential for "ruining the environment" through the overconsumption of natural resources, the pollution created as a by-product of mass production (Diener & Oishi, 2000, p. 186), and an overall lack of concern about environmental issues (Good, 2007). Based on their research, Diener and Oishi concluded that "the educational challenge is to convince people that other pursuits may sometimes lead to greater fulfillment than does the pursuit of more money" and material objects (p. 215).

That so many negative outcomes have been attributed to materialism suggests that material *gain* involves *loss* in other areas—relationships, spirituality, environment, finances, and so on. Likewise, in coming to recognize that "it isn't bad being poor," Joe seems to challenge an American cultural perception that being poor is necessarily bad or lacking. It also calls into question the meaning of such terms as rich and poor as well as how self/Other are judged on the basis of those terms.

Re-reading Reverse Culture Shock I: Postmaterialism and Playing the Game Differently

In re-reading Joe's story, which focused on the negative aspects of materialism, I look at ways in which spirituality may balance out materialism (and vice versa) while still enabling a connection to the material world. I also note Inglehart's (1971, 2008) belief that achieving some degree of material security ultimately gives way to "postmaterialist" goals of human development. Addressing the relationship between materialism and spirituality,

Swati Desai (2010), director of Psychological Services at Akasha Center for Integrative Medicine, reasoned that materialism and spirituality can be used to "balance" each other in the pursuit of a "good and fulfilling life." She advised,

> Allow the practice of spirituality to monitor the greed and envy, which seem to be at the heart of why materialism gets excessive, leaving the world around us a worse place....Use materialism to stay in touch with the realities of daily life, recognizing that amassing resources is a source of security, survival and freedom to experience life.

Desai also pointed out that a sole focus on spirituality could lead to "forced austerity, and eventually bitter dogmatism" as well as causing one to "become self-centered and deny the realities of the daily life." Similarly, Belk (1985) claimed that the "willful self-denial of material sources of satisfaction" may be related to the "psychopathologies of masochism, self-hatred, anorexia nervosa, and other self-destructive urges" (p. 266). This is not to suggest that rampant materialism is beneficial, rather that extreme materialism and extreme spirituality may ultimately prove detrimental.

Interestingly, Inglehart (2008) believed that it is the achievement of material security that enables a "shift from survival values to self-expression values" (p. 10). In 1971, Inglehart theorized that, "value priorities in advanced industrial society will tend to shift away from *materialist* concerns about economic and physical security toward greater emphasis on freedom, self-expression, and the quality of life or *postmaterialist* values" (In Inglehart & Abramson, 1994, p. 336).

More recently, Inglehart (2008) pointed to some of the trends that appear to bear out his theoretical assertions. These include: a decrease in voting along social class lines and an increase in voting "around lifestyle issues" (e.g., abortion and same-sex marriage); the proliferation of various social movements dealing with concerns for the environment, "gender equality," "gay liberation," and other social issues; and a "rise in challenges to corporate power" (p. 142). To Ingelhart's point, there have been recent challenges to corporate and political power, most notably in the ongoing "Occupy Wall Street" movement, which began in New York in 2011. The movement is described as "a leaderless resistance movement with people of many colors, genders and political persuasions" with the common creed that "We are the 99% that will no longer tolerate the greed and corruption of the 1%" (Occupy Wall Street, n.d.). Others have also linked the Occupy Wall Street movement to the "conscious-raising" goals and the social importance of gay rights and feminist movements (Guatney, 2011).

Regarding the environment, recycling stations are popping up everywhere (including schools and universities), and according to the Environmental Protection Agency (EPA) (2011), recycling has steadily increased from just 6.4% in 1960 to 34.1% in 2010 (p. 2). That these social movements coexist alongside materialistic pursuits appears to support Inglehart's (1971, 2008) theory of postmaterialist shift to the extent that having a greater sense of economic and existential security seems to create an opening for publicly addressing environmental and human rights concerns.

Additionally, Joe's decision not to "play the game," because he didn't like the competitive focus on making money and materialism in the U.S., suggested that he could escape from participating in the American value system. However, Foucault argued that "one escapes...not by playing a game that" is "totally different...but by playing the same game differently" (In Butin, 2001, p. 172). Therefore, in rejecting what he saw as American materialism in favor of other pursuits, it wasn't that Joe *wasn't* playing the game, he was playing the game from a different perspective than he had before. Both sets of values (relational/spiritual and competitive/materialistic) represent different facets of American culture. That one facet may be emphasized over another does not diminish the existence of the other. It also means that other cultural values may be emphasized at a later time or in different contexts.

Identity Shift II: Taking on a New Identity and Caring as Self-Sacrifice

In addition to becoming less materialistic, Joe also believed that his experiences in Moldova made him a more caring person. He argued that being a teacher in the Peace Corps meant that you "really have to care." He asked rhetorically if it were possible to spend 2 years teaching in another country, especially a poorer one, if one didn't care. He explained,

> For one, you're not making any money...that I think was instrumental because for me it was...like, "Are you stupid or what? You've been working all your life trying to make something of yourself and now you're gonna go work somewhere where they hardly pay you?"

He also made a comparison between Americans and Moldovans. He noted:

> ultimately I think I became more of a caring person and, and people in the United States don't care. I don't think they do. I think they care about themselves more than anything else, but I found a lot of people in Moldova that would help each other.

Along these lines, Joe theorized that it was the experience of "surviving as a native" in another culture that made him "a different human being" because he "had to be a different human being to be there." In a sense, Joe had to become a Moldovan—he had "to become them." He said this enabled him to make a "transformation" in which he no longer thought about when he would be getting paid or when school was out because there was little else to do but focus on work and spend time visiting others.

With regard to taking on a new identity, Jannson (1975) explained that a person who lives abroad and returns home is,

> confronted not only with a different world from the one he knew, but also with a different identity, in his own eyes and others'. All these changes...compounded by the loosening of social bonds caused by absence, can produce anxiety in the re-entrant and in members of the social system. (p. 137)

Joe described his anxiety in the Reverse Culture Shock I story in terms of the "painful" and "awful" feelings he felt after his return to the U.S., as well as his negative views on materialism, waste, and, in this story, the lack of caring on the part of other Americans. That Joe's American friends were shocked by his rejection of TV, air conditioning, and other comforts after his return to the U.S. (as noted in the previous story) implies that they experienced some anxiety as well.

Part of the identity shift Joe described was that his intercultural experiences in Moldova made him a more caring person. His perception of his role as a Peace Corps teacher seemed related to the notion of caring as a form of "self-sacrifice" as he pointed out that leaving the material comforts of the U.S. for the poverty he faced in Moldova meant he "really" had "to care." Heathwood (2011) argued that "Self-sacrifice has to do with *actions*" (p. 20) and that an act exemplifies self-sacrifice "only if performing the act makes the agent worse off than he otherwise could have been" (p. 21). Joe noted the monetary sacrifice he made in joining the Peace Corps as a volunteer, and in other stories he wrote about the challenges he faced learning a new language and adjusting to a new social system, so in the monetary and comfort sense, he was certainly worse off.

This notion of self-sacrifice is also somewhat formulated as "motivational displacement" in Noddings' (2010) relational ethic of caring. She explained that for motivational displacement, the caring person "puts aside" her or his "own values and projects" and the "motive energy" of the carer "flows towards the needs or projects of the cared-for" (p. 391). In order to complete the caring relation, Noddings added, the "cared-for must somehow recognize the efforts of the carer" (p. 391). It seemed that Joe shared a caring relationship with the Moldovans because he felt his role in Moldova was one of self-sacrifice and caring, and Joe's caring was ultimately reciprocated. In contrast, although Joe cared about Americans (especially his students, as shown in the Pedagogy I story) after his return to the U.S., he felt that Americans were more concerned with materialistic pursuits than developing personal relationships. In short, his caring was not acknowledged by Americans the way it had been by the Moldovans, causing him to feel that Americans were uncaring.

Re-reading Identity Shift II: Adding New Layers of Identity and Caring as Self-Gain

Joe felt that by living as a "native" in Moldova, he had taken on a Moldovan identity and become more caring. In contrast, he described Americans as uncaring and focused on satisfying their selfish "little comforts" through materialistic pursuits. Yet, while I agree that living and teaching abroad can be life-changing, I question the ability to take on a completely new identity, especially one derived from another culture. I also have doubts that it is possible to live as a "native" in another culture or that joining the Peace Corps involves complete self-sacrifice.

Speaking to the notion of identity, Wang (2004) suggested that while living in a different culture may help one "reach another level of the self or add another layer of the self," one could "never be totally different from" what one was before (p. 47). She also added that because identity was characterized by both "nonchange and change," it was "impossible and unnecessary to claim a totally new self" (p. 48). This implies the multiplicity of identity (multiple levels and/or layers) and that living within a different culture may enable different aspects of identity to be emphasized while other aspects are de-emphasized. And, likewise, even though new layers may be added, the old layers remain underneath, making a total conversion of identity impossible. In Joe's case, he seemed to be expressing the desire to highlight the more caring aspects of his own identity and to delimit the more competitive, materialistic, or selfish aspects, which he felt were in conflict.

In addition, while it is true that Peace Corps Volunteers are expected to live in similar conditions as their host country counterparts, I don't think it is possible to live as a "native" in the way that Joe suggested. In my own experience, the host country nationals I lived among treated me as part honored guest and part intruder, but I certainly do not think they treated me in exactly the same way they treated each other. Likewise, I and the other Peace Corps volunteers I knew responded to our surroundings not with the knowing of a native, but—even allowing for individual differences—like Americans. That Joe said he felt "uncomfortable" the entire time he was in Moldova in his first culture shock story indicated that Joe did not completely embrace Moldovan culture while there, but that his perceived Moldovan identity developed, in a sense, after his return to the United States.

With regard to Joe's identity shift in relation to caring, he stated that being a Peace Corps teacher meant "you" really "have to care." On second reading, this statement seems a bit ambiguous in that it doesn't make clear who it is Joe cares about. Is it the Moldovans? Is it himself? That Joe offers his material sacrifice as evidence of his caring is interesting. Using Nietzsche's critique of ethics based on "modes of sacrifice," De Marzio (2009) explored the idea that sacrifice "can actually be a way in which one practices self-care" (p. 169). According to De Marzio, the notion of sacrifice implies turning away from the self and forgetting the self as part of an ascetic ideal designed to make one feel morally "superior" (pp. 169–170). In other words, sometimes casting oneself as a caring person may be an attempt to elicit caring on the part of others and may enable the caring person to feel morally justified in their actions toward others or their judgments of others. Further, Kittay (2007) argued that,

> Total *self-sacrifice*, the annihilation of the self in favor of the cared for, is neither demanded by the practice of care nor is it justifiable, for one can see that a relationship requires *two* selves, not one self in which the other is subsumed and consumed. (p. 478)

This research suggests that within a caring relationship there is both "give" and "take." In a sense it also calls into question neat categories of "carer" and "cared-for" to the extent that the carer may also be the cared for. Although Joe did make sacrifices in joining the Peace Corps, he also enjoyed a good deal of self-enrichment in return. He learned a new language, travelled not only to Moldova but to other parts of Europe, gained a new perspective on the world, became more caring and less materialistic, felt a sense of healing, felt a sense of closeness with others, and overall felt a sense of excitement and adventure. In other words, despite his sacrifice, Joe flourished (De Marzio, 2009) in other ways.

Pedagogy I: Rote Learning and the Need to Teach Creativity

With regard to his pedagogy, Joe talked about the differences between his style of teaching and the Moldovans' style. Joe explained that the Moldovans used "the Russian method," which "was to memorize all materials presented and there was never any room for creativity." Joe said that this difference initially caused him to think that his students were cheating because their answers were so uniformly alike. He said his students were also "shocked" when he "asked them to write a creative piece" about their own lives. Joe soon realized this was challenging for the students because they couldn't do it "without being told specifically what to do." Joe continued that he ended up doing a lot of writing so that the students could follow his "thought processes." He felt that teaching the Moldovan students to be creative was "the most amazing part because [he] got to open up their minds to other possibilities." Joe also added that he translated the technique to his students in the U.S. because "they have the same problem," especially when it came to answering open-ended essay questions on the year-end state-wide exam. He said his students in the U.S. would get a prompt such as "what was the best time you ever had with a family member…and it's too vague for them and they can't seem to narrow it down to something specific." He added that "being in Moldova helped me to realize that if you've never been taught to be creative it's a very…difficult thing to do."

According to Joe, the Moldovan educational system is based on the Russian method of rote learning, which focuses on the "accumulation of knowledge" but does not "encourage problem-solving, innovative thinking and creativity" (Fretwell & Wheeler, 2001, p. 2). Surprised by his Moldovan students' inability to write a creative essay about themselves, Joe used his difference in teaching style to open up new learning possibilities, especially in the area of creativity. Referring to "creativity" as the "current icon of the educational world" (p. 149), Gibson (2005) noted that an important theme in the field of education is the linking of "creativity to the needs of individuals, where education promises the flourishing of individual potential" through a "concern with the creative needs of individual" students and "the personal growth of their imaginative and aesthetic lives" (p. 153). This seems to fit with Joe's belief that by teaching his Moldovan students to write creatively, he was "opening their minds."

Following this line of inquiry, Ferrari, Cachia, and Punie (2009) described "creative learning" as "any learning which involves understanding and new awareness, which allows the learner to go beyond notional acquisition, and focuses on thinking skills. It is based on learner empowerment and centeredness…[and] is seen as opposite to the reproductive experience" (p. iii).

This definition refers to creative learning in much the same way that Joe did, in opposition to rote/reproductive learning. Similarly, Novak and Cañas (2008) made the distinction between rote and meaningful learning and argued that "Creativity results from very high levels of meaningful learning" (p. 5), although they saw the "rote-meaningful distinction" as a "continuum" rather than a "simple dichotomy" (p. 4). Further, Gino and Ariely (2011) argued that "Creative thinking allows people to solve problems effectively and also to remain flexible so that they can cope with the advantages, opportunities, technologies, and changes that are a part of their day-to-day lives" (p. 3). It seems then that creativity is a positive trait related to personal development.

Joe's realization that creativity needed to be taught and practiced also helped make him more aware of his American students' needs with regard to writing. One of his techniques was to be creative himself and model creativity for his students. According to Sternberg and Williams (in Fasko, 2000–2001), "modeling creativity" and "building self-efficacy" are prerequisites for developing student creativity. Other tips on their 25-point list include: questioning assumptions, encouraging sensible risk-taking, allowing mistakes, and imagining other viewpoints (p. 324). While I agree that these are useful tools for stimulating creativity, they also pose certain risks for teachers and students. It is my experience that few people like to have their assumptions questioned, and in many places (including the U.S.), teachers and students may be punished for questioning certain cultural values. Likewise, to the extent that creativity involves risk-taking and making mistakes, this poses challenges for student work that must be graded and approved by another entity—a teacher or an exam board. Westby and Dawson (1995) explored this paradox, that even though teachers may espouse creativity, they do not always appreciate the personality traits associated with student creativity. For the authors, this suggests that "to be creative and still be liked by the teacher, children must also display the properties that make them easy to manage in the classroom" (p. 8). Perhaps, then, creativity, when framed as risk-taking and questioning assumptions, is not in the students' best interest. In many instances it seems that conformity and compliance with the teacher, the school system, or examination board is what is most often rewarded.

Re-reading Pedagogy I: Rote Learning as Meaningful Learning and Creativity as Cultural Reproduction

With regard to teaching styles, Joe pointed out the Moldovans' use of rote memorization in contrast to his use of creativity. He seemed to cast rote memorization in a negative light by saying that "there was never any room for creativity." On the other hand, he equated creativity with opening his students' minds. For me, Joe's belief in the value of creativity supports a Western cultural perspective. For example, a European Commission Report for the Department of Education (2009) noted that,

> Creativity is a powerful catch phrase. In Western societies it epitomises success, the modern, trends for novelty and excitement. Whether linked to individuals, enterprises, cities or regions, creativity establishes immediate empathy, and conveys an image of dynamism. Creativity is a positive word in a society constantly aspiring to innovation and "progress." (p. 3)

In contrast, "rote" learning is defined as "the use of memory usually with little intelligence" and "mechanical or unthinking routine or repetition" ("Rote," 2012). Tan (2011), however, argued that such a "narrow conceptualisation of memorisation, that is, rote learning which leads to nonlearning" (p. 137) is a Western misperception. Through her research on Adult Asian learners, she concluded that "Memorisation perceived from the East Asian culture is more than just rote learning. Memorisation can transcend to the level of understanding and meaningful learning" (p. 137). She also explained how, from an Asian cultural perspective, the learners in her study could "memorise and understand simultaneously" (p. 138). Specifically, she pointed to both the rote memorisation and understanding one needed in order to grasp the complexity of the Chinese alphabet (p. 138). This also supports the earlier findings of Kember (1996), who noted that Asian students used understanding and rote memorization techniques strategically, in the sense that "Without some attempt at understanding, students would have a limited basis for determining what to memorise" (p. 352). In addition, for Mayer (2002), rote learning could also lead to creativity when "remembering knowledge is integrated within the larger task of constructing new knowledge or solving new problems" (p. 228). To the extent essay writing involves the memorization of letters, sentence structures, certain stylistic rules, and teacher modeling (as in Joe's case), it appears that creative writing also requires an element of rote learning. These perspectives point out that rote learning can also be meaningful and lead to, or coexist alongside, creativity despite Joe's claim that rote learning did not leave room for creativity. In addition they point to a cultural influence on beliefs regarding the value and effectiveness of learning and teaching styles.

While the perspectives offered above work to counteract a negative view of rote learning, others challenge the notion that creativity carries singularly positive meanings. For Gibson (2005), creativity is a "hurrah word," a happy, rallying word that everyone seems to support, yet runs the risk of becoming a rational instrumental self-legitimizing term that "can be filled with any content and used in any cultural, political or moral context" (p. 149). In other words, its positive surface can be used to conceal its "dark side" (McLaren, 1993; Akinola & Mendes, 2008; Gino & Ariely, 2011). Drawing from the fields of art, technology, science, and history, McLaren (1993) provided that, "In our intoxication with the idea of divine principles, inspiration, and aesthetic characteristics, we tend to ignore the fact that much of human creative effort has been in the service of violent and devious stratagems" (p. 137).

Some examples include creative technological advances in weaponry, the creative cruelty of various groups throughout history who have intentionally inflicted pain on other human beings, and the image of creativity gone awry evoked by Mary Shelley's *Frankenstein*. In this vein, Gino & Ariely (2011) found empirical support for their supposition that the "divergent thinking" and "cognitive flexibility" that characterizes creative thinking may help "dishonest" people to "develop original ways to bypass moral rules" and "reinterpret available information in a self-serving way...when justifying their immoral actions or choices" (pp. 5–6). Further, Akinola & Mendes (2008) linked heightened creativity with "intense negative emotions" and "mood disorders" such as depression. I think the importance of this research is that creativity is not a static term, that it may have different sources, intentions, and outcomes that are not inherently positive, and that it may mean a variety of things to a variety of people, including students and teachers.

Additionally, after exploring the cultural emphasis as well as the positive and negative aspects of rote learning in Asia and creative learning in the U.S., Kim (2005) believed that "each approach has benefits from which the other could learn" (p. 337). Yet, Novak and Cañas (2008) argued that "People often confuse rote learning and meaningful learning with teaching approaches" (p. 4). They say that despite the teaching approach used, the way in which the information is learned depends on other factors including the "disposition of the learner" (p. 4). For educators, this implies that despite their best efforts, there can be no guarantee of outcomes. For instance, one might reasonably assume that with all of the emphasis on creativity, out-of-the-box thinking, and so-called nonconformity in American culture, creativity would be second nature to American students. Yet, Joe observed, "they have the same problem" as his Moldovan students and struggled when it came to creative essay writing. This might lead one to wonder if American culture is as creative as has been portrayed or if what has been called creativity is simply the reproduction of culturally approved forms of "creative" expression.

INTERPLAY 1

A "Subject" in Motion

> For an instant he was overcome with surprise: then since he was moving quickly and knew that he was getting somewhere, all his fury and fear left him.
>
> Flannery O' Connor (1995) from *The River*

With every step I took down the airport ramp, I got a sinking feeling in my stomach. I had no idea whether I could keep moving forward or if gravity would snap me back to where Mama and Daddy waited to catch a long last glimpse of me before I disappeared into Africa for the next 2 years. I just kept picturing a passage in my sixth-grade science book: "An object in motion will remain in motion unless acted upon by an outside force," and I hoped to God an outside force wouldn't act upon me until after I could collapse into my airplane seat.

I also repeated to myself, "I'm doing it. I'm actually going to get on that plane and I am moving to Africa!" It helped knowing this would be the end to all the waiting and planning that had led to this point, and for now, all I needed to do was "be." Actually, I hadn't planned very much at all. Every time I started to imagine what Cameroon would be like, or what the people would be like, or the conversations we would have and the clothes we would wear and how I would feel, etc., I would try to get my mind to change the subject. I also tried very hard not to read too much about Cameroon either. Why should I strenuously read every travel book known to man on the subject of Cameroon only to be disappointed if the book was wrong, which they almost always were. I pictured myself wandering around with my mouth hanging open all slack-jawed saying, "It didn't say *that* in the book!" Well, forget the books!

Therefore, I decided to experience Cameroon for myself instead of taking the word of others. I would try as much as possible to rid myself of any preconceived notions I had and accept Cameroon for what it was and not what I could have imagined it to be. This would be tough because Mama always did say I had a big imagination, and this time Mama was right.

When I walked into Georgetown University in Washington, D.C., which is where we started out for the first week before going to Cameroon, the other 30-some-odd Peace Corps volunteers looked at me as if I were a huge ignoramus. To be completely fair, I dressed for the part in hiking boots, jeans, a green plaid shirt and a replica of the hat Indiana Jones wore in the *Raiders of the Lost Ark*. I also hadn't shaved for the last few weeks because I thought razors might be scarce in Cameroon so I had better get used to doing without.

I charged into the first meeting, fresh off the plane and terribly late because I had received the worst possible advice about how to get to Georgetown from the airport. I stormed into the room huffing and puffing, with sweat dripping from my forehead and an enormous backpack strapped to my back. Everyone in the room sat staring at me and frowned as if they smelled rotten cauliflower. They were all 5-to-10-years younger than me, neatly dressed, freshly scrubbed, and clean-shaven.

For a moment, I didn't know if I had stumbled into the right room or not. I tried to picture this group fighting for their survival in the wilds of Africa, but I could only picture them sipping wine coolers at a picnic thrown by Tommy Hilfiger. The look in their eyes told me they put me right down at the bottom of the social scale without much hope of rising very high in the ranks. I had come to know this look well. All through my life, I had gotten the feeling that people thought I was something less. As if the very things I had to offer weren't good enough or didn't count for anything. I suspect this is why I never cared much for group dynamics. There always has to be an upper group and a lower group and you can tell by the way people look at you whether they put themselves higher or lower than you.

In addition, people always seemed really nice one-on-one, but put them into groups and their behavior seemed to change. I thought maybe the Peace Corps would be different. I thought Peace Corps people would be kind and generous to each other and not subscribe to the same pecking order the rest of society subscribed to. This turned out to be misconception #538. I would describe many of the people in my Peace Corps group as competitive and self-centered. Who knew the most French? Who had already taught English? Who had travelled the most? Who had read the most about Cameroon? (See above if you think I would be impressed by that one.) Who could throw a Frisbee the farthest? Who could drink the most booze without barfing? The only award I would have won was the award for looking like a buffoon for showing up late in a knock-off Indiana Jones costume. This had the effect of making me feel unsure about myself, and when I felt unsure of myself, my usual defense was to shut up for fear of making everything worse.

Once we arrived in Cameroon, we were doled out to home-stay families with which we were to live for the next three months, and we began our training from day one. The Cameroonian family I lived with comprised a mother and a father and their three small children, along with a young nephew and an illegitimate daughter on the father's side who did all of the housework around the house and who took all the brunt of the mother's anger. Shortly after I moved in, the mother told me that they had decided NOT to be part of the Peace Corps home-stay program because their home was too small (I did notice that all of the children slept in the parents' bedroom) and that they were only doing this as a favor to someone else. Well, welcome to Cameroon! I tried to stay out of the way and help out as much as I could, but they always had a pained look on their faces when they looked at me. This was possibly due to the fact that my French sounded like pure gibberish.

When I arrived at the Peace Corps training center, I was put in the lowest level of French speakers in our group, which was a definite blow to my ego. Hadn't I been valedictorian in high school and college and voted most talented? Wasn't this just another way for the others to feel superior over me? How was I supposed to stick a whole new language in my head and have it come out sounding half-way normal in a matter of weeks? I quickly tried to remind myself that I didn't have to be an expert at everything, especially French, a language I had little experience with until fairly recently. I also figured that if hundreds of other people could meet the language requirements, surely I could. And furthermore, if I brought one good thing with me from Oklahoma that I could use, it was a pioneer spirit—no matter how unhappy Oklahomans are, they just figure it's par for the course and just keep plugging along. So basically, I decided to get over it as much as I possibly could. Besides, what I lacked in linguistic perfection I tried to make up for by catching people off guard and making them laugh with my bumbling French.

During our training we were invited to the harvest celebration of a tribe that made its home at the base of a remote mountain. While we were in the village, I noticed a little incident that probably no one else noticed, but it made me want to cringe just the same. As we were being led all through this village, I was lagging behind to see what I could see. Everywhere we went there were groups of little children following in our footsteps. I watched the children watching us with curiosity and fascination. I also noticed that one small boy had sidled up to one of the male volunteers. While they were walking, the little guy put his hand in the hand of the volunteer. They walked on like this, hand in hand, for a little while and I thought, "ahhhh Peace Corps, this is what it's all about." That was until the volunteer looked down to see that a child dressed in practically rags was holding his hand and he let go of this child's hand with a palpable force and a scowl that looked as if the child had given him a deadly disease. Why did I have to see that? That put an ugly twist on my beautiful and perfect dream.

And, if you don't believe me when I say that Peace Corps people could be self-centered, then I'll let you be the judge. Once, we had this seminar where they kept drilling into us that we were each other's support system and lifeline. In other words, we needed to be able to count on each other and watch out for each other, and to work together as a team. Yes indeed, everyone nodded their heads and acted like they had discovered world peace. HOGWASH! After the meeting broke up, we all went hiking up this small mountain that was close by. As we almost reached the half-way point, one of the girls became extremely sick to her stomach and said she needed to go back down the mountain. I happened to be in the very back of the line taking photographs and observing things, and I watched as each person walked right by this sick girl who could have had God knows what illness, just so they could say they reached the top. I'm not very proud to say that I was thinking roughly the same thing. Why shouldn't I trek on up to the top? I'm here in Africa and I'm doing this for me. Who cares if some strange girl can't keep up? It's not my problem. I kept imagining how the sick girl would feel walking down the mountain by herself, and unable to assuage my guilt, I felt obliged to go with her even though I surmised that the others would judge us as pathetic quitters. As it turns out, it gave me and the girl a chance to get to know each other a little better, and we stopped to take pictures of each other and the gorgeous panoramic views on the way down. So, as it turned out, I hadn't sacrificed anything and the mountaintop would still be there for another day. I was also beginning to learn how to care about others.

Another part of our training involved teaching summer school while being watched, filmed, and rated by each other. After trying to learn a foreign language, this is the best way to get rid of any shred of ego that you may have had. After sitting in the back of your class watching you make a complete fool of yourself, the other PCVs (Peace Corps Volunteers) filled out a little feedback sheet and picked you apart from one end to the other. Spelling mistakes, nervous ticks, muddy grammar explanations, and lack of student discipline techniques were all fair game. Most of the negative comments they made about these first classes that I taught had to do with things like my voice level, which was just above a whisper—well, I had no idea if what I was saying was the right thing or not so why just yell everything out? They also pointed out the words that I misspelled, the slow pacing of my class, the fact that I had prepared too much material or not enough, and they even pointed out that I made one talkative student move to a seat that was surrounded by a pool of vomit that some kid had puked up when I wasn't looking.

I often felt embarrassed and humiliated, but I kept reminding myself that this was all new to me and I would be stronger if I could just hold on for one more day without going completely berserk. What I really found difficult was trying to follow the cookie-cutter style of teaching English that I told myself I needed to emulate instead of following my own natural teaching instincts. I don't know how or where I got the impression that my way of doing things was wrong and everyone else's was right. Didn't I used to be in advertising? What was the difference between selling a tangible product and promoting an idea? If I could draw pictures of some of these ideas, couldn't I get the point across even faster? So, I picked up some paper and magic markers from the Peace Corps Center and went to work at home, at night, in secret. Since I felt more comfortable teaching my way, I thought the students would feel more comfortable and would be able to follow me a lot better. Then, the feedback I was getting started to improve: "Excellent voice," "Great variety of exercises and cool game," "Great presence! Great management techniques, voice, and rapport," "Your hand-writing is delicious," and "(You are the) fucking VA (Visual Aid) king." I hadn't perfected my teaching method yet, but I had found my niche, my persona, my road map, and my self-esteem.

After a day of teaching what I thought was a pretty good round I went home and waited for dinner. I had felt a little funky off and on all day long, but whatever was wrong, I just couldn't put my finger on it. Have you ever seen a movie in which they show a sick or drunk person from the sick or drunk person's point of view? Well, when my home-stay Mom called me in for dinner, that's how I felt. I walked into the living room and the room started tilting up on one end. Then I looked the other way and the whole room seemed to tilt the other way. After that, complete darkness as I fell to the ground in a dead faint. I was quickly moved to my bedroom, while someone was sent to get the Peace Corps nurse. Meanwhile the children were having a conniption fit because they thought I had died. When I finally managed to get revived, I understood that I had succumbed to the effects of malaria.

Malaria! We had been taking a malaria prevention medication since before we even got to Cameroon in addition to being injected for every God-awful disease known to man. Fortunately, the malaria seemed to me to be somewhat like the flu. The nurse gave me some medicine, Lord knows what, and said I needed to eat something. They brought me a big bowl of rice with fish heads sticking up out of the top of it. Now I'm not too keen on fish heads and rice on a good day, so you can imagine what I was thinking when they put the bowl up to my face. I managed to get a few bites down before spewing rice all over the bed and myself. But I guess I survived, and not wanting to dwell on the whole ordeal, I went back to teaching the next day. It probably helped me build up antibodies or something because I never really had any major sicknesses after that. And, in many ways, I would be healthier in Cameroon than I was in the United States, with all the fresh food we ate that wasn't cooked up in a chemistry set, having to walk a great deal, and drinking lots of water to stay hydrated.

So, after three months of practice teaching, adjusting to Cameroonian culture, suffering through tropical illnesses, coping with our own and each other's insecurities and mood swings, we were all ready to get the hell away from each other and into our own villages. The village they were sending me to was called Olawati and it was in the northern part of Cameroon. I was really excited to be going to Olawati, which reminded me of the dry sandy mountainous terrain of New Mexico. It was a small village populated by several different ethnic groups who were mainly Muslim. There was also a Peace Corps Volunteer named Sara who lived in a nearby village. She had already lived there for a year and we became friends when she visited my training group. She had also lived with the same family I did when she went through training so we were already related in a way.

Before the other volunteer trainees and I left for our new posts, the students we had taught as part of our Peace Corps teacher training got together to sing us songs of encouragement. They sang stuff such as the following, and added dance steps and dramatic gestures:

> Move on, Move on,
> Don't be frightened
> Our dear volunteers
> No turning back.
> Move on, Move on,
> Don't be frightened
> Students are waiting
> No turning back.
> We say move on!

Seeing these young African children trying to encourage *us* big brave American volunteers not to be frightened, not to give up, and not to turn back, well wouldn't that make you want to bawl? It did me. But they were right—it was time to *move on* and by this time, we were ready!

· 3 ·
TOWARD A PEDAGOGY OF NON-PREJUDICE

Introduction

Harley was a 33-year-old Filipino American woman who was working as an associate director of International Programs and Services at a Midwestern university when we met for our interviews. She also taught a class called "Transitions," which was a freshman experience course designed to help newly arrived international students adjust to American culture. In addition, she also offered intercultural communication presentations not only for international students, but also for local students and community members. For her Peace Corps service, Harley taught English at the primary and secondary levels and held conversation classes for local teachers in Kazakhstan from 1999 to 2001. Additionally, she was the first volunteer to serve in the small rural village where she taught. After completing her Peace Corps service, Harley also taught English for a total of 9 years in four different countries: Thailand, Japan, Poland, and Kyrgyzstan. She recently received her PhD in Education & Human Resource Studies.

I first met Harley at a local coffee shop in the small Midwestern university town where she lived and worked. As I sat waiting for Harley in the coffee shop, I was slightly annoyed by the people at the table next to me who appeared to be two grandparents minding a child of about three. The grandparents kept saying things like, "What do you want to drink, Bonnie? Bonnie, do you want milk or do you want a soda? Come on please tell us, Bonnie." And, "What do you want to do after we leave? Do you want to go swimming or do you want to go to the zoo, Bonnie? Come on, sit up and tell us, Bonnie." For her part, Bonnie didn't seem to know what she wanted and looked as if she didn't really care. I thought to myself about how children are often placed at the center of attention in American culture, whether they choose this role or not, whereas in some of the other cultures through which I have travelled, children's wants and needs are often secondary to those of their parents, also whether they choose that role or not.

As I sat thinking about what Bonnie would ultimately choose to drink and what she wanted to do later, Harley arrived. I admit I was taken slightly off guard when a woman dressed in black leather cycling gear riding a Harley-Davidson motorcycle adorned with miniature skulls pulled up in the parking lot. Moments before she arrived, a balding middle-aged white man that looked an awful lot like the way I had described myself to Harley sat down just outside the door of the coffee shop. As Harley approached the shop, I noticed that she was trying to make eye contact with the man, but that he seemed rather reluctant to return her gaze. Realizing that it was not me, she entered the shop and upon finding that I was the man she was to meet, she greeted me with a large, warm hug. We had some coffee and shared a laugh about our mistaken identities—that while she seemed to break a stereotype, I fit mine so closely that another person could be confused for me. Along these lines, Harley mentioned that among her group of friends she was "always the unique one."

During our subsequent interviews at her office and her home, it became clear that experiencing different cultures and riding her motorcycle were a large part of Harley's identity. Both her office and her home were filled with mementos of her travels through 50 countries as well as Harley-Davidson memorabilia. She said that what she loved about living overseas was "the travel, the different cultures of people you meet, the different languages, food, all of that" and that she felt sad that living in the United States she would have to give that up. But since buying a Harley-Davidson motorcycle upon her return to the U.S., she has become a part of a new culture—biker culture. She explained, "I was learning about something new...because just the different culture of being with bikers and symbols, signs, different language, everything that I loved about living overseas and learning about other cultures, I got through this." She also learned, through riding her motorcycle through some 30-plus states (she keeps a map with each state she visits highlighted), about the diversity within the United States. She noted, "I realized from state to state, from North to South, East to West, how it's very different. There are a lot of different foods, different types of people, different accents, different atmosphere, different restaurants" that she would not have experienced had she not become a biker.

Interestingly, Harley described riding a motorcycle and having intercultural experiences in similar ways. She considered both as experiences that made you "feel" something. In a roughly nine-minute student-created video-biography juxtaposing Harley's role as an educator and her identity as a woman and a biker, she said that in biking, "You really feel everything that's happening around you…you feel all the bumps in the road, you experience all the weather…it just gives you a heightened sense of life and travel." Likewise, she said of intercultural experience, "it makes you feel, whether it's that you feel good or you feel bad, but you feel." She added that intercultural experience can "really jolt you" because "you start to really feel and reflect on life…who you are…what you believe…what you didn't believe and what you believe now." Accordingly, she viewed culture shock and reverse culture shock as learning experiences even though it sometimes took considerable time and reflection to determine what lessons may be learned from those experiences. She often used the lessons she learned abroad and at home to relate to the international students and the minority students she mentored.

In her stories, Harley often returned to issues surrounding the ways in which her bi-cultural (Filipino American) identity played a part in her culture shock. Because she felt that some of her shock experiences are the result of racial prejudice and because she uses those experiences to inform her pedagogy, I have titled her chapter "Toward a Pedagogy of Non-Prejudice." In this chapter I have included two culture shock stories, one reverse culture shock story, and two pedagogy stories. I did not include an identity shift story in Harley's chapter because she seems to have already developed an attunement to identity issues through her early travels to the Philippines, and her identity struggles during and after the Peace Corps seem to go beyond those of recognizing the ways in which different cultures may shift one's worldview. In her first culture shock story, Harley talks about the differences in cultural orientations between America (where she was born), which she describes as individualistic, and the Philippines (where her parents are from), which she feels is more collectivistic. In re-reading this story, I question the categories of collectivist and individualist as representing singular concepts and note that national cultures may not easily fit into these categories. Although this story is not directly related to Harley's Peace Corps experience, I feel it expresses an important culture shock experience in Harley's identity development. In her second culture shock story, Harley talks about the visible corruption in Kazakhstan as she wonders how the country can ever develop. In re-reading the story, I look at corruption in a different light and suggest that corruption may coexist with development as it does in the U.S. In her reverse culture shock story, Harley explores the different uses of time in Kazakhstan, where people take time to build relationships, and the U.S., where time is limited and people focus on other things, such as watching TV, rather than building relationships. On second reading, I suggest that building relationships can take different forms, even by watching TV, for example. Next, Harley's first pedagogy story deals with the racial prejudice in both Kazakhstan and the United States and how she helped students confront their own prejudices. In re-reading the story, I look at the potential benefits of being bi-cultural and the way in which Harley thrives in spite of the prejudice. In her second pedagogy story, Harley talks about her techniques for cultural adjustment. In the first reading, I examine these techniques through a cultural lens. In re-reading the story, I look at the same techniques from a different perspective.

Culture Shock I: Philippines = Collectivism, America = Individualism

Harley's parents were from the Philippines and began taking her to visit the Philippines when she was 10 years old. Even though she had grown up with Filipino cultural values, going to the Philippines could still be a source of culture shock for Harley. For instance, Harley said she "would always get into trouble in the Philippines" because she wanted to do things by herself but that the Filipinos were a more "collectivist society." She detailed that you couldn't go for a walk by yourself in the Philippines; if you wanted to go for a walk, others would have to go with you. If you were hungry, you had to wait until others were hungry too; eating alone would be considered rude. Everyone had to watch the same TV show together in the same room. She said this didn't reconcile with her American upbringing in which you could take a walk or go for a jog by yourself, eat whenever you were hungry, or watch whatever TV show you wanted on your own TV in your own room. It wasn't that she didn't appreciate and enjoy other aspects of Filipino culture, but that at home, in

America, she "would always have a little more freedom." This gave Harley a sense of independence that clashed with Filipino values.

Harley added that her mother also developed her strong sense of independence by explaining to Harley that,

> you're going to have to work twice as hard, not only because you're a woman, but because you're Asian, and...I want you to get the highest degree that you can...I want you to work as hard as you can, I want you to be independent and I never want you to feel afraid to do anything or to go anywhere, or that you have to depend on somebody for something.

So, when her mother complained about how independent Harley was, Harley would remind her mother that she had taught her to be independent. Her mother joked in response, "yeah, but I think I did it too much."

When I asked Harley to clarify what her mother meant when she said that as an "Asian and a woman" she would need to work harder, she explained that as the oldest of nine children and the first child to come to America, her mother had a lot of "expectations that were placed on her" such as being a role model for her siblings and sending back money to help the family. Her mother also had a master's degree in nursing from the Philippines, but it was not "considered good enough" in the U.S., and therefore she was paid less and treated differently from American nurses even though they only had bachelor's degrees. Harley also felt her mom was treated differently because of her accent, which some Americans associated with not being "as smart or not as knowledgeable," therefore she always had to work harder to prove herself. Likewise, Harley also worked hard to prove herself in the eyes of others, while striving for independence at the same time.

In this story, Harley pointed out two differing and apparently conflicting cultural orientations: the Philippines as collectivist and the U.S. as individualist. Kulkarni et al. (2010) described both individualist and collectivist orientations as follows:

> *Individualism* orientation refers to an emphasis on individual goals, individual rights, autonomy, self-reliance, achievement orientation, and competitiveness. *Collectivism*, on the other hand, refers to an emphasis on collective goals, collective rights, interdependence, affiliation with the larger collective, cooperation, and harmony. (p. 95)

Noting the importance of understanding individualist and collectivist orientations, Fischer et al. (2009) indicated that "Individualism-collectivism (IC) has dominated cross-cultural research...is the most commonly applied construct to explain and predict cultural differences" and is a dimension that appears highly stable across cultural groups (p. 188). They further asserted the unlikelihood that people can work toward individualistic and collectivistic goals simultaneously. In addition, although Rothstein-Fisch and Trumbull (2008) believed that "every culture has both individualistic and collectivistic values" (p. 9), they also offered a framework for clearly identifying the traits associated with each type of cultural orientation, such as equating self-expression, individual achievement, and self-reliance with individualism and cooperation, respect, modesty, and a focus on group success with collectivism (p. 9).

The image that this research creates is that individualism and collectivism are powerful constructs in the field of cross-cultural research, and that as relatively stable constructs across cultures they may be easily delineated for the purposes of cross-cultural comparison. Likewise, when I read Harley's story, the differences between the Philippines as collectivist and the United States as individualist became exceedingly clear. All of the individual "freedoms" Harley took for granted in the U.S., such as taking a walk, eating, and watching TV by herself would be considered rude in the collectivist society of the Philippines, where she was expected to perform each of those activities as part of a group.

Additionally, when Harley's mother said, "I want you to be independent and I never want you to feel afraid to do anything or to go anywhere, or that you have to depend on somebody for something" she appeared to be instilling in Harley an "individualistic drive to separation, autoarchy, and self-reliance" (Simmel, 2007, p. 68). But in complaining about Harley's over-independence and expecting her to behave in collectivistic ways, her mother may have been sending a mixed message to Harley to the extent that mingling collectivist and individualist orientations may prove exceedingly difficult.

Re-reading Culture Shock I: Individualism (?), Collectivism (?)

In re-reading Harley's story with respect to collectivism and individualism, there seems to be a fair amount of research that calls into question the stability of each of these constructs. For example, Simmel (2007) demonstrated that the concept of individuality could have different meanings by comparing the "expressive differences" between a "Germanic" and a "more typically Latinate

Romanic" notion of "Individuality" (p. 66). He explained that while the Germanic idea of individuality was expressed in terms of the "incomparable deeds of a person," the Latinate concept of individuality made "reference to a general or universal formal principle of some kind" (p. 66). In explaining the Latinate version of individuality further, Simmel wrote that although there were no particular standards for male fashion in Florence, Italy, during the Renaissance period, the painted portraits of men from that time period show a certain "uniformity" of clothing style and added that,

> It is this element of commonality, despite all individualization, that in the end leads individuals to present themselves as bearers of a type, with a more or less generalized character or temperament...All individual freedom, distinction and excellence are sought within these limits, and are in fact nothing other than particularly pure and strong manifestations of typical nameable attributes. (pp. 66–67)

Simmel's essay demonstrates that individualism is not a single, unitary category but can be described and experienced in different ways. I think it is especially interesting that in the Latinate manifestation, individuality was experienced in terms of similarity. In present-day America, this helps explain how one can buy mass-produced products and copy fashion trends as a way of asserting one's self-proclaimed uniqueness.

Other research has examined the extent to which cultures that have been labeled collectivist or individualist actually exhibit behavior or attitudes consistent with their label. Takano & Sogon (2008) discovered no significant differences in the in-group conformity rates (in-group conformity being a trait linked to collectivism) between Japanese and Americans, which they believed challenges the commonly accepted view that Japan is a collectivist culture and America is an individualist culture. Additionally, Kulkarni et al. (2010) cited research that characterized Indian culture as collectivist in some studies yet individualist in others (p. 95). In attempting an explanation, they argued that part of the problem is that individualism and collectivism are seen as "*bipolar, unidimensional*" constructs rather than as "*multidimensional*" (p. 95). For their study, Kulkarni et al. surveyed a total of 587 people across five countries (Bulgaria, India, Ireland, Israel, and the U.S.) on seven dimensions related to individualism and collectivism, such as beliefs about "competitiveness," "self-reliance," "supremacy of individual interest," etc. Their findings indicated that people from each of the countries shared a mix of both collectivistic and individualistic attitudes. Interestingly, when compared to the other countries listed in the study, the U.S. scored highest or next-highest in terms of collectivism on five of the seven dimensions and next-highest in individualism on two of the dimensions. Accordingly, the authors argued that their results are "suggestive of the co-existence of competitiveness tendencies and sacrifice for the group," and "It would be too much of a generalization to suggest that individualism as a cultural pattern tends to emphasize competitiveness; and collectivism as a cultural pattern tends to emphasize cooperation" (p. 106). Both of these studies seem to call into question the way in which collectivism and individualism have been conceptualized as an either/or proposition and accordingly how labels of collectivism and individualism may be misapplied, which in turn influences the ways in which individuals are perceived. This research also calls into question neatly labeled dichotomized lists that reduce whole cultures to a list of decontextualized cultural traits.

Addressing the need to understand the individual as both individualistic and collectivistic, Bell and Das (2011) argued that,

> Culture is no longer monolithic, as in individualistic or collectivistic. The person–culture relationship is no longer one that can be captured by independent and dependent variables. Instead, identities are both social and personal. Dynamic processes take the place of static states. Questions of how identities emerge and are maintained come to the fore. (p. 242)

Instead of focusing on broad cultural categorizations to understand the notion of identity, they look at how identity develops in relation to one's culture through dialogue with the self, which is "envisioned as a multiplicity" (p. 244), as well as dialogue with others. Bell and Das also felt that these ongoing dialogues with selves/others create "conflicts or tensions" that can "trigger system reorganization" (p. 244). This suggests that while perhaps different cultures claim (or are judged to have) certain fixed orientations, individual identities are under constant negotiation based on contextual and individual variables, making it problematic to predict how each person relates to cultural values.

Using Bell and Das' (2011) technique to examine the notion of a multiple self in dialogue with self and others in Harley's stories, I first looked at the ways in which Harley narrated her multiple selves in this and other stories, and then I looked at how Harley seemed to be shaped by her mother's "independence" narrative. Exploring her multiplicity, Harley sometimes referred to herself as Filipino ("proud that we were Filipino," "being Filipino," and "I'm Filipino"), sometimes not completely Filipino ("not fully Filipino"), sometimes as American ("I'm American," "The American"), and also as a Filipino

American ("having been brought up Filipino American"). She also referred to herself as a "woman," an "Asian," a "PhD" student, an educator/administrator, and a "biker." In addition, she indicated certain roles that she played, such as those of dutiful/rebellious daughter (in that she both accepted and rejected some of the responsibilities given by her parents) and caring sister/dutiful son (in the sense that she both took care of her brother who was in a coma and also took on some of his traditionally male duties within the family). These multiple parts of Harley's "self" seemed to appear and re-appear depending on the topic we were discussing.

Additionally, one of the dialogues that seemed to shape Harley's self-understanding was her mother's insistence that Harley, as a woman and an Asian, would have to work harder than others because she herself had to do so, and yet be independent of others. In Cohen (2007), two cultural narratives were identified as driving Asian American women to work harder in order to perceive themselves as successful. The first is Baylor psychologist Dr. Dung Ngo's suggestion that due to "cultural expectations," Asian American girls are treated more strictly than boys and they feel family responsibilities more acutely (In Cohen, 2007, p. 1). The second, according to California State University Associate Professor Eliza Noh, is the American cultural "myth that Asians are smarter and harder-working than other minorities" (In Cohen, 2007, p. 2). Noh further suggested that although this pressure to work harder has led to high levels of depression among Asian American women, these women likewise show "resourcefulness" in locating their own "diverse healing strategies (In Cohen, 2007, p. 2).

For Harley's part, she seemed to both accept and rebel against her mother's notions of responsibility and independence in that she applied the narratives to her own life in a seemingly extreme manner, so much so that her mother stated that she had promoted Harley's independence "too much." In order to challenge her Mother's seemingly cultured narratives, she joined the Peace Corps against her parent's wishes and took up motorcycling, a typically male pastime, when she returned to the States. This suggests a more complex process of identity development that is neither completely cultural nor individual. For DeKorne, Byrum, & Fleming (2007), "individual and national cultural identities…can no longer be viewed as the permanent structured foundation of the self" but rather are based on a "vast array of choices making up myriad cultural identities" (p. 292). Whether Harley chose her various individual and cultural identifications consciously or subconsciously is difficult to say, but she did emphasize different individual/cultural relationships depending on the story she was telling, as noted above, which indicated that she was choosing between identities (or between facets of her identity) in constructing her narratives.

Culture Shock II: Corruption in Kazakhstan as Survival and a Lack of Development

Harley said that prior to teaching in Kazakhstan, she thought that the "expectations of students were going to be the same" as in the United States. She was therefore stunned to find that teachers would accept bribes to inflate student grades. She said that after the first time she graded student work, the students were upset and demanded that she give them higher scores. Recalling her own experiences when she was a student, she said,

> I remember thinking when I went to school I couldn't go to my teacher and say give me an A, like if the teacher gave me a C, because that was my fault...and I'm not just going to change it because you came in here to ask me, and the next time you come you bring me chocolate, I'm not going to change it again. After that point I realized that that's how it works, that a lot of students get these high marks not necessarily on their own merit, but because that was the system there.

She added that she was especially astounded because the Kazakh teachers would "blatantly" change student grades in exchange for gifts or favors.

Harley did confront her English-teaching Kazakh counterpart about why she changed the students' grades. The other teacher explained that it was the "system" there, that if she didn't do it the community would be upset with her, and it was "easier to conform." She also told Harley, "you can come here, do your teaching, be here for two years and you leave, but I don't get to leave, and this is how it is." Harley said that although she "never got immune" to the daily corruption she witnessed nor adopted the practice of changing student grades, her counterpart's statement that Harley "got to leave" made her stop "questioning" and being so "condemning." She also reflected that the corruption at the school was likely related to survival, but she wondered how the community would ever "move ahead" if there was so much corruption.

With regard to corruption in the United States, Harley saw it more in the "realm of politics." Within academia, she related corruption to "dishonesty"—that sometimes educational leaders made decisions based on their personal or financial self-interests rather than the needs of the students. She pointed out that in the U.S., corruption wasn't,

> blatantly up in your face…but it's a little more malicious…almost dangerous because it's hidden here, as opposed to there. Like I could see it every day and here it's like hidden in a way, and you're working at a place that's apparently supposed to have the mission to take care of the students and take care of the people that are working for them, but they're just better and smarter at covering it up and hiding real reasons for doing things.

When I asked her how she dealt with this understanding, she said she thought about her Kazakh counterpart and, like her, felt there was nothing she could do about it. Harley also said she felt "helpless" because she wasn't the "one in power" making the decisions.

Harley's story about corruption reminded me of my own struggles with corruption as a teacher in a small village in Cameroon, Africa. At the end of my first year of teaching, all of the teachers and administrators gathered to discuss the standards for passing a student on to the next level. After developing the standards, we discussed each student in detail and each student's name was written in a book along with their overall grades and a notation indicating that they had passed to the next grade level or they had to re-take the same grade level the following year. This was a long and laborious process and seemed very official. Imagine my surprise when almost all of the students that were required to repeat their grade level had advanced to the next grade level! When I asked about this, the discipline master became very defensive. When I located the end-of-year grade book and pointed out specific names of students who had advanced despite the notation of "re-take," he exploded. He yelled that Americans always thought they were better than everyone else and that they were always trying to change things. His thunderous voice could be heard reverberating through the tiny open-air school yard for all the teachers and students to hear. I felt like I had started World War III, set the Peace Corps mission back 100 years, and put myself in physical danger. I seriously considered leaving the Peace Corps, since my teaching would obviously make no difference to the development of the country. I even took a few days off to mull the problem over. The students, sensing my frustration, explained that they had paid bribes to go to the higher level and that this was normal. They didn't like it, but it was part of the system. They also said that if I didn't continue teaching, the school would not hire another English teacher and they would be the ones to ultimately suffer. I, like Harley, also confronted my

English-teaching Cameroonian counterpart about this practice. My counterpart asked me, "Do you think that the students are poorer than me?" In truth, I did, but I was wrong. Even though my co-worker taught as many classes as I did, he was often not paid for his services or paid a fraction of his salary while some of our students had parents that were well-off by comparison. Both my students and the other teacher made me feel selfish and spoiled. Later, I did at times loan students money (through an intermediary student) to pay the bribes they needed to pay to avoid being kicked, or kept, out of school, and they always paid me back. Did that make me corrupt as well? I didn't think so at the time.

In her story, Harley linked corruption in Kazakhstan to survival and a lack of development in that she was concerned about how Kazakhs would ever "move ahead" in light of their blatant system of corruption. Her teaching counterpart also noted that bribing teachers was part of the "system." Exploring this link between development and corruption, Leiken (1996–1997) wrote that while "In most developed countries, corruption remains a violation of the rules of the game; in many developing and postsocialist countries it is the game itself—corruption is systemic" (p. 61). Adding support for this perspective, Economics professor Daniel Levy (2007) explained the reasons for his family's participation in corrupt practices (which included bribing teachers, doctors, and government officials) during his youth in Georgia (the Eastern European country not the American state). He wrote,

> First, we had no choice. There was no other way a family could live and survive in Georgia without being engaged in these types of illegal activities. Second...it was *the norm*. Everybody was doing it, and that provided ethical and moral justification for our actions without feeling too much guilt or embarrassment about it. (p. 440)

For Levy, corruption served a dual purpose—survival and maintenance of norms. Likewise, Harley related corruption to survival and norms in Kazakhstan, and while the bribing of teachers violated her "expectations" of how students were supposed to earn grades, for her counterpart, it was clearly the custom.

There was also support in the literature for Harley's assumption that corruption was a detriment to economic and social development. Leiken (1996–1997) argued that corruption represented a "hazard to free trade and investment, a threat to democracy and development, and...a danger to national security and public health and safety" (p. 55). For Mauro (1997), corruption could also be tied to lowered economic growth, potential misappropriation of aid for purposes other than those intended, misdirection of talent away from productive work due to time spent maintaining the system of corruption, loss of tax revenues, and inferior public infrastructure and services (e.g., substandard construction of buildings) (p. 87). In addition, Gupta, Davoodi, & Alonso-Terme (2002) linked corruption to income inequality and poverty (p. 40). Corruption also seemed to lower the levels of investment and entrepreneurial incentives as well as weaken the judicial systems in some countries (Jain, 2001, p. 72). Further, the International Council on Human Rights Policy (ICHRP) (2010) argued that corruption was essentially a human rights and social justice issue. Their report, *Integrating Human Rights in the Anti-Corruption Agenda,* focused on the human cost of corruption. Some of the issues they considered are the ways in which corrupt practices in specific cultural and social contexts work to block access to health services, education, clean water, and housing for certain marginalized groups, as well as how they promote human trafficking, violence against women, racism, and other forms of discrimination. Certainly, there are bound to be emotional and psychological repercussions as well. Based on this research, it seems clear that corruption precludes economic and social development and works to undermine both human dignity and social justice.

Re-reading Culture Shock II: Corruption in the U.S. as Hidden Amidst Development

In re-reading Harley's story on corruption, two things stood out to me—the shift in her moral stance regarding the Kazakhs' participation in corruption, and her perception that corruption in America seemed more "hidden," "dangerous," and "malicious." For Leff (1964), a major difficulty in researching the role of corruption in terms of economic development is that corruption "is almost universally condemned," and the criticism of it, especially when applied to others, "is based on moralizing—explicit or latent—self-interest, or ideology" (p. 8). He also argued that "Foreigners living in underdeveloped countries…have condemned corruption on moral grounds and criticized it as both a cause and a characteristic of the backwardness of these countries" (p. 8). This seemed to be the case in Harley's story. She appeared to take a moral stance against the corruption at her school and condemned her Kazakh students and colleagues for their participation in it. Although, she did not ever become "immune" to the corruption she experienced, Harley did become less "questioning" and "condemning" of the students and teachers after speaking with her Kazakh counterpart. She also seemed to become more empathetic to their plight after feeling powerless to confront the "hidden" corruption and academic "dishonesty" she experienced later in the United States. Again, this is not to suggest that Harley condoned corruption in any way, but she recognized the challenge of addressing it at an individual level and began to judge others less harshly.

In considering the way in which corruption can be hidden, I note Leff's (1964) assertion that condemning other countries and cultures as corrupt can act to serve "self-interest." This implies that focusing on the corruption of other countries can conceal the corruption in one's own country's participation in helping to create the conditions for corruption to occur. I think a poignant example illustrating this concept exists in the economic and social relationship between the United States and Mexico. On January 1, 1994, the United States, Canada, and Mexico signed the North American Free Trade Agreement (NAFTA) with the expectation that "trade, employment, and wages" would increase while Mexican migration would decrease (Martin, 2005, p. 7). And although trade has increased, illegal immigration has also increased significantly. Uchitelle (2007) explained,

> When Nafta finally became a reality, on Jan. 1, 1994, American investment flooded into Mexico, mostly to finance factories that manufacture automobiles, appliances, TV sets, apparel and the like...[However] Mexican manufacturers, once protected by tariffs on a host of products, were driven out of business as less expensive, higher quality merchandise flowed into the country....As relatively well-paying jobs disappeared, Mexico's average wage for production workers, already low, fell further behind the average hourly pay of production workers in the United States....Something similar occurred in agriculture. The assumption was that tens of thousands of farmers who cultivated corn would act "rationally" and continue farming, even as less expensive corn imported from the United States flooded the market. The farmers, it was assumed, would switch to growing strawberries and vegetables —with some help from foreign investment—and then export these crops to the United States. Instead, the farmers exported themselves.

Note that the Mexican farmers were expected to "act rationally" despite the threat to their livelihood. Additionally, Hernández Flores and Lankshear (2000) suggested that the unequal power status between Mexico and the U.S./Canada played a role in the agreement, as they point out that at the time of the agreement, Mexico "ranked 48 on the United Nations Development Index" while Canada and the United States ranked 1 and 2 on the same index (p. 240). They also submit that the "low wage 'reality'" in Mexico makes it an attractive source of low-cost labor but also "undermines in diverse ways the process of developing a well-educated, highly skilled, quality-oriented workforce" (p. 241).

This research suggests that NAFTA was an unequal economic arrangement designed to serve (North) American desires for low-cost goods and not to serve the Mexican workers' interests. In order to keep costs low, wages and human development were kept at a minimum. While the governments of the countries involved in NAFTA may have agreed to this inequitable arrangement, the Mexican workers who were asked to "rationally" accept their poverty did not. Many chose to "illegally" immigrate to the United States. They engaged in a number of "corrupt" activities to do so, including human smuggling, bribing, and border crossing. North Americans routinely condemn them for such acts yet seem oblivious as to how their desires for cheap goods and their government's self-interests helped create the conditions for such corruption to occur.

In addition to helping create the conditions for corruption to occur in other countries, there is also evidence that American culture owes some of its own development to corruption. From a historical perspective Bardhan (1997) noted that, "In the U.S. "gilded age" of 1860s and 1870s widespread corruption of state legislatures and city governments by business interests and those seeking franchises for public utilities is reported to have helped rather than hindered economic growth" (pp. 1328–1329).

More recently, Cohen (2012) argued that, owing to a mix of "cultural, political, and economic factors" (including catering to the "interests of the wealthy"), corruption is a "staple of American life." Supporting this assumption, Glaeser and Saks (2006) offered that in the United States between the years 1990 and 2002, "federal prosecutors convicted more than 10,000 government officials of acts of official corruption," leading the authors to assert that "Corruption is not just something that happens to poor countries" (p. 1053). Given that the U.S. is an economically well-developed country and given its apparent widespread corruption both past and present, it seems that economic development can co-exist with corruption but at what social and psychological costs to ourselves and others?

Reverse Culture Shock I: Clock Time Versus Event Time

The first thing that Harley noticed upon her return home was that Americans had "so much stuff," even stuff they didn't need that was kept in storage buildings. She said this was a "big eye opener" because she "didn't remember... noticing that American's had a lot of stuff" until she returned to the United States. Cultural differences in the way time was utilized in Kazakhstan and the United States also created a sense of reverse culture shock for Harley when she returned to the States. In the following passage, she talked about how life in Kazakhstan was slower and how time was used to develop social relationships. She said,

> I felt like when I was in Kazakhstan, that things were just slower or there wasn't as much to do or as many distractions per se, so I felt like there was more time to create relationships with people, because there was more free time to just hang out and talk....It wasn't like looked upon as you're being lazy or you're not doing something with your life, but that time together doing something simple, you're bonding and spending time together and just hanging out....People still worked hard, still got all the domestic duties done, did everything that we still do here....So people would come and stop by and it wasn't considered like a nuisance...it was just nice, because I knew that I could just go stop over at someone's house whenever I wanted and I wasn't going to be interfering with anything, because it was just like they were happy that you were there.

Consequently, when Harley "first moved back" to the U.S., it "kind of tripped [her] out" because she didn't feel that she could spend as much time with people as she could in Kazakhstan. In the next passage, she explained how the use of time differed in America:

> in the States, I feel that, because everyone is so busy with their family or with work or spending a lot of time commuting in their car, like even just to try to make time to like hey, let's go and get some coffee, like you have to schedule it. It's not like there's some random free time to just go hang out....I was always like intruding on their time or I had to be conscious of time and looking at my watch....There was always a definite cut off time, as opposed to just like relaxing for as long as we wanted. I never felt that here in the States....I feel in America that people don't make as much time for these times to build connections or time to build friendships.

In addition, when Harley did try to build relationships with other Americans after her return from overseas, she felt a sense of "rejection" in that most people failed to ask her about her travels abroad. For example, she found it odd that when she mentioned that she had just returned from Kyrgyzstan (her last overseas teaching post with a private company), most people showed little interest in the country or her experiences there. She complained,

> dude, I just said I lived in Kyrgyzstan…and you're looking at me as if I just said something like I went down the street to the store, but then the…person next to me will talk about oh yeah, did you see that show on TV, it was so good, and they'll totally be all animated talking about that, and I'd be flustered, because I'm like you care so much about some stupid TV show, when I'm just telling you where I had just come from and that was of no interest to them.

After receiving the same response a number of times from different Americans, Harley stopped talking about her experiences abroad and began giving the generic answer that she had spent some time living overseas when asked where she had worked or lived previously. She found that people who really cared about her experiences would ask her more questions and then she would give more concrete answers. She also mentioned that she felt she was returning to a place where she was supposed to feel "comfortable" because she grew up here, "but then at the same time all these things were happening and how I had changed, it was like people around me never changed or never saw outside of their bubble."

Harley's story about time reminded me of Michael Ende's (1985) novel *Momo*, which was originally published in Germany in 1973. In the novel, a young homeless girl named Momo turns up in an unnamed city and takes up residence in an abandoned amphitheater. She soon develops friendships with both children and adults through her special talent for listening. She "listens for the words behind the words," which appears to have "magical effects" on those around her who, in turn, begin to listen to themselves and to one another (Brotto, n.d.). Yet along come the "MEN IN GREY" who "live off the stolen time of others" (Brotto, n.d.). They convince the adults that they can save time if they work harder instead of wasting it by relaxing with friends or spending time with their children. Eventually, even the children get caught up in the time trap and Momo appears to be the only person left who is immune to the desires of the Grey Men. I won't spoil the ending, but the shift regarding the uses of time in the novel from having free time to lacking free time after the arrival of the "Grey Men" seemed an apt metaphor for understanding Harley's story as well.

Likewise, in her story, Harley seemed to address the different ways that time was allocated in Kazakh and American cultures. According to Gross (1984), the study of time allocation is useful in "cross-cultural" studies because it provides "primary data on many kinds of social interaction and provides the basis for defining social groups by behavior" with regard to "attitudes, values, cultural style, and emotions" (p. 519). Likewise, Brislin and Kim (2003) also noted cultural differences in the uses of time, and they made a distinction between two types of time allocation, "clock" time and "event" time. They explained that, "A time schedule symbolized as 'clock' represents official, formal, and task-oriented temporal concerns. This contrasts with event time, which gives attention to interpersonal relationships among people" (p. 365).

They also added that in clock time cultures, the "Emphasis is on time" and being "time sensitive" and the "Schedule evolves around the clock," whereas in event time cultures, the "Emphasis is on people" and being "time insensitive" and the "Schedule evolves around events" (p. 370).

Brislin and Kim's (2003) descriptions of clock and event time appear to mirror Harley's observations about the different relationships to time in Kazakhstan and the United States. In Kazakhstan, the pace of life was slower, there were fewer distractions, people were the focus, dropping by unannounced wasn't seen as being a nuisance, and time flowed from one event to the next without a definite ending. On the other hand, in the United States, the pace of life was faster, people were busy, Harley had to always be conscious of time, felt that she was intruding on other people's time, and there was a definite cut-off time for events. Consequently, Harley felt that people in the U.S. didn't make time to build relationships. This suggests that relationships to time are culture-bound and that time systems are mutually exclusive and don't overlap.

Another thing that made Harley feel rejected was that the Americans seemed more focused on "some stupid TV show" than on getting to know her. To the extent that Harley implied that TV was a barrier to building social relationships, there was some support for this view in the literature. In their review of time allocation studies spanning the time period 1965 to 2003, Aguiar and Hurst (2007) found that both leisure time and TV watching have increased. They wrote,

> More than 100 percent of the increase in leisure can be accounted for by the increase in the time spent watching television, which totals 7.4 hours per week for the full sample, 6.7 hours per week for men, and 8.0 hours per week for women. This increase in television is offset by a 3.9-hour-per-week decline in socializing (going

to parties, bars, etc.) and a 3.1-hour-per-week decline in reading (books, magazines, letters, etc.). (p. 987)

The authors further argued that this change in trends denoted a "sharp decline in socializing" (p. 987). The findings also supported Putnam's (1995) review of historical and longitudinal research regarding civic engagement, club memberships, and social interaction habits. He stated, "TV watching comes at the expense of nearly every social activity outside the home, especially social gatherings and informal conversations....In short, television is privatizing our leisure time" (p. 679). This research indicated that TV watching interfered with, and in some way precluded, social interaction. That Americans seemed to care about TV shows rather than making time to get to know Harley certainly appeared to be a frustrating experience for her.

Re-reading Reverse Culture Shock I: Intermixing Clock Time and Event Time Through the Use of Media

In re-reading Harley's story, I question the notion that Americans don't take time to build social connections, that the U.S. is strictly a clock-oriented culture in which social relationships aren't important, and that TV watching prevents social interaction. Oehlberg, Ducheneaut, Thornton, Moore, & Nickell (2008) shared Harley's belief that busyness and scheduling concerns can interfere with social interaction. They wrote,

> Urban sprawl...can make travelling to a friend's house for a movie night inconvenient; domestic isolation and scheduling constraints prevent gatherings (e.g., for a mother taking care of young children); and increasing mobility often separates family members (e.g., a child living away from his family to attend university). (p. 1)

But they also added that "Sociability is becoming more and more distributed in this context as technology enables diverse remote interactions" (p. 1). Perhaps, then, because of the differing contexts between Kazakhstan and the U.S., the ways of interacting socially took on different shapes. In Kazakhstan, living in a small village with few distractions enabled long periods of face-to-face bonding. In the U.S., because of busy schedules and physical distances, Americans use technology and media for the purpose of social interaction. So, it wasn't that Americans didn't make time to interact, but they learned to interact socially in different ways.

With specific regard to television, Oehlberg et al. (2008) claimed that TV watching can "foster multiple forms of sociability" either directly "when chatting with friends and family during a "movie night" at home" or indirectly "when discussing previously viewed programs with colleagues at the office water cooler" (p. 1). Williams et al. (2009) offered similar observations and also gave the example of a study participant who "reported frequently watching shows while texting and phoning her friends as a running commentary on what was being viewed" (p. 25). They also believed that families and social groups used TV and other media to "strengthen their bonds" (p. 25). This appears to indicate that conversations about TV shows were not necessarily about the shows themselves, but served an underlying bonding function. I know that in my circle of friends, we spend time socializing by watching or commenting on TV shows. I even sometimes text message friends during certain shows (*American Idol*, for example) when I need to be separate from my friends but also want to feel connected to them. And while the television show might be the catalyst for our conversation, other thoughts and observations invariably come up that lead our conversation in other directions. So when I watch television alone in my home, it is often a social act.

In addition, despite the claim that the U.S. is a clock-oriented culture focused on "official, formal, and task-oriented temporal concerns" Americans do also give "attention to interpersonal relationships among people" (Brislin & Kim, 2003, p. 365). I notice, for example, that myself and my co-workers text, e-mail, and instant-message friends, family, and other co-workers throughout the day as a means of interacting that is neither formal nor task-oriented. I see some colleagues toggling between work screens on their computers to Facebook and other social media. I see other colleagues taking time during the work day to share family photos, share artwork they have created or purchased, play computer games or games on their cell phones with friends and strangers across the country, and discuss the TV shows they watched the night before. Again, it seems that sociality is woven throughout the day in a mix of face-to-face and more long-distance interactions made possible through the use of technology as a means of building or maintaining social relationships. Along these lines, it seems that at least some Americans inter-mix facets of both clock (task-oriented) and event (relational) time through the use of media and technology.

In Harley's story, although she seemed frustrated about the focus on TV, the problem seemed more related to a lack of shared experience. In their research on the ways that participants introduced topics into a conversation,

Maynard and Zimmerman (1984) noted that "participants...rely on shared experiences to provide sense and make sense in topical introduction" (p. 305). To the extent that Harley had had 9 years of experience living and travelling outside the U.S., I think most people might have difficulty sharing or making sense of that experience at least initially, just as she had difficulty connecting with her friends' shared excitement about television that seemed to bind those friends together. For me, then, one question that develops from this story is how to communicate and interact socially with culturally different others despite the lack of shared experience.

Pedagogy I: Identity Shock and Being Treated as an "Extra Foreigner" and "International Student"

In this pair of stories, Harley experienced similar "identity shocks" in both Kazakhstan and the U.S., which she later used to inform her intercultural communication classes. For Harley, moving from a large and diverse city on the West Coast to a small village in Kazakhstan with a population of about 500 people was "a little bit of a shock." She says she not only felt the difference of being an American in Kazakhstan, but also the difference of moving from a city in the U.S. where she didn't necessarily stand out as different to living in a very small village where everybody stared, watched, and paid attention to her every move. But for Harley, it was the Kazakhs questioning her American identity that gave her the greatest feeling of culture shock. She felt that the Kazakhs thought of her as an "extra foreigner" because even though they knew she was from America, she "didn't look American" to them. She said that because she didn't have "blue eyes, white skin, and blonde hair" she was treated almost as if she were a "fraud" and had to constantly explain her identity and where she came from. She said that it felt like an "attack" on who she was, what she "stood for," what she had previously felt "secure in," and now she had to constantly "prove" who she was in a new environment where nothing was "comfortable."

In exploring the reason why the Kazakh's treated her this way, she believed their limited exposure to other Americans (recall that she was the first volunteer at this post) and their limited access to diverse media images of Americans (they relied heavily on the TV show *Dallas* for their image of Americans), led them to develop an unrealistic picture of what Americans looked like. When I asked how she handled the situation, she said she did a lot of "repetitive story-telling" about the diversity of people in the United States and explained to them that the limited American television programs they watched were "not a good representation of all the United States."

Harley added that although the Kazakhs did eventually accept her, she's not sure that they ever believed that she was really an American. Despite this, she related that once her Caucasian American Peace Corps friends began to visit her, the Kazakhs began to appreciate her difference from what they saw as "traditional" Americans. She intimated,

> I always felt funny because I felt like how their views had changed and how at one time they were, oh, you're not a real American, we're going to be distant until you prove to us you are, but then when they saw other, what they thought were real Americans, oh wait, we like [Harley] because she understands and she'll eat our food, she speaks to us in Russian, or she does all these things with us because she understands us better.

For her part, Harley didn't blame the Kazakhs for their views because she felt they "didn't know any different" due to their limited exposure to Americans and American culture.

Ironically, Harley had a similar culture shock experience after returning to the U.S. and accepting her current position in a small Midwestern town. Harley said she was surprised to find that even though she was an American, she was often treated as an "international student" because of the way she looked. She remembered in particular getting complimented on her English several times. She explained,

> the first 4 months when I lived here...I can remember five times at least that I got complimented on my English...people would come up to me and be like wow, your English is so good...where did you study or you're almost sounding just like an American...and I was really shocked. I called my mom and I'm like mom, I don't know where the hell I moved to. They're complimenting me on my English and I was thinking like, dude, I'm from [the West coast]!

She also noted that during community presentations, community members often assumed that she was a graduate student rather than the Assistant Director of International Programs. "Why couldn't it be that that I worked in the office?" she questioned, and "why don't you say, what do you do in the office?" rather than make these assumptions. In answer to these questions, Harley concluded that perhaps the people in this small town either felt "shocked" or "intimidated" by her because the various parts of her identities—Asian,

Female, PhD student, biker—didn't "necessarily mix into what a stereotype of a person getting a PhD should be, or a person who's working as an associate director should be, or someone who's riding a Harley [motorcycle]."

Harley noted that when she shared the story above as part of her intercultural communication presentations for international students and also for domestic students at the university where she works here in the United States, they tended to "laugh," and she was concerned that they didn't "recognize" the "prejudiced" thinking behind the assumption that she was seen as an international student. Therefore, she engaged the students in various "interpersonal" exercises so that they could

> reflect on some of the prejudices that they have and ones that they may not know that they have, and to try to help them see, at least recognize that just because someone is different or just because you have some sort of opinion in your mind about this person...you can't think about that being true, without getting to know, or figure out what else is behind them.

She also pointed out to them that even though people lived in the same country, their experiences and points of view could be very different. She confided that learning to negotiate other cultures and the shock(s) she experienced made her feel more "confident," "freer," "more compassionate and appreciative of people," "more open and more loving," and more "curious" about others, which in turn enabled her to "relate to people differently."

Harley's story reminded me of the experience of a young woman in my Peace Corps group in Cameroon. Her heritage was African and Native American. She was excited to be going to Africa as a way of affirming her African roots. However, once we arrived there, the Cameroonians referred to her with the same term that they used for all of the volunteers—"nasara" which we had been told meant "white man" or "white foreigner." As we sat discussing this she began to cry. She said that she had had to fight for her identity as a black woman in the U.S. and now she would have to fight for her identity as a black woman in Africa. Although her story and Harley's are not exactly the same, they both point to ways in which culture shock can be a shock to one's identity. Within the culture shock literature a number of writers have noted that culture shock can have a strong influence on one's sense of self (Adler, 1976; Bennett, 1977) because it challenges the "stability" of one's "psychic organization" (Garza-Guerrero, 1974, p. 410). Zaharna (1989), who referred to culture shock as a form of "self-shock," explained further that intercultural encounters are "dominated by unknowns, uncertainty, and ambiguity" and therefore the intercultural context creates a "double-bind of *increased need* to confirm self-identities, with *diminished ability* to do" so (p. 516). However, the experiences of both my Peace Corps group mate and Harley seem to express something beyond culture shock in that they experienced similar identity struggles in both host and home cultures. While I have certainly had to reflect on notions of identity, I have not had to defend my skin color, gender, nationality, or language ability. Likewise, when the Cameroonians called me "white man" the term fit me so it didn't feel like an attack on my identity, even though I tired sometimes of having the term "nasara" flung at me almost everywhere I went. The point is that for people whose identity draws on two or more cultural backgrounds, they seem to face an ongoing form of identity shock in that whether in the host culture or home culture, they are always in an intercultural context. The notion of culture shock also fails to address the prejudice that underlies certain inter- and intra-cultural judgments.

Similarly, Sonu and Moon (2009), one of whom is Korean and the other Korean American, wrote about their feelings of alienation from both their "home" and their "homeland" because they do not fit easily into the categories of Korean or American. They also both share Harley's experience of being complimented on their English in the United States. For Moon, a Korean working in the U.S., he first felt that the compliments regarding his English ability were a "reward" for his hard work in learning English, but after a while, he began to see such compliments as recognition that, despite his fluency, he had failed to assimilate into American culture (p. 142). Describing her experience of being complimented on her English ability, Sonu, a Korean American, noted the seeming "*mismatch*" between her "*Asian face*" and her "*seamless American accent*" (p. 142). She wrote, "*A piece of me dies every time I am forced to explain where I learned English. This has not been once, but so many times. Is my face that deceitful, elusive, exotic, betraying?*" (p. 142).

These authors also drew on Frank Wu's notion of the "perpetual foreigner" to describe the Asian experience in America and to point out the racism behind the apparent belief that Asians cannot also be Americans (whether by birth or by choice) as evidenced by compliments of English ability and questions about one's country of origin (p. 154). The notion of Wu's "perpetual foreigner" recalls Harley's feelings of being treated as an "extra foreigner" and a perpetual "international student." Further, Sonu and Moon's (2009) autobiographical accounts illustrate that despite the perhaps well-meaning intention of compliments on the surface, compliments may also serve to highlight racial differences and underscore racial prejudices.

There is also additional support for the view of Asian Americans as "perpetual foreigners" in America in writings dating back to the first half of the 20th century. In a 1914 publication by the American Sociological Society regarding racial assimilation in American culture, the report noted that the Asian

> bears in his features a distinctive racial hallmark, that he wears, so to speak, a racial uniform which classifies him. He cannot become a mere individual, indistinguishable in the cosmopolitan mass of the population...[but] is condemned to remain among us an abstraction, a symbol...of the Orient and that vague, ill-defined menace we sometimes refer to as the "yellow peril." (In Park, 1928, pp. 890–891)

Stonequist (1935) added that in the American melting-pot, it is the minority groups that are "expected to do most of the melting" (the "adjusting, conforming, and assimilating") (p. 2), but that racial differences compound the problems associated with assimilation for second generation Asian Americans whom he described as "neither Orientals nor Americans in a full sense" who represent an "undetermined status" (p. 8). This implies the near impossibility of Asian American assimilation due to racial differences, cultural biases (the "yellow peril"), and the American cultural desire for all people to fit into singularly and narrowly defined cultural frameworks.

Stonequist (1935) also argued that once the bicultural person becomes aware of the conflicts arising from her or his differing cultural orientations, he or she may enter into a "crisis" phase involving "confusion, even shock, restlessness, disillusionment, and estrangement" (p. 10). For Park (1928), this crisis phase is "relatively permanent" and is marked by "spiritual instability, intensified self-consciousness, restlessness, and *malaise*" (p. 893). For these authors, the bi- and/or multi-cultural experience in America, in general, and the Asian/Asian American experience in particular, is replete with various forms of prejudice, racism, conflict, crises, and alienation—and because of racial differences and biases, the feelings of crisis are potentially ongoing. It is also interesting to note that Park (1928) and Stonequist (1935) both used the term "restlessness" in discussing the bicultural experience, to the extent that Harley's need for constant travel both within the U.S. and abroad seems to exemplify a certain restlessness and a desire to escape the small Midwestern town in which she currently resides.

The culture shock(s), identity shock(s), and racial prejudice that Harley experienced both in Kazakhstan and the U.S. served as teaching tools for Harley here in the United States. In Harley's case, both the rural Kazakhs and rural

Americans called Harley's American identity into question by focusing on her Asian appearance. In the U.S., she felt insulted when complimented on her English since it was her first language, and angered for not being recognized as a leader/administrator, which she felt was indicative of racial prejudice. Both cultures seemed to link being American with whiteness. To have her American identity rejected, not once but twice, was painful and alienating for Harley. Her experiences being treated as an "extra foreigner" and an "international student" also lent credence to her mother's suggestion that as an Asian woman she would have to work harder (see Harley's Culture Shock I Story), in the sense that she had to go to greater lengths to prove that she was American—something that neither I nor other white Americans have to do, whether at home or abroad. These experiences gave Harley a "double-consciousness"—an awareness that the white majority does not have (Balfour, 1998)—which she used in her teaching to expose and confront prejudice.

Re-reading Pedagogy I: The (Potential) Benefits of Bi-Culturality

Despite the negative aspects associated with being bicultural, such as "identity confusion, dual expectations, and value clashes" (Nguyen & Benet-Martinez, 2007, p. 106) and "dealing with the implications of multiple racial stereotypes and pressures from different communities" (Benet-Martinez & Haritatos, 2005), there is emerging research that suggests that bicultural people may possess certain skills that are particularly beneficial in a rapidly globalizing world (Stonequist, 1935; Benet-Martinez & Haritatos, 2005; Nguyen & Benet-Martinez, 2007; DeKorne et al., 2007; Friedman & Liu, 2009). For example, Stonequist (1935) wrote that the bi-cultural "individual's dual contacts may give [her or] him an advantage, making him [or her] a leader… conciliator, reformer, teacher" and "The stimulus of the situation may create a superior personality or mind" (p. 11). This suggests that somewhere amid the tension created by differences, the bicultural person may use that tension in order to gain new insights and to fruitfully thrive.

Additionally, through their interviews with nine long-term immigrant women (four in the U.S. and five in the U.K.), DeKorne et al. (2007) found that "identifying with more than one culture" (p. 301) can bring other benefits, such as increased understanding of self, others, and home culture as well as becoming more tolerant and accepting of others yet more critical and analytical at the same time. Benet-Martinez and Haritatos (2005) also suggested a link between bicultural identity and a sense of "openness (i.e., tolerance of and interest in new values and lifestyles) and emotional stability (i.e., resilience, flexibility)" (p. 1022). In addition, Friedman and Liu (2009) argued that two skills that bi-culturals seem to develop out of necessity—adaptability and the ability to connect people and ideas from different cultures—may serve them in becoming stronger organizational leaders.

In Harley's case, although she certainly felt the sting of racial prejudice in Kazakhstan and the U.S., she also felt that her experiences made her "more compassionate and appreciative of people," "more open and more loving," and more "curious" about other people, so that she was able to "relate" to them "differently." Her extensive travels both overseas and in America seem to demonstrate her curiosity and openness to others. Yet, like the women in the DeKorne et al. (2007) study, she also became more critical and analytical, especially in the area of racial prejudice, which she used to inform her teaching. That the Kazakhs ultimately appreciated Harley more than the other "real" Americans also suggests she was able to develop "assurance" in herself "apart from cultural identification" (DeKorne et al., p. 2007, p. 304). I have also seen other evidence of Harley's self-assurance, her leadership abilities, and her openness in bringing friends, students, and co-workers from differing cultural groups together in order to share a meal, discuss broad-ranging cultural and interpersonal issues, and to play video games involving dancing or simulating a rock band. For Thanksgiving 2011 and 2012, for example, she hosted a group of more than 100 people (international students, friends, and those with no place to go) at her home. In other words, Harley did not let the prejudice she has experienced (and may continue to experience) prevent her from connecting with others or from reaching her goals as an educator and a leader.

Pedagogy II: Cultural Adjustment as "Context" or "Consistency"

Harley also shared with her international students some of the tools she used to negotiate other cultures in order to help them adjust to American culture. In the following passage, Harley highlighted the need to constantly evaluate one's efforts in trying to adjust to another culture. She explains that she and the other foreigners teaching abroad, would see if there was something that we did, that we're like oh-oh, that's not going to work, back track, what should we do? We're like oh, wait, that worked this time, so we do it again in another situation, oh, that didn't work again, back track, like that constant confusion, and I say there is never going to be a time that you're not evaluating. It's never going to ever be the same, sometimes it might have worked in this situation, but it might not work in another.

She added that the constant evaluation was "sort of tiring...you'll never know completely the right answer." Still, she told the international students she didn't want them to "be afraid to try" to interact with American students or teachers and she didn't want them to feel bad after they left the U.S. because they "didn't try."

Harley also had her international students reflect on their comfort level and how far they were willing to step out of their comfort zone in order to participate in their classes or befriend American students. She explained to the students that "Anything that's new and different" would "never feel comfortable" and that there would always be "a little bit of nervousness and a little bit of anxiety." She also told them it was "good" to feel those feelings in that if "you're always comfortable with things, it's just mundane and nothing ever changes" and these feelings "make you know that you're still alive." She even used the international students' sense of culture shock to help them understand why it may be uncomfortable and "scary" for American students to get involved with them. She said,

> I tell them, think about when you came here when you were trying new food and when you were trying to go to the bookstore or go to Wal-Mart, that was kind of a little bit new and different for you and it's a little bit scary, but you guys have to do it in order to survive, because you need to do that and you're able to overcome that and that shows a lot of strength, just the fact that you're here and you're wanting to do this, but you were still scared...from the [American] students' point of view, like they're scared and they don't push themselves to try to explore and experience that, unlike you guys are pushing yourselves to explore and experience things. There's just not that extra push, so it will always stay at a certain level.

Harley also explained to the international students that they may have to help American students get over their fear by being the first to reach out, otherwise the Americans may not be willing "to try" to get to know them.

When I asked Harley if she was always able to appreciate the negative emotions she experienced through culture shock, she said that if I would have asked her that during her "first 6 months in the Peace Corps" that she "wouldn't have been able to show the positive at the end." She said that finding the positive often takes time, distance, and reflection. She also said this was something she discussed with the new international students coming to her university, that "sometimes you have to feel all these negative feelings in order for it to be good, or in order to be positive you have to feel the negative, because it just balances each other out." Harley also noted that it took students different lengths of time, sometimes months, sometimes a year or more, to find this balance.

While Harley believed that cultural differences affected the ways in which international students adjusted to American culture, she felt that "people's perceptions and personalities" also played a part in intercultural interaction. She noted, for instance, that while some international students felt a "disconnect" between themselves and the other American students or teachers, other international students felt that American students and teachers were very approachable and welcoming and so they "were able to integrate and find a way that they were a part of a group." Overall, she felt that one couldn't "generalize" about what would or wouldn't be helpful for students and that one couldn't "force...relationships to happen." Still, she believed intercultural interaction "doesn't happen...naturally...someone has to be proactive about it and make an opportunity for it."

Helping international students adjust to American culture formed a major part of Harley's pedagogy in her "Transitions" class. Sifting through the literature on cultural adjustment, scholars from Project GLOBE (Global Leadership and Organizational Behavior Effectiveness) which, as its name suggests, studies leadership and intercultural interaction on a global scale, made a link between cultural adjustment and identity. They wrote,

> Cultural adaptability refers to the mental and psychological ability to move from one situation and country to another...The dexterity to adjust one's behavior is a critical requirement. Not everyone can do this; to many people it may bring into question one's own identity. (Javidan, Dorfman, De Luque, & House, 2006, p. 85)

For Maertz, Hassan, and Magnussan (2009), "stress," "discomfort," and "internal conflicts" are created when the new culture demands behavior that is inconsistent with the sojourner's identity, therefore adjustment "involves resolving [these] internal inconsistencies" (p. 67). However, some argue that the need to resolve these "inconsistencies" is a Western or European American cultural preference (Suh, 2002; English & Chen, 2011; Kim, Peng, & Chiu, 2008). Reviewing the psychological literature from the 1950s to the present, Suh (2002) noted that in Western culture "psychological well-being" has unfailingly been linked with "developing and maintaining a consistent identity" across differing social contexts (p. 1378). Suh further argued that the notion of self in East Asian cultures is less concerned with consistency, is more "malleable" and dependent on the context, and is more tolerant of dissonance (pp. 1378–1379). English and Chen (2011) related this tolerance for dissonance to the Eastern philosophical concept of "dialecticism," which they explained is "a system of thought characterized by acceptance of contradiction, expectation of change and dynamism, and holistic perception" (p. 479). Additionally, Kim et al. (2008) suggested that Asians may be more attuned to change as exemplified in the Confucian philosophy of *"yin and yang,"* which posits that opposing forces (dark/light, evil/divine, etc.) will eventually take the place of the other (p. 113). This implies that an awareness that conditions will change can assist one in tolerating dissonant situations.

While it is not clear to what extent Harley's Asian heritage influenced her philosophy on cultural adjustment, her beliefs seemed to fit more closely with the East Asian paradigm. Her notions of "back tracking" and "constant evaluation" suggested the need to adjust behavior based on the context rather than attempting to maintain a consistent approach to all circumstances. Likewise she implied the necessity to tolerate and appreciate the anxiety and nervousness created by internal conflicts because they make one feel alive. This recalls a passage from Laozi's (2009) Tao Te Ching, which reads,

> "Value your calamities as part of your being…
> What makes it possible for me to have calamities
> Is treating myself as having a being…if I had no being
> What trouble could I have?" (p. 63).

Further, Harley appeared to recognize that situations were constantly changing and that perceptions of events or interactions could shift from negative to positive with time and distance. Overall, she noted the need to adjust one's behavior according to the context since the outcomes of one's efforts were not "generalizable."

Yet, although these techniques were helpful for Harley during her travels in other countries, adopting or maintaining a contextual self may prove frustrating in adjusting to American culture, which seems organized around the belief in the autonomous, decontextualized self. As Suh (2002) argued, "Within this highly self-centered cultural scheme, it comes quite naturally that the self, the principal source of personal meaning and guidance, needs to be highly organized and consistent" (p. 1378). Further, there appears to be an American cultural belief in a single "right" answer, unlike Harley's insistence that "you'll never know completely the right answer." If this is the case, then it may also be beneficial to share the cultural expectation of autonomy and consistency with students and others as a point of potential intercultural conflict.

Re-reading Pedagogy II: Cultural Adjustment as an Ability to "Flex"

While in the previous section, adjustment to new cultures was related to notions of identity from a cultural perspective. Bennett (1977), however, seemed to blend elements of the cultural perspectives presented earlier and to look at the personal skills that can aid one in the adjustment process. Although Bennett agreed with the research presented in the previous section that culture shock is a "reaction to cognitive inconsistency" (p. 47) and is related to identity, she posited that having a stable identity can both help and hinder the adjustment process. For example, she wrote that in the culture shock experience, which she refers to as a type of transition shock, "the quandary is frequently: 'Who am I?'" (p. 48) and that

> The individual who is most likely to master this situation is the one who has a firm sense of self-identity....However...a strong sense of identity could also be a hindrance if we are inflexible and become threatened too quickly by conflicting stimuli. (p. 48)

This suggested the need for both firmness and flexibility during the adjustment process and tolerating or reinterpreting the perceived threat to one's identity.

Additionally, Bennett (1977) drew upon Sargeant's model of psychological adjustment to new environments to suggest the notion of "flex," which she feels "does not imply a surrender of world view" but denotes various "adaptations which may be employed to reduce dissonance in the new culture" (p. 48). Some of these adaptations involved immersing oneself in either the host or the home culture, assimilating both cultures, or selecting and mixing parts of each culture. She further argued that some of the "personality characteristics" that helped promote the ability to "flex" included "self-awareness, non-evaluativeness, cognitive complexity, and cultural empathy" (p. 48). Overall, Bennett believed that overcoming the need to "flee" feelings of discomfort, as well as reflecting on one's own personal adjustment process from prior transition experiences, enabled one to cope more effectively with culture shock, aided one in tolerating intercultural differences, and led to personal growth.

In revisiting Harley's story through Bennett's (1977) "flex" perspective, I noted areas of similarity and difference. Like Bennett, Harley pointed out that people's "personalities" played a role in their ability to adjust to a new culture. Harley also similarly promoted both self-awareness and cultural empathy when she asked the international students to recall their culture shock experiences coming to the U.S. as a way of relating to the American students' fear of things that were new and different. She also pointed out that while the international students were motivated by survival in a new culture, the Americans did not share the same motivation, which seemed to be Harley's way of depersonalizing any rejection the international students may have felt.

In addition, Harley's perspective on the need to "backtrack" or use various techniques in order to adjust to a new culture, to overcome one's fears, to see that the positive can grow from the negative, and to avoid generalizing, demonstrated a good deal of cognitive complexity. However, while Harley stressed the importance of evaluation during the adjustment process ("there is never going to be a time that you're not evaluating"), Bennett (1977) argued that "evaluation" actually increases culture shock and that "among the first skills we need to develop are the abilities to withhold evaluation, to refrain from cultural absolutism, to accept rather than reject." While I agree with Bennett's suggestion that learning to accept a new culture is an important skill, it seems unlikely that anyone could accept everything in a new culture (or everything in one's home culture, for that matter) without rejecting some part of it. Yet, constantly evaluating every interaction might be "tiring," as Harley noted, and may ultimately prove futile. Still, there seemed to be at least some aspects of the "flex" perspective in Harley's own experience and in her pedagogy for helping international students adjust to American culture.

INTERPLAY 2

Who Am I (Becoming)?

"I am not," she said tearfully, "a wart hog. From hell." But the denial had no force.
Flannery O'Connor (1995) from *Revelation*

The first house I moved into looked like a cream-colored African adobe. Another house had been arranged for me by the Peace Corps but had been rented out to someone else before I arrived. The solution that was worked out (not by me) was for me to displace the landlord who had rented the first house to someone else, and he would move into the compound inhabited by his four wives. How awkward! The house had concrete floors and cinder block walls, a small living room, two smaller rooms, and a modern bathroom with a modern toilet and faucets—none of which worked. The toilet I had to use was a hole in the ground out back. For the water, I would have children gather it from the community foot-pump well for a few francs and then I would boil and filter it on my gas bottle stove. I had also brought a bed given to me by the Peace Corps (although they had given me the wrong bolts for it and it kept falling apart), a mosquito net, a medical kit, and the clothes and assorted junk I had brought from home. I had no furniture and no cookware. It took me probably all of 30 minutes to get moved in, and I thought, Well, what am I supposed to do now?

It didn't take long before small groups of curious children started to gather to try and figure out just what the heck I was. I had stretched long sheets of fabric across the barred windows, but that didn't keep their tiny hands from reaching in and pulling them to one side in order to catch a glimpse of me. I felt like a big blonde baboon stuck in a cage for the entire world to gawk at. Fortunately for me, at some point during the day they decided they might need to feed their new pet, and tiny hands reached through the bars of my cage with some freshly boiled corn and bananas sent over by their mothers. To me, both the realization that I was a human being and that I might be hungry was tangible evidence that I was welcomed to be in this strange place, and more than anything that had happened so far, it gave me a little hope to hang onto for the future.

At some point, I decided to explore the village and see what I could see. I started out walking until I heard some music and decided to follow where it led. I came upon a teeny-tiny little tin-roof shack with a sign on it that said "discotheque d'Olawati." Music was warbling from two large beaten-up speakers sitting outside. Turns out in French, a discotheque is where you buy music, not necessarily dance to it. The little shack had a few small shelves of well-worn cassettes that you could listen to and then choose the songs you wanted to record on your own blank cassette. Don't even ask about copyright laws. I figured that anyone who ran a music store had to be fun, open-minded, and definitely in the know, so that's where I would start. And as it turned out, I was right.

The proprietor of the little music shop was called Niko, although why, I don't know, because his real name was something completely different. He was also jokingly called "monsieur le mayor," which means Mr. Mayor, but I don't know why he was called that either, except it seems that Cameroonians are extremely fond of nicknames. Anyway, Niko and I had a nice long visit and we became instant friends. We talked about the previous Peace Corps volunteers in Olawati from years past. Seems there had been no new volunteer for the past few years. We talked a bit about Cameroon and the United States and Olawati. He even produced a cassette of music for me to take home and listen to. I told him I would bring it back soon, and he said that there was no hurry because he knew that white people didn't steal things. Boy had he got that one wrong, but I was too tired to argue and I probably forgot how to say it in French that he couldn't be further from the truth. As I got to know Niko better, I could always count on him to give me the inside scoop about all of the scandals going on in Olawati. He was somebody everybody told their secrets to.

Anyway, over the next few weeks I began to meet the assorted characters that inhabited Olawati. Most of the townspeople of Olawati were cotton farmers, but there were also politicians, teachers, businessmen, prostitutes, missionaries, picture-takers, taxi drivers, market sellers, animal herders, crazy people, and various assorted passersby. I was most impressed by the handicapped people in Olawati. The handicapped aren't given any special consideration whatsoever. They were neither helped nor hidden away from view. They just were. This one guy I called "spaghetti leg" had this leg that curved in three places just like a limp spaghetti noodle. He had fashioned himself a little skateboard-type contraption to wheel his leg around in. I thought that was pretty bright.

I also became especially fond of the deaf people. There were two deaf people in Olawati. I never knew their names, but Olawati being a small village, we'd bump into each other, have an exchange, and then go our separate ways, each of us happier for the meeting, or at least I'd like to think so. I think we liked each other because we were on a sort of equal footing, they not being able to speak very well due to forces of nature and me not being able to speak very well because I was linguistically a dorkus. That being the case, we developed our own sort of sign language although our repertoire of signs was somewhat limited.

One of the deaf people was an old man who always pretended to steal my knapsack. He'd come near me and pretend to grab the shoulder strap and I'd grab my bag, step back and wag my finger at him and then we'd both laugh in our own ways and he'd invite me to go pray at the mosque, always with gestures, mind you, and I'd gesture back that I'd prayed at home and couldn't go, which all seemed to amuse him terribly. The other deaf person was an older lady who lived along the path that I took on my way to the school. She'd always be furiously brushing the sand in her front yard and we'd give each other a hearty wave if she thought to look up. One day she came running out with some snack that she had made, probably something made out of peanuts (dear God I hope it was peanuts!) and that seemed to make her happy. When I was leaving Olawati, I decided to give her the fabric that I used as my front door and my curtains. The fabric still had a lot of life left in it and could be re-used or re-sewn into a charming house frock, as nothing is wasted in Cameroon, and besides, it had worked for Scarlett O'Hara in the movie *Gone with the Wind*. As I handed the fabric to the woman, she made it clear that she thought it was pretty but that she didn't have any money to pay for it and then she cried and thanked me profusely when I gave it to her anyway. Amazing what a few good scraps of fabric can do. I wasn't thinking or I'd have given my bag to the nice deaf man who was always pretending to steal it.

There was also a group of 4–5 very old men that always met to gossip under a shade tree near my house. They always stood up and greeted me and then asked me for money and patted down my pockets. When my keys would jingle they would say, "Ah-ha!," and then they would fake being seriously disappointed when I pulled out my jingling house keys. I credit them with motivating me to learn more of the local language (called Fulfulde), because when they started harassing me in their own loving way, I wanted to have a good variety of comebacks ready for them, which made them laugh in hysteric fits. I could say stuff in their language like, "There is no money. I am a poor man and I only have a little change that I'm saving for tomorrow." That may not seem very funny in English, it was a big hoot in Fulfulde. I guess the real joke was that they knew that I was lying and that I had millions of dollars stashed away somewhere, which of course I didn't.

One of the strangest people in Olawati was a young fellow I referred to as "Vampire Boy" because he went around telling everyone that I was a vampire and that the reason I was white and not black was because I had no blood and therefore I had to suck out everyone else's. He also tried to touch my arm or shoulder when nobody was looking as if to see if I was really real. But even though Vampire Boy kind of gave me the creeps, he was not my least favorite person in Olawati. The one person that I truly despised was named Mr. Ndu-du and he was the discipline master at our school. He had extremely large nostrils and such a turned-up nose that if you looked at him, you felt you were looking at a skull. His nostrils were so big that whenever anyone in the village had anything derogatory to say about him, which they often did, they would finish with, "And him with his big nostrils." He was the meanest person I ever met in Cameroon. His favors, such as final grades and national exam scores, could be bought for a price, and if the students couldn't pay up, he made them work in his onion fields.

On my first encounter with Mr. Ndu-du, he was rifling through the students' pen-pal letters from America, taking out all the cassettes and good stuff and keeping it for himself. On our second encounter, he made a tacky remark to me in front of the other teachers. We were all sitting in the teacher's lounge, a sparse room with a big square wooden table and some rickety creaking old chairs. There were about six or seven other teachers waiting for their next classes to start when Mr. Ndu-du loudly and proudly asked me had I ever "tasted a Cameroonian woman?" Now does that sound like an appropriate question to you? The other teachers sat there awestruck until one of them said something like "Oooooooooh, the red question," only he said it in French. I thought of a nasty retort to his filthy question but then again, I imagined him sneaking into my house under the cover of darkness, just like some African ninja, to slit my throat with a rusty knife. So I decided to play it cool, pretend that I didn't understand what he was saying, and I went about my business. This wouldn't be our last confrontation though—he was what you could call my arch-nemesis.

In the opposite corner, on my side, was Mr. Bonti. Mr. Bonti was a nice polite young Cameroonian who would be my English-teaching counterpart. Mr. Bonti was great. His English was surprisingly good, although one time in a class of his that I was observing, he referred to the forearm as the "before arm" and the belly button as the "belly nostril." He seemed different than most Cameroonians and I had the sneaking suspicion that he was a Euro-phile. In addition to English, Mr. Bonti taught German and he cut out pictures of white people and put them on the wall of his one-room house. Mr. Bonti helped me with everything, all with patience and a good sense of humor. But ultimately, I think what made Mr. Bonti such a good friend was the fact that he wasn't 100% sure of what to think about his own culture, so I could definitely relate.

And besides Mr. Bonti, the one person who made my coming to Cameroon absolutely worth it all was a student of mine named Sunny. He sat far in the back of the 11th-grade class and was always skinny, sickly, and pathetic. He never raised his hand or tried to answer a question, but he always refused to let me clean the chalkboard myself, and if I tried he would always take the eraser from me and clean the board himself. Still, for the first three months, I had very little idea that he even existed. It wasn't until after I came back from Christmas break the first year that I noticed a change in Sunny. He started trying to answer as many questions as he could. He was usually wrong, but he tried very hard. He studied, he participated, and he began to learn English. One day he came to my house and begged my assistance in procuring for him a small French/English dictionary that he could pay for in installments.

After me trying to keep a proper Cameroonian household with very little experience, I quickly hatched a plan. I had plenty of French/English dictionaries and I told him he could have one if he was willing to do a few chores around my house. But Sunny said that was his and the other students' responsibility anyway, that in their culture, students were supposed to help all of the teachers. That was news to me, especially since I previously hired this one kid who was the nephew of some bigwig in town, who kept asking for more and more money and spent most of his time in the kitchen gobbling up what little food we had until I asked him not to come back after he began disrupting my class with hoots and screams at odd moments. So when Sunny came along and I was one week into cooking for myself and doing my laundry by hand, he seemed like a blessing in disguise.

Even after Sunny had more than repaid his debt, he still came around to help me with anything that I needed. He was always formal and serious, which never failed to amuse me. He was fairly tall and very, very thin. He had a straightforward deadpan look in his eye and you'd have thought after coming over to my house several times that he'd kind of loosen up, but he was always real scrappy—chin up, eyes straight ahead, that sort of thing. Even my attempts to joke around with him failed miserably. He would always come over, cook, leave and then wait until I and any guests had eaten and then return, put away the leftovers, do the dishes and then leave without eating. I told him that the reason there were leftovers was that they were leftover for him to eat. But he said he wasn't there to eat, he was there to do his job. Can you imagine that, in a country of starving people, this hungry-looking teenager says he wasn't there to eat?

Over the next few months, our little arrangement worked out really well for me—hot meals, clean clothes, and a well-manicured sandy lawn, I was set. Then it occurred to me that in all the time that Sunny had been taking care of me and my needs, I knew little about his life, nor did I know where or how he lived. I asked if I could see where he lived and he took me to a very small, low hut, just big enough for two people—he and his younger brother. They had a small gas cooker and a bag of millet that was supposed to sustain them for four months. They slept on hand-woven mats without any sheets or blankets. During the winter, it did get very cold at night but would warm up after 10 a.m. the following morning. At these times, many of the old and weak die because the temperature change is such a shock to their system.

I felt guilty as I walked home to my gigantic house, where I had a bed and pillows, and blankets to keep me warm. On the walk home, I passed a small shack that sold dry goods and other necessities. I was overjoyed to see a large peach-colored blanket for sale. Trying to conceal my joy, I asked Mr. Bonti to bargain for the blanket and deliver it to Sunny. Later, Sunny modestly thanked me for the blanket, and then one night after I had gone to bed and he was leaving the house after doing the dishes, he passed by my room on his way out, and through the door he said he was leaving. I said "okay," and then in rough English he stammered, "I...love...you." "I love you too," I quickly replied and rolled over with a big smile on my face. I had made a difference in someone's life, I had done something good!

These life-affirming occasions notwithstanding, I don't mind telling you that living in a place like Africa can do a real head-trip on you if you are not paying attention. There were some days that I didn't know who I was any more. I certainly began to relate with all those celebrities who act as if they just want to be left alone by their adoring fans. So many people would look and stare at me, that I began to think that I was weird or something. Now I know what Madonna feels like. Well, perhaps not exactly.

Not only did it seem as if everybody was looking in a fish bowl and I was the fish, but everyone that I knew had a different name for me. The following is a short list of some of the names people called me by, at least to my face:

1. Jon
2. Mr. Jon
3. Nasara (Fulfulde for white man)
4. Baba nasara (father white man)
5. Baba bikkoy (father of the children, based on me being a teacher)
6. Nasara Manga (big/important white man)
7. Yaya (the muslim equivalent of Jon)
8. Le blanc (French meaning 'the white')
9. Teacher (but it came out more like teacha)
10. Banderas (as in "Antonio Banderas," but only from a distance when I wore my black turtleneck and put my hair in a ponytail)
11. El Hadji Mandawadji (roughly translates to "Mr. Peanut"...hey, I liked peanuts!)
12. Junginowo (Fulfulde for a teacher in a Muslim school)
13. The Coca-Cola salesman who worked for the FBI (I had my skeptics)
14. Le grande blaguer (the big joker, LOL)

One thing I caught myself doing on a regular basis was running to the pit toilet, not only to relieve the constant swirling in my bowels that I had acquired since arriving in Cameroon, but also just to have a long look at myself in the mirror. I felt like a parakeet in a cage with its own little mirror to keep itself company. Sometimes I just checked the mirror to make sure that I was real... that all of this was really happening. This may sound strange, but after being surrounded by black folks 24 hours a day, I often just thought of myself as black and half-expected to see a black man staring at me from the other side of the mirror. Until, of course, someone reminded me of my whiteness. I'd be walking along minding my own business when inevitably someone would scream out, "nasara!" Nasara, we had been told, was the word for "white man," and evidently, it referred to the fact that the people of Nazareth (as in "Jesus of") were lighter-skinned than the other people of the region. Once, a Cameroonian friend even said I reminded of him of images of Jesus because I let my hair and beard grow out real long and I wore this long robe, and with all the children following me, he thought I resembled Jesus. Of course, after I shaved my beard and was left with the long hair and a smooth round pink face, sometimes strangers had a hard time telling whether I was a boy or a girl. I heard them whisper, "Na debbo na, na gorko na?" which was their way of asking "Is it a girl or a boy?" I had half a mind to walk up to them and say, "Hi. My name's Tammy, wanna wrestle?" And yet, I liked that feeling of ambiguity—of not being able to be placed into a specific category and therefore not having specific gendered expectations forced upon me. So why does this same feeling of gender ambiguity bother me so much in the U.S.?

But, just when I thought I was like everyone else, someone had to point out the fact that I was pigmentally challenged. How rude! This was usually done by, but not limited to, the pack of small children that roams around every small village in Cameroon. At first it was very cute to have a small choir of children chirping "nasara," like munchkins from the movie *The Wizard of OZ*, as I walked around town. This became less cute after hundreds of times of hearing the same thing over and over again. After a while, I realized that the social structure of the village did not allow children to taunt adults in this way, and well, me being an adult, I wanted my share of respect. So I asked my friends, "Why do they speak to me this way?" Their reply: "They do that because you don't beat them...beat them and they will stop." I was a bit stunned. I imagined pitchfork-wielding villagers chasing me if I even thought about beating their precious little angels. That would not be good for world peace or my pitchfork-riddled ass. Fortunately, though, you often only have to go through the motions to get your point across. I quickly realized I simply had to make an upward tree-limb-grabbing motion, which is evidently the universal sign for "somebody's about to get their butt beaten," and the children would scatter, thus keeping world peace, and my hindquarters, intact.

When adults called me nasara, however, they seemed to mean it. I can say with certainty that I understand that feeling of being called out by my skin color, and it's an uneasy one. It's as if you are walking around unaware, and maybe even happy, and somebody slaps you in the face and says, "Don't feel too safe, you're not one of us!" I guess I was different. And for every child that followed me chanting "nasara! nasara!" There were just as many who ran away from me shrieking in terror. I distinctly remember a hut along the path that I took to school where some naughty little boys lived. As I walked toward their house I could see them race to the backyard to fetch their baby sister and rush her to the front gate, then laugh uproariously as I entered her field of vision. Every time she saw me, she became terrified and desperately ran into her house, crying all the way. After repeating this same episode many times, I decided to teach the boys a lesson, and once, after the little girl had run away, I pretended to go crazy and I chased the boys, who in turn ran away in fright. In case you are keeping score: Jon Smythe 1, world peace 0.

Parents also liked to get in on the act of frightening their children. They would dare their kids to walk up and shake my hand and laugh loudly as their children held onto their parents' legs in utter horror. One parent had the foresight to mention to his little tot that I made a habit of eating little black kids. Great! Now I was going to be known as the guy in the village who ate babies, and couldn't get a tan.

· 4 ·

TOWARD A PEDAGOGY OF SOCIAL JUSTICE

Introduction

Ryder, a 46-year-old white male, was an assistant professor of English at a Midwestern university at the time I conducted his interviews. For his Peace Corps service Ryder taught English in forms 1–4 (basically ninth–12th grade) at a rural boarding secondary school in Kenya from 1987 to 1990. He also stayed on in Kenya an additional year and taught on his own. Later, after returning to the U.S. and completing a master's degree, he taught English in a college preparatory program for a large oil company in Saudi Arabia for approximately 6 years. Although his teaching in Saudi Arabia was unrelated to the Peace Corps, we talked about some of those experiences and I have included references to his experiences teaching there in this study.

I met Ryder in his university office, which was small and sparsely decorated except for a few bookshelves filled to capacity, a few older-looking rolling chairs that squeaked loudly every time we shifted our weight in them, and a handful of gifts from students and colleagues. For example, there was a braided ornament from a Chinese student, a small paper bag decorated with a face so it could be used as a hand puppet, which was a gift from an American student at Halloween, and an international-looking letter holder given to him by a world-travelling colleague. There was also a "jumbo-sized" pink eraser still in its packaging hanging on the side of one of his bookshelves. Ryder explained that it was a gift from an American student in a recent applied linguistics class and that it related to a culture shock story from Kenya that he told in the class that had to do with the difficulty of shared meaning even in the same language. In the story, two young female Kenyan students asked him for a "rubber." Ryder was shocked that these two girls were asking for a rubber, which he thought referred to a condom. When he questioned why they needed a "rubber," they said they needed it to "rub" the chalkboard so they could write on it, which made him realize that a "rubber" was the American English equivalent of "eraser." A few days after telling the story in his American linguistic class, a student gave Ryder the jumbo pink eraser that I saw hanging on his bookshelf. Ryder said he kept the eraser hanging there to "celebrate" the fact that someone was paying attention in his class and that it reminded him of the two Kenyan girls whose request made him reflect on how words in the same language could have a "double meaning."

When I asked Ryder how he chose his pseudonym for the study, he explained that Ryder was a character from Sir Arthur Conan Doyle's short story "The Adventure of the Blue Carbuncle." In the story, the fictional detective Sherlock Holmes deduced that a man named James Ryder had committed a crime (in this case he had stolen a gemstone) and blamed it on another person. But rather than sending Ryder to prison, Holmes forgave Ryder and told him to "go forth and sin no more." Remarking on this notion of forgiveness, Ryder (the professor, not the character from the story) noted, "I suppose all people should be punished if they commit a crime but sometimes there's something to be said for being forgiving," and asked, "Don't we all need to be forgiven?" This question lingered with me as I listened to Ryder's stories.

During our interviews, Ryder continually returned to issues of social justice, which he says he developed through his experiences in the Peace Corps and afterward. He referred to social structures as "hierarchies" and "pecking orders" and alluded to their effects on the lives of stigmatized populations around the world, especially the poor. When I asked if he held certain social justice beliefs prior to his travels overseas, he said that before serving in the Peace Corps, he "didn't know what [he] thought." But since his return to the U.S., he has decided that "Wanting the world to be a better place is not bad" and that "probably the biggest thing I learned from the Peace Corps" was that the world "should" and "could" be a "better" place. When I asked Ryder how the world could become a better place, he said that he didn't have the "solutions" but that the problems were "pretty obvious." He also felt that most people wanted to "know what's right and wrong" because living in the "gray" area between right and wrong made people feel "uncomfortable," yet he believed that "people who think they know what is right and wrong are actually just pushing their moral agenda on me or on others." He added, "I'm aware of these things and I'm constantly…trying to figure out what the right thing to do is. And sometimes it's very frustrating because I don't know. Or I've decided what the right thing is and then I realize I've done something horrible."

I think this brings up an important moral dilemma in an age of globalization—having the desire to help others who are disadvantaged yet discovering that one's efforts have unintended consequences. This implies that there is no single right thing to do. It also suggests that one person alone cannot decide what is best for others. I think that for social justice to be viable, multiple voices must share in the meaning-making process.

Because Ryder turned to issues of social justice in nearly every story he told and because it formed such a large part of his pedagogical goals, I have titled his chapter "Toward a Pedagogy of Social Justice." In this chapter, I have included two stories related to culture shock, one identity shift story, one reverse culture shock story, and one story regarding his pedagogy. In his first culture shock story, Ryder talks about the differences between the Western and Kenyan perceptions of time and he points out an element of fatalism within the Kenyan approach. In re-reading the story, I draw on other research and my own experiences teaching in Africa to look at fatalism in a new light. In the second culture shock story, Ryder talks about the generosity he experienced in Kenya and the lack of generosity in American culture. Using reports of American generosity and non-generosity in the popular media, I first read Ryder's story in terms of generosity as measurable in dollar amounts or percentages, and later, drawing on Derrida's "aporia of the gift," reread the story in terms of generosity as an impossible practice due to an underlying component of self-interest. In the identity shift story, Ryder expresses his shock at finding homosexual practices in Saudi Arabia, which he considered a conservative culture, and the condemnation of homosexuality in America, which he thought would be more liberal, as well as how this shock led him to be more tolerant and supportive of homosexuals. I first read his story in terms of moral hypocrisy at the cultural level and reread the story in terms of the difficulty in using such labels as conservative and liberal or homosexual and non-homosexual.

Next, for Ryder's reverse culture shock story, he shares his frustration that while the Kenyan poor exemplify reality, middle-class American culture is built upon and in some ways bound by non-reality. In rereading Ryder's story, I challenge these assumptions and look at reality as multiple rather than monolithic. In his final story related to his pedagogy, Ryder discusses the way in which his experience of language stigmatization by other Peace Corps volunteers, as well as his Kenyan and Saudi students' experiences of language stigma by others, led to his realization that standard and non-standard language usage is tied to social power. In reading the story, I look at the need to affirm and appreciate linguistic diversity in the classroom, and in re-reading the story I challenge the notion of a clear distinction between standard and non-standard notions of language.

Culture Shock I: Western Time as Linear/Control, Kenyan Time as Cyclic/Fatalistic

Ryder noted that issues related to "time" would sometimes make him feel "annoyed." He said that from an American perspective, "When we're told [a specific] time…and it happens three hours later, we're a little upset." In contrast to the American meaning of the word "tomorrow" as the day after today, Ryder reflected on what "tomorrow" meant in Kenyan culture: "It means sometime in the future. I don't know when. It doesn't mean the day after today."

Unlike Americans who seemed to get "angry" and start "shouting" when things didn't go as planned, Ryder noted that he never saw the Kenyans "get angry," or at least they "didn't register anger" the way that Americans did. When things did not happen at a specified time, Kenyans often said that things would happen "When God wills it." He continued, "Maybe it's because they know that getting upset is not going to change anything" and that sometimes you "have to accept" life as it is. He also felt that the Kenyans' sense of time was related to "fatalism," which he described as a "reflection of living a life in which you know you're not in control." With regard to Americans, Ryder felt that "we think we have more control and that's where a lot of the culture shock comes from."

In terms of time orientation, Gannon and Pillai (2010) argued that while Western cultures prefer a more linear orientation to time, African time is more cyclical (p. 559). Samples (1993) described the differences between cyclic and linear time as follows:

> Cyclic time is the time image that best applies to nature. Seasons, days, seeds and birth-death cycles are all part of the rhythmic pulse of nature. Linear time is an abstraction. It is the invention of humans who arbitrarily divide up cycles into units... [which] are more addable, subtractable, and certainly more abstract. Cycles on the other hand vary....As a result, they pose problems to those who measure them in linear time...They pose no problems to those who accept cyclic time. (p. 28)

From a linear perspective, it seems that time is "controlled" in the act of dividing, adding, subtracting, and so on, whereas from a cyclic perspective, the control of time is ceded to nature or a deity or deities. Also, as noted in the Samples quote above, cyclic time poses a problem for the linear thinker because the cycles vary and are unpredictable. For Ryder and other Americans, it was a source of culture shock.

Time issues also provided me with the greatest sense of culture shock in my own Peace Corps experience, so I found it easy to relate when Ryder said Americans get upset when given a specific time for some event and then it happens "3 hours later." My students, colleagues, and friends also seemed to underscore the sense of "fatalism" or the "doctrine that events are fixed in advance so that human beings are powerless to change them" ("Fatalism," n.d.) noted in Ryder's story. They would often tell me that while a man may make plans, it is God who decides whether or not they will come into fruition. Another popular saying when there didn't seem to be an option or a solution to a problem was, "Oh well, what's one going to do?" One of my former students has also noted in our email correspondence since my return to the U.S. that "nothing is sure in Africa," "time is still not money," and "I could not do anything to change my destiny." This student certainly sounds fatalistic and seems to represent the type of fatalism Ryder also noted in his experience.

Re-reading Culture Shock I: Fatalism as Self-Management and Humility

In his story, Ryder associated Kenyan time with "fatalism" as a "reflection of living life where you know you are not in control." Fatalism is a word I often hear associated with Africa. To me, it has a negative connotation in that when something is "fatal" it causes "death," "failure," or "brings ruin" ("Fatal," n.d.). The term "fatalism" also creates the impression of African powerlessness and passivity, which is seen as negative in the Western active/passive framework.

It seems like an insult and a label applied from outside African culture rather than from inside the culture. In re-reading Ryder's story, I challenge this notion of fatalism and look for other possible meanings.

I think of what has been called fatalism as an approach for managing one's negative emotions. For example, Gannon and Pillai (2010) wrote that "fatalism helps people to wait patiently or react calmly" when things do not go as planned (p. 558). In Ryder's example, when things did not happen as planned, he/other Westerners became upset, got angry, or shouted, whereas the Kenyans didn't seem bothered, or at least they didn't express their anger publicly, as Ryder noted. It is possible that the Africans were indeed bothered and angry but they were managing their emotions in a more inconspicuous manner.

With regard to using the phrase "when God wills it" as a sign of fatalism, I recall similar sayings from American culture, such as "I'll be there, God willing" or "Lord willing." I also attended a meeting recently in which an administrator at my institution expressed a certain powerlessness in enforcing pre-established rules by stating "That's just the way it is and there's nothing I can do about it." For me, the "God willing" or "when God wills it" sayings can serve as linguistically polite ways of saying "let's wait and see." Likewise, the phrases "What's one going to do?" and "That's just the way it is and there's nothing I can do" are ways to express frustration in the moment. One cannot know everything that will happen in the future. Circumstances may change. Cultures use linguistic tools to express emotions in indirect ways. If both Western and African cultures use similar linguistic techniques, why is African culture often labeled as fatalistic when American culture is not?

I would also challenge the belief that African fatalism is tantamount to passivity or futility. My African students were neither forced to go to school nor simply allowed to go to school; they worked for the privilege. They grew cotton entirely by hand to earn enough money to go to school. In that sense, there were no passive students in my classroom. They worked hard to get into school even though their money could have gone toward taking care of other necessities. They expressed their hopes and dreams to me in quiet and subtle ways. The African teachers I worked with not only taught, but also almost all had little side businesses in order to earn extra money. They had goals and plans for the future but they didn't share those plans publicly. Everyone in the village worked to maintain close relationships with others, not just for fun, but also in case they needed help in an emergency. They were generous and social but also frugal and private. In short, the Africans I knew were active when the situation called for it, and likewise quiet and passive when needed. This suggested to me that "fatalism is not complete futility; rather it means dignity in the face of adversity and humility in the event of prosperity" (Gannon & Pillai, 2010, p. 560).

In the first reading of Ryder's story I mentioned a student who claimed he could do nothing about his destiny. That student, who represented one of many, had 13 siblings and grew up without electricity or running water. The school where I taught was not in his village, so he and his brother rented a small hut normally used to shelter goats. They ate millet every day for 4 months until they could return to their village at the end of the semester and get more. Sometimes friends or villagers would invite them for meals or to share snacks. This student grew and harvested cotton when he wasn't in school and took on every odd job under the sun to make ends meet and help provide for his siblings. In the time that I have known him, he has suffered numerous bouts of malaria and has had little-to-no healthcare or dental care. He has also gone on to earn his bachelor's and master's degree. He recently accepted his first government post as a history teacher. He has hopes and dreams and he does everything he possibly can to make them come true. Sometimes he gets frustrated when things do not go as planned. That he says there is nothing he can do to change his destiny is more an act of modesty and frustration than fatalism. In an email I received just the other day he wrote "if we just hope without effort we fail." So while it may seem that Africans have a fatalistic vision of the future on the surface, what lies underneath, in my experience, is something very different.

Culture Shock II: Generosity as Measurable

According to Ryder, the experience of Kenyan generosity made him feel "shame" for American "avarice." In one example, Ryder was invited to the home of his school's night watchman. Ryder wrote:

> When I arrived at his homestead late morning one hot Saturday, I recall the scene rather well. Two mud-brick, cylindrical huts with grass-thatched roofs sat before me. The yard was hard dirt that had been recently swept with homemade hand brooms to make it look well-maintained. A skinny dog greeted me with a wag of a weary tail, and about 15 chickens ran about clucking and chasing insects. [The watchman] came out of one of the huts and greeted me and welcomed me to his home....He [said] that this was his home and what I saw God had blessed him with. Though what I saw was poverty, I saw [a] man without greed.

Ryder seemed to feel especially touched when the man's wife cooked one of the 15 chickens he had seen running about the yard earlier, especially since the couple had so few possessions. He said that the generosity he had experienced that day was "a generosity [he] had never experienced in the United States." Explaining his perspective more fully, Ryder offered,

> What I had experienced reminded me of the biblical story in Mark 12: 41–44 about the widow and her giving two mites [a monetary unit of measure during biblical times] in comparison to what all the rich in the temple had given: "For all they did cast in of their abundance; but she of her want did cast in all that she had, even all her living." Americans love to think that they give more than others, and monetarily we probably do. However, percentage wise we don't even come close. I have never visited an American and had them serve me a meal worth one-15th of their world possessions.

While Ryder felt that Kenyans were much more generous than Americans and that Americans were not as generous as they thought they were, several articles within the popular media have extolled the virtues of American generosity (Tripathi, 2006; Brooks, 2009; Wilson, 2011; Bennett, 2011; Chao, 2012; Klotz, 2012). Wilson (2011) said that the view that Americans are not generous is a distortion of the "media and liberals" who "portray Americans as selfish Scrooges." He made the case that "America is the most generous country in the world" based on its ranking on the World Giving Index 2011, which was developed by the U.K.-based Charities Aid Foundation (CAF). To create the World Giving Index, the Charities Aid Foundation (2011) used information gathered through Gallup poll interviews from 153 countries to look at three specific behaviors: giving money to a charity, volunteering, and helping a stranger (p. 2). Although the U.S. did not have the top score in any one category, its overall score earned it the top rank of "most charitable country globally" (p. 11). Using the same measures, Kenya ranked 62nd (p. 36). Further, the United States ranked first on the Hudson Institute's Index of Global Philanthropy and Remittances (Adelman, Spantchak, & Marano, 2012), which placed the total amount of American aid to developing countries in 2010 at $165.2 billion (p. 16), which included Official Development Assistance (ODA), private philanthropy (through foundations, corporations, universities, volunteer agencies, religious organizations, etc.), and remittances (described as money sent from "migrants living in the United States to their home countries") (p. 8). These data seem to contradict Ryder's assumptions that Americans aren't as generous as Kenyans or that the belief in American generosity is misplaced.

On the other hand, just as Ryder asserted, some argue that despite the U.S. giving more in terms of dollars, other countries actually give a larger percentage of their overall economy, often referred to as GDP (Gross Domestic Product) or GNI (Gross National Income) (Somberg, 2005; Riley, 2005; Eisenberg, 2008; Moylan, 2010; Chronic, 2011). Somberg (2005) blamed the media for inflating American generosity by making "Americans think they live in an extremely generous country." For example, he contested one article comparing America's and Britain's pledges of aid related to the Indian Ocean Tsunami in December 2004 that noted that America's pledge of $350 million was three times that of Britain. Somberg (2005) pointed out that the article failed to mention that the "U.S. has 5 times Britain's population and six times its GDP." Additionally, in reviewing the aforementioned Index of Global Philanthropy and Remittances (Adelman, Spantchak, & Marano, 2012), although the U.S. ranks first in giving when looking at dollar amounts, it ranks 12th when looking at percentage of aid in relation to GNI (pp. 16–17). When looking strictly at Official Development Aid (ODA) alone, the U.S. drops from 1st to 19th place (pp. 6–7). The general impression these data give is that despite the U.S. donating the most money, the money given represents a smaller percentage of its economy, thus making the U.S. appear less generous.

Overall, it would seem that perceptions of American generosity depend upon the scale used to measure that generosity. Because of this, some argue for a dual view of America as both generous and non-generous (Efron, 2004; Benton, 2009; Cohen, 2012). Benton (2009) and Cohen (2012) added that while America is generous in many respects, it may not be especially generous to its own poor. For instance, offering his British view of American generosity, Cohen wrote that

> despite America's brutal treatment of its poor, there is an undercurrent of extreme generosity that I personally have not seen in any other country. Americans give an astonishing amount of their own money to charities....On a personal level there is a culture of kindness and understanding that is not manifested on a societal level—a strange contradiction that could have interesting outcomes.

For Ryder, who emphasized his poor upbringing in his biography, it is perhaps this sense of America's lack of generosity toward its own poor that enables him to emphasize the belief that Americans are not generous, while ignoring the other ways in which Americans might exemplify generosity.

Re-reading Culture Shock II: Generosity as Self-Interest and Impossible

In the previous section, generosity was gauged in terms of measurable dollar amounts or percentages of money given. Ryder even wrote of the night watchman's meal as representing one 15th of his worldly possessions. There is some literature, however, that suggests the manner in which aid is offered is equally as important as the amount given (Korf, 2007; Minnicks, 2011; Neild, 2012; Bhala, 2005; Glennie, 2011). Korf (2007), for example, made the case that the "over-attention towards the virtues of Western generosity" in the media following the 2004 Indian Ocean Tsunami "produced a humiliating force upon aid recipients" (p. 5) by painting those affected as passive victims, downplaying the victims' own contributions toward self-help, and ignoring their input altogether. He argued further that gift-giving in which "the recipient is unable to reciprocate" creates "asymmetric" power relations (p. 4) and, following Bourdieu, acts as an "effective practice of symbolic domination" (p. 7) especially when the giver seeks constant affirmation of their generosity or other favors in return. For Minnicks (2011), this suggests the importance of giving in a more discreet manner. Quoting Jesus from Matthew 6:3–4, she wrote:

> So when you give to the needy, do not announce it with trumpets, as the hypocrites do in the synagogues and on the streets, to be honored by men....But when you give to the needy, do not let your left hand know what your right hand is doing.

In this passage, Jesus suggested the importance of giving without the need to proclaim or be "honored by men" for the giving. Reflecting on the notion of gift-giving and generosity, I can personally think of times when I felt embarrassed or resentful when given a gift if I did not have the means to, or felt expected to, return the gesture (especially during the holidays). I can also think of other times when I, as the gift-giver, felt hurt at not having my "gift" acknowledged.

In their own ways, both of the authors above pointed out the problematic of self-interest in the process of giving. According to Derrida's "*aporia* of the gift," it is this element of self-interest that negates giving as an act of generosity (In Korf, 2007, p. 8). Exploring Derrida's position, Barnett (2005) reported that

> As soon as a gift is given knowingly as a gift, the subject of generosity is always anticipating a return, already taking credit of some sort, if only for being generous.

> This relationship between giving and taking, anticipation and return, therefore inscribes the gift within a circuit of utilitarian exchange that it is supposed to exclude. On this view, the ethical content of the generous act is annulled in the very moment of its enactment. (p. 10)

Additionally, Barnett argued that for an act/gift to be generous, it could not be "recognised as a gift by either party" (p. 10). This suggests the impossibility of claiming generosity by either the giver or recipient, in that once generosity is claimed, it loses the quality that makes it generous. In other words, by claiming the act as generous, it becomes a tool of self-interest.

In Ryder's case, his dissatisfaction with American culture enabled him to deemphasize American generosity while highlighting and perhaps overstating Kenyan generosity. For example, Ryder appeared to indicate that because the night watchman was poor, he could not also be greedy or have self-serving motives in inviting Ryder to lunch. It is possible, though, that the watchman may have been interested in developing a social relationship with Ryder for reasons that may not have been known to Ryder at the time. In portraying the man as poor, without greed, and as being thankful for being "blessed by God," Ryder re-inscribes the asymmetries of power (Korf, 2007), in a sense, by casting the man as innocent, passive, and righteous (in the biblical sense) and not seeing the man in light of his potential totality. Likewise, he seemed to paint all Americans as greedy and avaricious.

Staying with this theme of self-interest at a cultural level, while I don't think that self-interest is necessarily a bad thing, I do think it is important to recognize how seemingly generous foreign aid to developing countries may be considered a form of self-interest. Neild (2012) argued, for instance, that because of the "strings attached" to aid, it often becomes "more of a transaction than an outright gift." He suggested that aid is often given in return for supporting political or military interests in other countries and that reports of American "government philanthropy" dollars includes aid that is "earmarked for military purposes." Likewise food donations actually support "American agribusiness" by requiring that aid be spent on American agricultural products, thereby increasing foreign dependence on American goods. Somberg (2005) noted too that while large pledges of money may make a country appear generous, those pledges may turn out to be empty promises that do not represent actual aid given. Glennie (2011) also observed that "Aid buys things donors want (such as political support and economic advantage, whether directly for donor businesses or indirectly through policy change)." He proposed that for wealthy countries to become "truly generous" would require more than monetary donations, such as reducing their consumption and adopting fairer tax, trade, and accounting practices. Overall, these writers give the impression that looking solely at generosity in terms of numbers may hide the ways in which giving to others may be tied to self-interests. It also brings into question whether or not one can speak of so-termed generosity at all.

Identity Shift I: Sexuality as Moral Hypocrisy and Social Control

Ryder's culture shock experiences in Kenya and later in Saudi Arabia also made him reflect on issues related to sexuality. He noted in Kenya that men held hands "all the time" and that he "had to learn" that it was not sexual in nature. When I asked how he reacted when Kenyan men tried to hold his hand, he said that he was "freaked out by it" at first and pulled his hand away. But after a while, he said he began to realize that the Kenyan men were not "gay" or "looking for sex," that holding hands was more a demonstration of friendship and human closeness. Later, as a teacher in Saudi Arabia, he also found that men not only held hands but often kissed as a show of friendship. I should note that although his experiences in Saudi Arabia were not with the Peace Corps I have included the story here because they added to his culture shock and are related to his overall theme regarding male sexuality. Speaking of his experiences in Saudi Arabia, he relayed that "I have been kissed nose to nose by an Arab and it wasn't a homosexual act, it was a gesture of friendship, which is a big change for me." Ryder also reflected that Americans and Westerners in general tended to be more "homophobic" and would likely view such acts as homosexual.

Ryder was, however, surprised to discover that homosexual behavior existed in Saudi Arabia despite the social and religious prohibitions against it. He said that before he went to Saudi Arabia, he thought it was a "puritan culture where everybody abstained from everything. Everything is forbidden," especially homosexuality, which he understood was punishable by death. He was therefore shocked to find that one of his roommates and some of his co-workers who were from various Western countries had "overt" homosexual relationships with Saudis, Arabs, and other foreigners as well. He said that this "astounded" him because he "thought people would be more afraid to be a homosexual in Saudi Arabia than they are in the West." Yet since he has returned to the U.S., he has a different perspective. He argued, "My concept of America was that it was more liberal and tolerant than it actually is. We are very puritanical" and "very conservative." He added that even though homosexuality is not considered a crime punishable by death in the U.S., he felt that many Americans would "certainly condemn you to death."

Ryder also shared a poignant story in which he had rejected a brother who was gay. His brother was living with him at the time in an apartment inside an elderly woman's residence. One night, his brother was followed to the apartment by some men who verbally and physically attacked him for being gay. The police were called to settle the disturbance, and due to the altercation Ryder and his brother were kicked out of the apartment. Holding back tears, Ryder explained,

> I told my brother, get…out and don't ever come back, you got me kicked out of my apartment. I don't care what the situation is. Those are probably the most hurting words….At the time I was angry and I meant them, because I was angry, but I didn't realize they would be the last words I would ever say to my brother.

They lost touch after that and Ryder never saw his brother again. Ryder went on to say that it was a "development" for him to overcome his negative beliefs about homosexuality and that through his intercultural experiences in which he worked closely with homosexual men, he had come to think of it as being natural as heterosexuality. He also pointed out that homosexuality existed in the animal world and he felt that sexuality was the product of cultural "programming" and "conditioning."

Ryder's story made me think about the notion of "moral hypocrisy" and how it may be understood at the level of national culture. Drawing on Batson et al.'s research, Tong and Yang (2011) described moral hypocrisy as a "behavioral response driven by the motivation to appear moral and yet, if possible, avoid the cost of being so" (p. 159). An important part of this description is the attempt to "appear" moral in whatever way moral may be defined. Additionally, in their research on the social nature of moral hypocrisy, Valdesolo and David DeSteno (2007) found that "Subjects readily excused other individuals' unfair acts if these others belonged to subjects' emergent social groups" thus helping to shape "group-level social identities" (p. 690). This suggests that moral hypocrisy can be understood not only in terms of individual behavior, but also as promulgated along social and cultural lines. In the story above, Ryder indicated how the cultural, moral, and legal prohibitions against homosexuality in Saudi Arabia gave the appearance that homosexuality did not exist there, hence he was shocked to find that it did exist. Being an outsider enabled him to recognize this inconsistency between appearance and actual practice. It also seemed to make him more aware of American moral hypocrisy after he returned to the U.S. in that he argued that Americans are more "puritanical" and "conservative" despite claiming to be "liberal" and "tolerant."

In addition to moral hypocrisy, Ryder also hints at the ways in which sexuality is subjected to social control. DeLamater (1981) believed that "social institutions, primarily the family and religion, are the source of both general perspectives and specific norms that govern sexual expression" (p. 264). He explained that social institutions control sexual behavior in three main ways:

> First, they provide a specific perspective...a set of assumptions and norms that defines reality for adherents and thus serves as a basis for self-control. Second, those who occupy institutional roles will utilize the perspective in interactions, as a basis for informal controls. Third, institutions may have sanctioning systems that are activated when norms are violated; fear of sanction is thus an additional source of conformity by participants. (p. 264)

These three elements of social control appeared to be present in Ryder's narratives. Both killing and condemning homosexuals seemed to be part of the sanctioning systems that the social institutions in both the U.S. and Saudi Arabia have used to control homosexuals. Likewise, Ryder himself became an unwitting participant in the social control of his brother by rejecting him, even though his brother was the victim of a crime and it was not his fault that Ryder was kicked out of the apartment. I would also suggest that schools, as social institutions, as well as teachers, may also be prone to engage in these forms of social control. Likewise, fear of these social controls may lead sexual minorities to suppress themselves through behaviors such as detachment from others, pretending to be heterosexual, and committing suicide.

Re-reading Identity Shift I: Social Control (?) and the Problem With Labels

While I appreciate Ryder's enthusiasm in fighting social and sexual injustice on behalf of gay people, his position seemed based on a heterosexual/homosexual dichotomy as well as the belief that sexuality could be completely regulated by one's culture. That homosexual behavior seemed widespread and overt in Saudi Arabia suggests that it was in some ways tolerated, that the social controls against homosexuality weren't working very well or weren't strictly enforced, and/or that people's sexuality and sexual behavior cannot be completely controlled, especially by governments. Likewise, in the U.S., which Ryder branded as homophobic and conservative, there are also pockets of liberality and acceptance. Witness the increase in states that are legalizing same-sex marriage. Look at the increases in religious institutions that welcome and support gay people. Observe the inclusion of gay characters on some of the most popular television programs. And, even at the time of writing, President Obama has come out in support of gay marriage. In my own life, I have sensed a shift toward greater acceptance of sexual minorities in the last few years. However, I am not naïve. Gay people still suffer the effects of social control through suicide, verbal harassment, isolation, depression, violence, and homelessness (GLSEN in Youth Pride Inc., 2010) both in the U.S. and in other countries. My point is that the picture is more complicated and that there seem to be pockets of tolerance amid intolerance.

I also question the categories of hetero- and homo-sexual. According to McIntosh (1968), thinking of sexual behaviors in fixed and mutually exclusive categories is problematic. She wrote,

> Many scientists and ordinary people assume that there are two kinds of people in the world: homosexuals and heterosexuals. Some of them recognize that homosexual feelings and behavior are not confined to the persons they would like to call "homosexuals" and that some of these persons do not actually engage in homosexual behavior. This should pose a crucial problem; but they evade the crux by retaining their assumption and puzzling over how to tell whether someone is "really" homosexual or not. (p. 182)

She also argued that the term "bisexual" was developed "to handle the fact that behavior patterns cannot be conveniently dichotomized into heterosexual and homosexual" (pp. 182–183). I think it is interesting that McIntosh wrote her article in 1968 and at that time there were three socially constructed categories—heterosexual, homosexual, and bisexual. Yet the labeling has continued. Note the acronym LGBTQQ, which stands for Lesbian, Gay, Bisexual, Transgender, Queer, and Questioning. There are other variants with additional letters for other categories as well. Although there seems to be a greater recognition in the diversity of sexual behavior in American culture, there also seems to be the belief that the totality of a person can be accounted for by an initial, or that their emotions and behaviors can fit into mutually exclusive categories.

This research suggests that such characterizations as conservative, liberal, heterosexual, and homosexual may be misleading to the extent that such labels seem to hide the existence of the other concept within those labels. By that I mean, there may be components of both liberality and conservatism in a single country or a single person. Similarly, there may also be elements of both hetero- and homosexuality in a single person. For instance, I know people who consider themselves gay who have engaged in "heterosexual" sex and people who consider themselves straight but who have engaged in "homosexual" sex. In those instances, labels seem to serve a more social or political function than to reflect the complexity of actual sexual practices.

Reverse Culture Shock I: Reality vs. Non-reality

For Ryder, seeing the "extreme level of poverty" in Kenya added to his "reverse culture shock" in the sense that he was "amazed" at how full grocery stores were even though there were hungry people in the world. He was also bothered by the amount of consumption here in America and pointed out how obese many Americans are. In addition, he felt that as a rich country there "should be no problems" in the U.S. because this is "America, it's the first world." But he did find problems that were especially annoying because he felt that Kenyans, as poor as they were, often did things "better" than Americans. Although he couldn't give a specific example of the type of the problems he encountered, he remembered "feeling intolerance for any little mistake that may have happened." He also suggested that his experiences with reverse culture shock "probably started some of [his] problems with Americans" in that they seemed to make him more aware and critical of American culture.

Ryder further noted that before he joined the Peace Corps he strongly believed in the Protestant work ethic, that "success or good comes to those who work hard," and that poverty was the result of "laziness" or "indolence." While he still believed in the value of hard work, he no longer believed that it necessarily equaled success. He explained that living among the hard-working yet poor people in Africa made him realize that they didn't deserve their poverty but rather their poverty was a circumstance of an unjust social structure. He thought, "these people [in Kenya] work as hard or harder than anyone I've seen in America. Why are they not where they ought to be? Why do they have less? It's certainly not because of something they didn't do."

In addition, Ryder said he felt like a "freed prisoner" after living outside of the U.S. for a number of years. He explained that most Americans were like prisoners in a cave looking at "shadows" on the wall. They assume these shadows to be real and choose to live "absolutely oblivious to [the] reality" outside the cave (I should note that Ryder's use of the cave metaphor is similar to, yet somewhat different from, Plato's *Allegory of the Cave*). Ryder explained that

> though [the Returned Peace Corps Volunteer] returns to the cave to explain to erstwhile former cell mates that the images on the wall are merely shadows and that the real world lies above and beyond their imaginations, he [or she] is not only frequently disbelieved but many times found to be the object of the contempt of [her or] his peers who are more than complacent about their lives and do not wish to know more or to seek change (i.e., they embrace willful ignorance).

In making his case that most Americans prefer to live in willful ignorance, he quoted two popular American aphorisms: "If you can't say anything nice, don't say anything at all" and "if it ain't broke don't fix it." He argued that the first saying meant that nobody had "the right to complain" or say something "negative" and that if you cannot point out the aspects of American society that were negative or broken, there was no reason to fix or change anything. Ryder also implied this sense of willful ignorance to explain why some Americans "can buy a five dollar cup of coffee when they know that four billion people are living on two dollars or less a day."

Applying the cave metaphor to Kenyan culture, he said of the poor subsistence farmers he lived among, "They are reality. They're the outside world." He also believed that it was the Kenyan middle class who "are seeing shadows on the wall." Specifically, he felt that it was their conspicuous consumption of certain luxuries (driving cars, "eating at their level") that made the poorer Kenyans "suffer."

According to Kauffman, "exposure to another culture and to other ways of thinking and behaving leads to new ways of looking at one's own culture" (In Voigts, 2008). For Ryder, this certainly seemed to be the case. Through his experiences in other cultures he gained insights into American culture and a broadened perspective on issues of poverty. This enabled Ryder to reflect on the nature of social structure and how language (such as popular aphorisms and the Protestant work ethic) is used to support the structure and shape cultural perceptions. Along these lines, Bazerman (1992) believed that "Knowledge...

is made up out of words and other symbols, that words are used by people, and that people have their own concerns to look out for" and can become "imprisoned by the words they use" (p. 61). He also argued that learning how these words and symbols "function" and "whose interests they serve" exposes the "choice making that lies behind the apparently solid and taken-for-granted world" and "forces us to address the ethical question of our responsibility for our world" (p. 62). Ryder's experiences enabled him to challenge the belief that hard work necessarily equaled success. He also gave examples of popular American sayings that supported a non-questioning and problem-avoiding attitude. He felt this use of language served the middle class, and argued that most Americans preferred to live in "willful ignorance" rather than face or change inequitable social problems.

I was especially intrigued by Ryder's use of metaphors to describe American and Kenyan middle class culture as a "cave" and the people within it as "prisoners" who accept the shadows they see projected on the wall as reality. Through these metaphors, Ryder equated wealth with imprisonment in a shadow world where nothing is real, and poverty with freedom and reality. In many ways, the United States seems like a shadow world, especially due to the increase and proliferation of the popular mass media. I recently read a magazine article featuring the pop star Lady Gaga who was talking about a magazine cover that she had appeared on without any makeup. She said "I think that artifice is the new reality" and she argued that the so-called "natural" photo of her looked more artificial than real. She added, "There's this idea that it's all natural, but everything's been staged to look natural" (Eggenberger, 2011). This seems to indicate that the artificial has subsumed the natural world and the social world is one that has been "staged" or constructed.

Similarly, De Zengotita (2005) believed that American culture has become engulfed in, and shaped by, media. He explained that *"mediation* means dealing with reality *through* something else" (p. 8). This implies an indirect relationship with "reality" through other means such as television shows, movies, video/computer games, advertising, etc. As an example, one of my best friends, "Julia," has a virtual horse named "Scout." The horse is part of a computer program stored on her iPad. I watched as Julia called Scout by tapping on a virtual fence surrounding a virtual pasture. The sky was blue and the grass was green and there were sounds of virtual birds chirping pleasantly in the background. I watched Julia feed, exercise, and groom Scout. By taking good care of Scout, Julia earned "gems," which she could trade for horse-feed or riding gear. Julia also received updates about Scout through text messages on her cell phone. Does this count as "looking at shadows on the wall" while other more pressing and "real" matters are being ignored?

Everything in the mediated landscape was designed to make Julia feel good and forget the challenges of the physical world. Yet, there seems to be an increasing dependence on media, given that the time and money spent engaging media is steadily increasing (U.S. Census Bureau, 2011) and that media "addiction" is also on the rise (McIlwraith, 1998; Kubey & Csikszentmihalyi, 2002; Seay & Kraut, 2007; Young, 2009; Caldwell & Cunningham 2010). This increase in media addiction perhaps signals that many Americans are indeed becoming imprisoned by their need for a mediated reality and that media acts as a form of escape.

In contrast to Americans or middle-class Kenyans, Ryder felt that the poor subsistence farmers he lived among were the "reality." They had a direct and close relationship with nature and their survival depended on that direct relationship. Ryder's classification of them as real and free is supported by De Zengotita's (2005) contention that "We are most free of mediation, we are most real, when we are at the disposal of accident or necessity" (p. 13). To the extent that the poorer Kenyans' survival was tied to nature, which included elements of both accident and necessity, American culture must seem like a shadow world in that the emphasis seems to be less on survival and more on creating the "appearance" of a certain type of social reality. For Ryder, the time and effort spent in attending to the shadow reality also has ethical implications in that it distracts from attending to the survival needs and very real suffering of others.

Re-reading Reverse Culture Shock I: Reality as Multiple

In Ryder's story, the notions of real and unreal were polarized, with poverty cast as "reality" and "freedom," whereas wealth represented a kind of shadowy "non-reality" and a "prison." His linking of the poor subsistence farmers and reality seemed to indicate the view that the physical and natural world was real whereas the social and mediated worlds constructed by Americans were not. Drawing on the psychological work of William James, Schutz (1945) offered a different view of reality. He wrote that "The origin of all reality is subjective, whatever excites and stimulates our interest is real. To call a thing real means that this thing stands in a certain relation to ourselves" (p. 207).

But rather than argue for a singular notion of reality, Shutz argued for the existence of "an infinite number of various orders of realities, each with its own special and separate style of existence," which James called "sub-universes" (p. 207). Some of those "sub-universes" or "subworlds" included:

> the world of sense or physical things...the world of science, the world of ideal relations, the world of "idols of the tribe," the various supernatural worlds of mythology and religion, the various worlds of individual opinion, the worlds of sheer madness and vagary. The popular mind conceives of all these sub-worlds more or less disconnectedly, and when dealing with one of them forgets for the time being its relations to the rest. But every object we think of is at last referred to one of these subworlds. (p. 207)

This gives the impression that there are multiple layers of reality and that although one may interact in multiple realities, it may be easy to forget the existence of these other layers when focusing on a particular aspect of one of those realities. In Ryder's story, the American and Kenyan middle class were portrayed as uniformly in the dark and oblivious to the suffering of others. There seemed to be no room for recognizing the ways in which the middle class could also be generous, insightful, and concerned with the plight of others. While it is true that many Americans live in a mediated reality, it is also true that they care about the well-being of others. Only recently I noted that my middle class co-workers generously and secretly donated enough money to buy two air conditioning units for a member of the contracted janitorial staff when it was learned that her air conditioner went out during 100+ degree heat. I have also seen them raise money for wildfire victims and donate clothing or other goods to the poor both in America and other countries. It seems possible that Ryder's painful experiences growing up in poverty made him feel resentful of the middle class. In many ways I can relate to his frustration, having grown up in a modest, rural, working-class home. But it does make me wonder why painful experiences sometimes seem more real than happy ones. Is it because happiness is fleeting and can be more easily taken away? Is it because pain seems more powerful than joy? Is it too difficult to support the tension of being both generous and greedy?

In applying the cave metaphor, Ryder also indicated that the middle class were prisoners of their material desires (in the form of shadows) and that the poor were free by implication. I'm not sure, though, that "poor" Kenyans would describe themselves as freer in comparison to middle-class Kenyans. In my experience working with poor Cameroonian farmers, they certainly felt constrained by the social system. In addition, it wasn't that they rejected the mediated and material world, they simply couldn't afford to engage in it to the extent that the middle-class Cameroonians could. One could further argue that the physical "outside" world in the form of nature can act as a "prison," with set laws and boundaries, whereas the imaginative and creative world is freeing in the sense that its landscapes are limitless. If indeed the poor Kenyans were free as Ryder indicated, there would be no need for Ryder to pursue social justice on their behalf.

Ryder also pointed out how language is used to support the social structure and benefit those who do not wish to seek change such as wealthy middle-class Americans. This recalls Bazerman's (1992) suggestion that people may become "imprisoned by the words they use" (p. 61). The examples Ryder gave were "If you can't say anything nice, don't say anything at all" and "if it ain't broke don't fix it." He also challenged the narrative of the Protestant work ethic that work equaled success. But I would argue that if words can act as prisons, they may also be used to find openings. Popular quotes can be read in different ways. There are also other counter-narratives that may be enlisted. The phrase, "if it ain't broke don't fix it" could be read as meaning its opposite as in "if it *is* broke, *do* fix it." In the movie *Steel Magnolias*, one of the main characters adapted the "say something nice" example by saying, "If you can't say anything nice, come sit next to me," which suggested that she wanted to hear the negative, especially about other people! As far as the Protestant work ethic that hard work equals success, I have overheard the saying "work smarter, not harder" on numerous occasions, which seems to challenge the goal of working hard. The point is simply that other sayings exist and other meanings exist within those sayings, and further, that the words used to socially construct reality may be deconstructed in order to create openings for other possible realities to exist.

Likewise, the same media that creates the beautiful images that buffer people from reality can also be used to cast light on reality in new or different ways. Books, films, and documentaries such as *To Kill a Mockingbird, A Passage to India, Schindler's List, And the Band Played On, Spanglish, The Motorcycle Diaries, Gandhi,* and *Getting Justice: Kenya's Deadly Game of Wait and See,* just to name a few, are examples of popular media that have been used to focus on issues related to social justice. This is not to suggest that social issues and suffering do not exist, only that the middle class is no monolithic group, and that words and media can be used to both support and challenge the status quo.

Pedagogy I: Teaching an Appreciation for "Dialect Diversity" as Social Justice

In considering how culture shock and reverse culture shock influenced his pedagogy, Ryder says he sometimes used his overseas experiences to "try to shock" his students by sharing some "provocative" stories in class. He said, "I'm thinking some of these students are sheltered little children. Let me see if I can shock them out of there." He continued,

> I have to be careful because I want to tell them things that I was surprised by, like the fact that I think that Saudi Arabia is very homoerotic, that astounds people to hear that. I think maybe I would have been astounded prior to my travels.

He also indicated that he needed to be careful when sharing his Peace Corps stories that had to do with sexuality and bodily functions in front of women "Because in polite society you don't talk about these things...despite what people say, men and women are treated differently."

For Ryder, one particular set of experiences with culture shock had a profound influence on his desire to learn about and teach linguistics. It also shaped his critical perspective with regard to his pedagogy. Ryder said that while he was in the Peace Corps in Kenya, he was persistently made fun of for the way he spoke English, not by Kenyans, but by the other American Peace Corps Volunteers. He explained that the other Peace Corps Volunteers imitated and teased him for the way he pronounced certain words in his "Ozark dialect" of English and this hurt Ryder even though the other volunteers may not have intended to do so. Ryder believed that if he had not joined the Peace Corps and met other volunteers from around the U.S., he "would never have been aware that [he] was speaking [an English] dialect...that was stigmatized." Ryder also discovered that some of the Kenyans he knew and some of the Arab students he taught also felt stigmatized because of their language use. The Kenyans felt stigmatized because their "English was not as good as that of the Americans or the British and...their Swahili was not as pure as that of the Tanzanians." "Paradoxically," Ryder's "rich Arab students felt stigmatized because their local dialect of Arabic was not the pure classical language of the Koran."

For Ryder, these experiences made him aware of "how much people were judged by their use of language." As a result of his new awareness, Ryder changed the way he spoke by adopting a more standard dialect of American English. In addition, he went on to earn a doctorate degree in applied linguistics as well as reflect extensively on how language use was socially constructed and prescribed. He said that through studying linguistics, he realized that he "wasn't doing anything wrong at all," that he was "speaking a dialect." He continued, "We all speak a dialect....If we happen to live in a majority we think that our dialect is better than the other one and it's not." Accordingly, Ryder's experiences and insights have enabled him to challenge socially prescriptive rules and language practices through both his research and his pedagogy.

Ryder explained further that he tried to demonstrate in his American linguistics classes how, from a cultural standpoint, behavior is both "learned" and "arbitrary" rather than "absolute" or "universal." He used the shifting notion of "etiquette" and behaviors that are accepted in some cultures but considered offensive in others to make his point. He said that to Americans, eating with one's bare hands may be "surprising" and "offensive" but it was acceptable in many other cultures. He also indicated that for Americans, "slurping soup" was considered "bad manners" but wearing shoes in the house was completely acceptable, yet from an Asian perspective, slurping soup was okay but wearing shoes inside the house was not. Additionally, Ryder also used a linguistic technique called "critical discourse analysis" in which students were provided with a "prejudicial but authentic text" and were asked to "examine how the text abuses social power, supports racism, [and] upholds inequality." He felt this would help stimulate cultural awareness as well as provide a framework for students to use in their textual analyses in the future. Along these lines, he argued that teaching for social justice promoted "tolerance" and "inclusion," reduced "marginalization," and enhanced "mutual understanding."

Ryder's experience being stigmatized by the other American Peace Corps volunteers for his non-standard use of English suggests that one's own culture can be a source of culture shock. It also points out the link between language and identity, which has pedagogical implications for student/teacher relationships in linguistically diverse language communities. Fought (2005) observed that "Language has always helped to signify who we are in society, sometimes serving as a basis for exclusion." Dubrow and Gidney added that, "Generally, those dialects spoken by people who enjoy social prestige, power, and wealth are more favored than the dialects of people of more limited power, wealth, and social prestige; the former come to be known as the standard dialect" (In Gallant, 2008).

In other words, language stigma is not simply about language but is wrapped up in social relationships of power and prestige. The way Ryder spoke was emblematic of his poor upbringing and his lack of social power. The other Peace Corps Volunteers appeared to use this lack of social power to make fun of him. Along these lines, Fought (2005) argued that language stigmatization often acts as a "stand-in" for other forms of discrimination. He wrote:

> Indeed, speech is a convenient stand-in for other kinds of stigma that we recognize but do not openly acknowledge. For example, in our society, discrimination based on appearance, race, sex, religion or national origin is TABOO and often illegal, whereas discrimination based on particular details of language use by men or women, people of different religions, people from other countries and so on is often allowed.

This indicates how discrimination can take on different forms that may not be readily apparent because they are subtle, symbolic, and socially sanctioned.

Fuertes, Potere, and Ramirez (2002) pointed out that the school is one of the social institutions where discriminatory language-related practices have been shown to occur. For Godley, Sweetland, Wheeler, Minnici, & Carpenter (2006), this signals the need to better prepare teachers for teaching in dialectally diverse classrooms. They feel that teachers, especially, can benefit from critical sociolinguistic training because they "are often positioned by institutions, students, parents, and themselves as privileged authorities on language" and because research has shown "strong connections between teachers' negative attitudes about stigmatized dialects, lower teacher expectations for students who speak them, and thus lower academic achievement on the part of students" (p. 31). As such, they envision the teachers' role as one of "social change" in that the "very act of affirming vernacular language runs counter to mainstream language ideologies" (p. 33). Further, they offer a number of tips for teachers to come to appreciate non-standard dialects and to reflect on their own beliefs about language learning. Clearly, the questioning of "mainstream language ideologies" shapes a great deal of Ryder's teaching in his linguistics courses. For other educators, however, recognizing their own language biases or teaching against the societal grain may pose no easy task.

Perhaps one of the strongest shows of support for linguistic diversity in education emerged from the Conference on College Composition and Communication, whose executive board published a resolution in 1974 titled *Students' Right to Their Own Language*, which "remains the official position statement of the guild of college compositionists on dialect difference" to this day (Zorn, 2010, p. 311). The resolution read,

> We affirm the students' right to their own patterns and varieties of language—the dialects of their nurture or whatever dialects in which they find their own identity and style. Language scholars long ago denied that the myth of a standard American dialect has any validity. The claim that any one dialect is unacceptable amounts to an attempt of one social group to exert its dominance over another. Such a claim leads to false advice for speakers and writers, and immoral advice for humans. A nation proud of its diverse heritage and its cultural and racial variety will preserve its heritage of dialects. We affirm strongly that teachers must have the experiences and training that will enable them to respect diversity and uphold the right of students to their own language. (in National Council of Teachers of English, n.d.)

This resolution seems to articulate Ryder's pedagogical assumptions to the extent that teaching a "standard American dialect" is linked to power and the exertion of "dominance" of one group over another—specifically mainstream teachers over nonmainstream students. It also expresses Ryder's pedagogical goals of promoting respect for linguistic diversity and greater tolerance and acceptance of those who speak non-standard dialects. Along these lines, "preserving" and appreciating non-standard dialects in the classroom is seen as a form of social justice.

Re-reading Pedagogy I: Questioning the Notions of Standard and Non-standard Dialects

Despite attempts to clearly delineate the differences between standard and non-standard English dialects, certain challenges arise. For instance, while the word "standard" implies something that is fixed and measurable, what may be counted as the standard in terms of language is shifting and ambiguous. Addressing the notion of "linguistic change," Trudgill (2011) noted, for instance, that because language features can dynamically shift from non-standard to standard and vice versa, it "is not always possible to say with any degree of certainty…whether a particular feature is part of Standard English or not" leaving some language features in an "uncertain and ambiguous" status (p. 11). This hints at the impossibility of classifying language in any definitive sense.

One of the most wide-ranging linguistic changes is the "internationalization" of English, which has "resulted in new contours of the language and literature, in linguistic innovations, in literary creativity, and in the expansion of the cultural identities of the language" (Kachru, 1992, p. 355). For Kachru (1992), this suggests the need to recognize that "English now has multicultural identities" and to think of English, not in terms of its singularity, but in terms of its multiplicity as "Englishes" in the plural, especially within curriculum (p. 357). Kachru's writings also challenge the notion that any one group has the power and ability to control the use of language. Confronting the notion of language standardization, Kachru wrote that due to the "global diffusion of English...the native speakers of this language seem to have lost the exclusive prerogative to control its standardization" (in Kalickaya, 2009, p. 36). Widdowson agrees and adds that to give sole ownership of a language to one cultural group would "arrest its development" and "undermine its international status" (in Kilickaya, 2009, p. 36). Loss of control over others' language use can feel threatening, especially for native speakers; however, sharing and appreciating language differences holds the potential for creating more ethical intercultural relationships.

Eckert (n.d.) also pointed out that definitions of standard and non-standard English are problematic in the sense that even if, for example, "an easterner" and a "midwesterner" were able to rid themselves of their "stereotyped regional features" and both were considered standard English speakers, "their speech will be far from identical" (p. 7). In Ryder's case, the fact that he classified himself as having adopted a standard dialect did not mean that he spoke with an accent that was the same as other standard speakers, only that his language differences had been deemphasized. This implies that even within the so-called standard, language differences still exist and cannot be completely suppressed.

Just as language is neither completely standard nor non-standard, language stigma is also not meted out in exactly the same ways, in the sense that "what is stigmatized is different from person to person...and from place to place" (Fought, 2005). Since what might be perceived as stigma shifts from person to person and context to context, I would argue that responses to stigma also vary. Ryder's response to being stigmatized was to change the way he spoke, to study linguistics, and to challenge linguistic rules. I note on the other hand, for instance how some have used their stigmatized language as a form of cultural identity and artistic creativity, as in the use of non-standard dialects in rap, hip-hop, and country music. I have also noted that the international students I have worked with over the years have employed a number of strategies to navigate language stigma. While some did try to change their accents, others used humor when confronted with language differences, and some ignored the stigma altogether and went about their business. The point is that language stigma is neither dealt out nor received in the same manner.

In general, it appears that language standardization serves to control and limit linguistic diversity. Noting that what is considered Standard English has more to do with social power and prestige than linguistics, Torghabeh (2007) pointed out that such terms as "bad English, non-standard English, sub-standard English, or corrupted English" are used to uphold the prestige of native speakers and limit the prestige of nonnative speakers. This implies that the categories of standard and non-standard have been constructed to serve other functions and have little to do with actual language use.

INTERPLAY 3

Chez nous c'est ne pas comme chez vous!

"Everybody is different," Mrs. Hopewell said.
"Yes, most people is," Mrs. Freeman said.
"It takes all kinds to make the world."
"I always said it did myself."
Flannery O'Connor (1995) from Good Country People

If there was one thing Cameroon taught me, it was the powerful influence that culture has on people. I'm not sure that you can get a clear understanding of this until you have actually lived in another culture yourself. If you've only lived in one place for all of your life, you may get the notion that the rules you grew up with were the only ones and the right ones, or maybe you never even realized that there were rules at all. I have come to the conclusion that culture has a high degree of control over people without them even knowing about it.

Basically, culture was waiting around every corner of Cameroon just to slap me in the face. Even when I could see it coming, there were times that I couldn't get out of its way. For example, I knew that if an event was to begin at say 1:00 p.m., it wouldn't actually start until at least 2 hours later. But try as I might, I'd sit and I'd squirm and I'd pace until I just couldn't stand to wait any more and I would rush to the agreed-upon meeting place to find nobody there; many times I'd return home and wait until I couldn't stand it any longer and I'd still end up being early. If you're from the U.S., you'd probably say that Cameroonians were always late, but if you're from Cameroon, you'd probably think that Americans were always early. My Cameroonian friends explained to me that in the U.S., "time is money," but that in Cameroon, "time is elastic" because it stretches out and back again. Neither of us was right, of course, we were just acting according to our respective cultures.

I received a good dose of "elastic time" on my first day of school. I was both nervous and excited. This was the day I would fulfill my purpose for learning French, suffering through Peace Corps training and home-stay, leaving my family and friends for 2 years, and even being in Cameroon in the first place. I had carefully prepared my lesson plans and had my little backpack all ready to go. I had about a 20-minute walk to school and I got an early start. I didn't want to be late and I knew that if I met any older villagers, it would take a while to exchange greetings.

When I arrived at school, I was a little taken aback to find that there was nobody there. I kept waiting and waiting and still there was no one. The teachers and students that I had met in the village during the previous weeks all said that today would be the first day of school. I felt a sudden twinge of panic. Am I at the right school? Am I in the right village? Am I even in the right country? What the hell am I doing here? I had walked up onto a large mound of earth at that point and I was turning around in a 360-degree circle just to get my bearings. I saw the village in the distance and the Olawati Mountains behind that. I saw the school and the mountains, and the huge fields of dried brown grass in between everything else. At that moment, the memories of the entire journey that led me to this point started to well up inside me, everything I had done and everything I had seen. As the tears began welling up from the total exhaustion and frustration I was feeling, it began pouring down rain. Out of nowhere came a scrawny Cameroonian boy that said, "Sir...sir, there is no school today—when it rains, there is no school," so I went home—soaked and confused.

I started asking around why I was the only one to show up for school. Where were the students and the teachers? They said that students wouldn't come back from their farms in their villages until the rainy/planting season was finished. Students earned money to go to school by working their own little plots of land, therefore school wouldn't start until the children showed up. The same was true of the teachers. They showed up when it was convenient for them to arrive. All this meant that school wouldn't actually begin for another 3 weeks and I was the first teacher to start teaching. I didn't mind being the first to start teaching. All of my classes were grouped together in the morning, and by noon my classes were done. So you can imagine my surprise when I came to school during the 3rd actual week of teaching to find other teachers teaching in my classrooms! They said, "Check the schedule, it's been changed." It sure had! Now, on some days I had one class at 7:30 a.m. and then one just before noon and one the very last hour of the day. Resenting my new schedule, I took my case to the principal who simply blew me off. When I complained to the other teachers, they taught me a new phrase "chez nous c'est ne pas comme chez vous" or "our place is not like your place" so it was up to me to accept the new schedule and move on.

At school, I had to adapt things that I had learned about Cameroonian culture in order to be an effective teacher. For instance, I initially taught the concept of bathing by raising my hand over my head and making a little showering gestures. They just couldn't get it. But after being in my village a while, I realized that they didn't take showers; they generally bathed in the river. Therefore, if I wanted to explain the concept of bathing, I would make a gesture like I was splashing water from a make-believe river toward my body, and they understood me clear as a bell.

I also had to get used to witnessing the physical punishment that was considered acceptable in the Cameroonian school system. Once, I came to school to find my entire ninth-grade English class sitting on their knees with their hands outstretched and their hands being caned by an enraged Mr. Ndu-du. Even the quiet, studious boys and girls were getting whacked and they didn't even flinch. Seeing the dead look in their eyes honestly got me choked up. What should I do? I was an outsider, but these were my kids too! I ran over to Mr. Ndu-du and asked what the problem was. He said, "Mr. Jon, they were disrespectful during the National Anthem and to beat an African is to feed him." What? "To beat an African is to feed him"—those were his exact words! And somebody else chimed in, "Yeah, an African's ears are in his ass." You're kidding right? "An African's ears are in his ass." Does the NAACP know about these people?

Fortunately, I never required the services of the discipline master as the students were generally respectful and well-behaved, although there were times that I cursed at them under my breath while I was writing on the chalkboard. See, that's one of the benefits of working in a place where they don't understand your language. As a form of punishment you could send the student out of the class by shouting "Go out!" Besides being told to "Go out!" other forms of punishment included having students sit on their knees in the front of the class, having them put their noses in a circle that I drew on the chalkboard, dusting the eraser on the student's uniform, or giving their hair a good chalk-dusting as well. These all seemed kind of tacky and humiliating so I basically stuck with "Go out!" on the few occasions that I wasn't in the mood to play.

I could see why the students were frustrated though—having very little experience with the English language and having this big white man speaking nothing but English to them. This was in addition to being squished, four to a hard bench, in a 100-degree-plus room under a tin roof. That's got to be frustrating. Something that I did to promote good discipline was to enter the classroom on the first day and write the word "respect" on the chalkboard. Then I asked the students to explain to me what the word meant in English. They sort of struggled with creating an actual definition, but fortunately the word is spelled the same and means the same in English that it does in French. These words are called cognates and we used them a lot to get our point across. Anyway, if they were unable to create a definition, I asked them, "Well, what can you do to show me and your classmates respect? They got the point. They would say, "Be on time," "No talking," "No cheating," and I added, "Try to do your best." And then I asked them to make rules for me regarding the ways I could show them respect. In every single class, their number one request was "Do not beat the students." I never did and never needed to.

Students were also required to attend a manual labor class in which all grades, including the seventh-graders, were issued matches and machetes to clear out the brush that surrounded the school. Would you give an American seventh-grader a machete and a box of matches? You would definitely need a school nurse and campus police on standby! Another weird thing that happened from time to time was school inoculations. I'd be teaching away and someone would scream that the Minister of Health had sent someone to inoculate everyone against who knows what. People would line up and just get their shots without knowing what they were getting a shot for or if they were allergic to the shot or if they had already had the shot. Absolutely no questions were asked and no records kept. I could have gotten a shot if I had gotten in line. Who knows if the needles were new or re-used?

Class was also disrupted from time to time for marching practice. Every now and again some bigwig or government holiday required us to march in parades. So at seemingly random points in the year, and without warning, students would be called out of class to practice marching, no matter what the teachers had planned that day. Sometimes this could be frustrating, but at times it was also a welcomed break.

Other than the occasional interruption, school was generally uneventful and very structured. I would enter the classroom and the students would stand. Then I would say, "Good morning class." They would respond, "Good morning sir." Me, "How are you today?" Them, "Fine thank you and how are you?" Me again, "Fine, thank you. You may sit." Then I would start teaching a lesson and I would try to keep a good pace so that they were a little distracted from how hot, tired, and uncomfortable they were. Halfway through the class I would have the students do a written exercise based on the lesson while I called the class roll. With 60–80 students on the roll, this was no easy task, so I always made sure to keep the kids occupied. Calling the roll was a linguistic mine field. The names could be long and complicated and my pronunciation made the students laugh. Students with the same name had their birthdate added onto the end of their name so that you could tell them apart. Other students that truly confused me had the same names in reverse, like Adamou Ibrahim and Ibrahim Adamou.

Teachers are also required to write down everything that was studied during a class period in a "cahier d'texte"—which I assume translates as "textbook." The book stays in the class and the teacher has to include the details of their lesson plans. These lesson plans are later reviewed by a government representative. Interestingly, nobody ever came to review my notes and it's a good thing too. My notes were sloppy and sparse. My friends' records were reviewed and this little bureaucracy was a means for the reviewer to demand a bribe. In fact, the teachers at my school said they were taught how to bribe through the French system of bureaucracy.

When I stayed home from school one day because I was feeling a little under the weather, I was up and down opening and closing the front gate, fetching my visitors glasses of water and laying there on my mat while they sat staring into space for 15 minutes or so until some unknown force would tell them that it was time to go, and they'd leave only to be replaced by someone else. At one point, one person said, "You should get some rest, you look sick." I thought to myself, "I would get some rest if everyone would leave me ALONE!" I even explained that in my culture, unless you are family, usually you leave sick people alone or if it's a serious illness you might send a card or make a phone call. They intimated that all of the diseases around those parts were potentially serious, that they may never have another chance to say goodbye to me again, and that I would think that they didn't care about me if they didn't stop by. Besides, according to them, everybody knew that it wasn't good to spend too much time alone. That's sweet, now get out!

Another thing that caught my attention with respect to Cameroonian culture came to light during my first few weeks of training at the Peace Corps center. I had become fairly good friends with my language instructor and as we were walking around the center he started holding my hand. OH! Hello! What did this mean? Were we married, engaged, or just dating? And what was I supposed to do, let go, hold on, or do nothing? I decided that passive acceptance would be my best defense and eventually he let go. Then I began to notice that males were close to males in their culture and females could be close to females, but with few exceptions they didn't really mix except in a family way. This was true on the streets where I saw old men walking hand in hand and it was true at school where even my teenaged male students held each other's hands or put their arms around each other. This seemed, well, nice in a way, that everybody had a friend to hold hands with. I never got the hang of the hand-holding thing though—I never knew when I was supposed to initiate the hand-holding, how much pressure to apply, or when to let go, so I just waited until somebody held my hand.

And of course these little differences in culture could lead to all sorts of misunderstandings. One time, a friend of mine stopped in to get out of the drenching rain. I told him that he could borrow, note BORROW, some dry clothes and I gave him a pair of jeans to put on, which he did. Weeks later, after still not having the jeans returned, I politely mentioned that he could return the jeans whenever it was convenient. Well, he had a strange look in his eye, but he returned them alright. When I went to put them on, I couldn't help but notice that they had been completely altered to fit a much shorter person. I thought it was clear that I was loaning him the jeans because he was soaking wet, we did this all the time when we were growing up in Oklahoma, but we knew that you had to give the clothes back. I thought, gosh, everyone knows that. Did I really need to spell everything out? As it turns out, I did need to spell everything out because we functioned under a completely different set of assumptions.

Fortunately, for me, many of the cultural differences I encountered produced smiles rather than pain and humiliation. When my class was preparing pen pal letters to go overseas to the U.S., they wanted to send photos to their soon-to-be newfound pen friends. I agreed to take their pictures. Keep in mind that I knew these students as happy, laughing, and jovial, but in their pictures, they looked so stern and so solemn that I was afraid that the children that we would be sending these pictures to might think that they were, well, scary. They told me that they were never supposed to smile in pictures because it would be phony and disrespectful and the viewer would think that they were being mocked. So we practiced gluing on our fake smiles so that when I took their pictures, they wouldn't look like they were on death row.

I even had another experience with the whole smiling issue when I visited Sunny's home village. We had brought plenty of gifts for his family, including fabric and housewares for his mother. She greeted me by bowing to me on her hands and knees, which bugged me because I felt that I should have been bowing to her, as hard as she had worked to raise 14 children. Anyway, when I handed her the gifts, she remained somewhat unfazed. I wasn't looking for a major show of emotion, but I couldn't tell whether she could give a flip or not. Later, Sunny came to my room and said, "Wow, did you see how excited my Mom was about the stuff we brought her?" She was about as excited as a rock, in my estimation, so I asked, "How could you tell she was excited?" Sunny thought a while but just couldn't come up with an answer that would satisfy me, so we left it at that. But, the next time I visited their village, out came this African lady painfully struggling to maintain a mile-wide smile whom I didn't recognize as being Sunny's Mom, until I realized that he had taught her to smile for my benefit. Oh, gosh—that wasn't my intention!

One of the most important lessons that I learned from Cameroonian culture, besides not to smile at everything, had to do with tolerating the differences in people. While it was obvious that they took one look at me and thought of me as an oddity, they always managed to make me feel as though I belonged. In that sense, they tried to find space for everyone and not just for an exclusive few. This point was driven home one day when I was complaining that a certain person in the village (Mr. Ndu-du) bugged me and was generally nasty to everyone so why didn't they just, sort of, well ask him to leave? Oh no…no, no, no, that wouldn't do. They explained, "That's just him, you know, that's just his personality. That's how he is." They didn't feel the need to CHANGE each other or cut people off socially, like I realized that I was trying to do.

Furthermore, no matter how poor everyone was, there was always music and dancing going on somewhere. No matter how starved everyone was or how little food they had to offer, they still offered it. No matter how little they had, they managed to live artfully and creatively. And, who doesn't appreciate random acts of dancing?

Don't get me wrong, I am proud of my own country and the wonderful things it has accomplished, but when I think about the U.S. in relation to many other parts of the world, I think of it as the place to make money and not the place to relax, be human, and have fun. There is nothing wrong with making money, but we seem to sacrifice everything for work so that we can have money to buy things that will enable us to distance ourselves from the natural world and each other. Doesn't it make you wonder why the so-called best country in the world is so depressed and needs some form of anti-depressant, whether it be pills, booze, processed food, or fantasies cooked up by the media, just to survive? What living with the Cameroonians taught me was that who I am is good enough and that I don't need to believe in a fantasy about myself in order to feel good. They accomplished this by greeting me daily, by giving me their time and attention, and by letting me be myself without trying to "improve" me. I wasn't too short, too tall, too skinny, fat, hairy, or bald and they couldn't care less if I had static cling or not. I was just me—a poor, pathetic human being, but perfectly acceptable just the same. Is it wrong to want this kind of acceptance for all human beings? Especially Americans? After all, Americans need love too.

· 5 ·
TOWARD A PEDAGOGY OF INTERCONNECTEDNESS

Introduction

Hyacinth was a 52-year-old white female who had been teaching English as a second language (ESL) at the middle school level for 11 years at the time of our interviews. She had also taught 13 years of ESL at the high school level in a U.S. city on the Mexican border following her Peace Corps service, and 2 years of teaching seventh- and eighth-grade language arts, 12th-grade remedial English, and ninth-grade Spanish at an inner-city school prior to joining the Peace Corps. For her Peace Corps service, Hyacinth taught English in a secondary school in a small town in the central highlands of Kenya for 2 years from 1984 to 1986. During her Peace Corps service, she met and married Richard, another Peace Corps volunteer who went to Kenya at the same time she did. At the time of our interviews, they had just celebrated their 25th anniversary.

My interviews with Hyacinth took place at her and Richard's home in the city where they lived. I spent an enjoyable evening sharing Peace Corps and other stories with both Hyacinth and Richard the night before we began our interviews. What I remember most about the interviews was the active atmosphere in which they took place and the seeming ease with which I was integrated into Hyacinth's busy schedule. Interspersed into our two days of interviews were: tending to two turtles that Hyacinth gleefully showed me (and other visitors) how to feed, attending to one of her children who had had money stolen from them at a swimming pool, meeting with a family of five and discussing how she would be introducing each of them individually (their likes and dislikes, their experiences, the things they excelled at, etc.) at church on Sunday, taking me and an elderly friend to see the movie *The Help*, walking the dog and feeding the guinea pig, taking me along to church and introducing me to some fellow church-goers who were from the country where I served in the Peace Corps, dealing with an oil stain on Richard's shirt, taking me and two young children from her church to the university waterpark for an afternoon of swimming, and then occupying the children with popcorn and a movie while we completed the interviews in the next room. It seemed like a lot to do in addition to taking care of me and reflecting on events that occurred over 25 years earlier. Yet, Hyacinth seemed to take everything in stride and even reflected how her intercultural experiences helped her learn to "interweave" people into her life without feeling burdened.

I have titled Hyacinth's chapter "Toward a Pedagogy of Interconnectedness" because of her desire to make intercultural connections with and between people from different cultures. In this chapter, I included one culture shock story, two identity shift stories, one reverse culture shock story, and one pedagogy story. In Hyacinth's culture shock story, she discussed the ways in which male privilege was constructed in Kenyan culture, and in re-reading this story I looked at the structure of male privilege in America. For her first identity shift story, Hyacinth talked about the self as a cultural product. For my re-reading of this story, I explored the self as a cultural process. For her second identity shift story, Hyacinth used the metaphor of "interweaving" to refer to the cultural practices of welcoming and hosting others in one's home in Mexico and Kenya. I re-examined these same practices as gendered practice. For her reverse culture shock story, Hyacinth talked about sameness and difference. In the first reading, she appeared to relate sameness with feelings of competition and felt that many parts of American culture were "directly related to nothing." For the second reading, I look at the conceptualization of difference/sameness at a broader level. And lastly, in her pedagogy story, Hyacinth talked about her teaching role in Kenya as that of ambassador and in America as that of bridge. In my re-reading of this story, I look at how the roles of ambassador and bridge may create distance in addition to connection.

Culture Shock I: Male Privilege in Kenya

Gender roles in Kenya seemed "disturbing" to Hyacinth at times. She related at least three stories that had gender roles as the focus. One had to do with women's role being to "carry" things, another had to do with birth control, and a third was related to the changing social status of a boy once he was circumcised. In the first story she told, Hyacinth had gone with one of the male teachers to the tea shop to bring back some Mandazis (similar to donuts) for the other teachers back at the school. After they bought the mandazis, the male teacher handed her the bag and said "sorry, men don't carry things in our culture, women carry, men don't carry." She said that although she found that practice "ridiculous," she tried to put it into perspective. She thought, "Really, I was there for the cultural experience, whatever that experience was. I was there to learn and for the most part I did not find myself being overly judgmental. I wanted to know and I wanted to understand."

In another story, Hyacinth talked about how "frustrating" and "sad" it was to see that Kenyan families were so large even though they were poor and growing enough food to support themselves often proved "stressful." Although there was some talk in Kenya about birth control and family planning, Hyacinth believed that most Kenyans were against it because it challenged the male gender role. She explained,

> family size was connected to a male self-esteem which had eroded in many ways since a more Western culture had emerged there, because men had traditionally been the hunters and did agricultural work. Men lost that role in life. Women maintained theirs as the farmers. So men didn't really have much to do because there weren't many jobs...one of the ways that a man proved his manliness within a tribe was to father many children. That was very frustrating to see people so poor, such large families and the plots of land that people grew their food on, what they were eating, was increasingly becoming smaller because it's passed down, divided between the children.

She also mentioned that at the time when they were in the Peace Corps, Richard had written a "scathing poem" in which he criticized "the family planning attitudes that were supported by the Pope and then reiterated by the [Kenyan] government." He was advised not to share it with anyone, to "get rid of it" or "burn it." Along these lines, for Hyacinth, this story also highlighted the lack of freedom of speech in Kenya.

In the third story, Hyacinth talked about how important male circumcision was in Kenyan culture. She said that around the age of 13 or 14, boys would be trained by village elders in the "ways of being a man." She recounted that after circumcision a boy was seen as a man and was "expected to give up childish ways." This meant that he could no longer make, play with, or even touch anything that was considered a toy. A man also wouldn't hold his children or even "relate" to a child until they were four years old. With regard to school, Hyacinth noted that becoming a man could cause a few "glitches" because "You could correct a young man before he was circumcised, afterwards he was seen as adult in the community and he really could not be criticized very much." She went on to say that in performing their roles, women were expected to be very "demure" and not criticize men.

According to Hyacinth, observing and experiencing the gender relations in Kenya was one of the experiences that made her realize how American she was. She said, "My values are very American...I feel men and women have equal rights." She reiterated this a second time during our interview and I asked if she thought women and men had equal rights in America and she replied, "yeah, oh yeah" and then changed the topic.

In this group of stories, Hyacinth explored the ways in which gender was socially constructed in Kenya. Lorber (1994) explained that from birth, human beings are taught how to enact socially constructed gender roles that have little to do with the genitalia one is born with. She noted that a "sex category becomes a gender status through naming, dress, and the use of other markers" and that once these gender markers are conferred on children "others treat those in one gender differently from those in the other, and children respond to the different treatment by feeling different and behaving differently" (p. 20). She also argued that gender roles are "legitimated by religion, law, science, and the society's entire set of values" (p. 21), that "Schools, parents, peers, and the mass media guide young people into gendered work and family roles" (p. 22), and that gender roles are constructed unequally according to "prestige and power" (p. 25). Some of the ways that gender was socially constructed in Kenya, according to Hyacinth, included the way that men didn't carry things, didn't play with toys, didn't hold small children, and couldn't be reprimanded by teachers or mothers. Men could also express their masculinity by fathering multiple children. On the other hand, Kenyan women were expected to be demure, non-critical of men, and act as the sole source of emotional and tactile support for their children because men didn't relate to or hold children until they were at least 4 years old. Both roles appeared to be constructed to support male privilege through social interaction at home and in public spaces, including the school. From an intercultural perspective, male privilege was also supported by Western religious practice vis-à-vis the Pope's position on the use of birth control, which gave male religious authority for the fathering of multiple children despite conditions of poverty.

Gender roles in Kenya were also enacted through work and the division of labor. Lorber (1994) offered that:

> One way of choosing people for the different tasks of society is on the basis of their talents, motivations, and competence—their demonstrated achievements. The other way is on the basis of gender, race, ethnicity—ascribed membership in a category of people. (p. 20)

Lorber also noted that the "gender boundaries" must hold "or the whole social order will come crashing down" (p. 25). In Hyacinth's story, she points out that the division of labor in Kenya was based on gender roles, where men were traditionally hunters and women were farmers. Changing economic and social conditions threatened the social order by taking away men's gendered work role. Male gender then was displaced and reaffirmed through fathering multiple children as visible evidence of manhood. Conversely, in Hyacinth's "American" view, men and women have equal rights, which suggests that the division of labor (and assignment of privilege) in the U.S. is not based on gender, but in the other ways described by Lorber (1994) through "talents, motivations, and competence" and "demonstrated achievements."

Re-reading Culture Shock I: Male Privilege in America

In re-reading Hyacinth's story, I question the notion that men and women have equal rights in the U.S. as I examine the system of male privilege that underlies American society. In the book *The Gender Knot*, Johnson (2005) pointed to the difficulty of unraveling male privilege in American culture because it does not take the clear-cut form of oppression that may be more obvious within other cultures. He wrote:

> Openly oppressive systems of privilege like Apartheid in South Africa...provide comforting clarity because it is easy to see who oppresses whom and how it is done. You can always tell one group from the other, differences in privilege are obvious, abuse and exploitation are public, and the entire system is organized around rigid segregation....It would be easier to see how patriarchy works if it fit into this kind of model, but it doesn't. (p. 163)

In other words, even though the examples of male privilege in the U.S. may not be as obvious as those presented in Hyacinth's story of Kenya, it exists nonetheless. I think that focusing more on the clearly defined examples of dominance and privilege in other cultures enables privilege of a more subtle nature in one's own culture to remain hidden because it is so easy to say, "Well, at least we are not like them."

Relatedly, Johnson (2005) argued that male privilege in the U.S. has been rendered almost "invisible" because it has become a part of the very fabric and structure of our culture. He wrote,

> Because patriarchal culture designates men and masculinity as the standard for people in general, maleness is the taken-for-granted backdrop, making it the last thing to stand out as remarkable. When we refer to humanity as *man*, for example, maleness blends into humanness, and men can enjoy the comfort and security of not being marked as *other*. (p. 155)

McIntosh (1989) also felt that male privilege was invisible. She argued that male privilege was "unacknowledged" and "unconscious" and that people (men in particular) "are taught not to recognize male privilege" within American society. Interestingly, by reflecting on the ways in which male privilege was systemically constructed and conferred, she began to understand how her own whiteness offered "invisible" privileges. She wrote, "Thinking through unacknowledged male privilege as a phenomenon, I realized that since hierarchies in our society are interlocking, there was most likely a phenomenon of white privilege which was similarly denied and protected."

McIntosh added that as a white person, she "was taught to see racism as individual acts of meanness, not in invisible systems conferring dominance on my group." Accordingly, in order to make the "invisible" nature of white privilege visible, she created a list of 26 ways in which white privilege was conferred to her personally. Some of the examples she offered included: "I can be sure that my children will be given curricular materials that testify to the existence of their race," "I can do well in a challenging situation without being called a credit to my race," and "I can take a job with an affirmative action employer without having co-workers on the job suspect that I got it because of race." I realize that this discussion of white privilege veers somewhat off the topic of gender (although I think the two are interrelated) and I appreciate McIntosh's technique for making the invisibility of privilege more visible.

Finding McIntosh's (1989) technique for revealing the system of white privilege both personally and socially illuminating, I decided to give it a try with regard to male privilege. Here goes:

1. I can visit the majority of places of worship in my city and "God" will be addressed in terms of male gender and the sermon will likely be delivered by someone who is male.
2. I can be relatively sure that the next American president, like all others before, will be a male.
3. I can be certain that the founding documents that form the basis of my government were written by men.
4. I can be certain that the majority of lawmakers (senators, representatives, etc.) are men.
5. If I call the police or other law enforcement agencies for assistance, it will likely be a male who responds.
6. I can turn on the TV and find multiple examples in which a man is the leader of a group or a team.
7. I am sure that if I open a history book, the deeds of men (our forefathers) will be represented throughout. (Note: Is there such a thing as a foremother?)
8. I can be aggressive, angry, and competitive without being called a "bitch" or "emotional." (A female colleague insisted I include this one.)
9. I can be relatively sure that the upper administration positions at a majority of schools and universities (as well as in the corporate world) are filled by men.
10. I live in a culture where "all *men* are created equal."

A female friend and educator also observed that the worst insult for boys/men is to refer to them in feminine terms and to question their masculinity. Certainly this is not an exhaustive list, but I think it offers a glimpse into the subtly obvious ways in which gender and privilege are structured in the U.S. and also how the feminine is made Other in American society.

For Hyacinth, experiencing the male privilege in Kenya made her feel a greater sense of being American, to the extent that she felt men and women had relatively equal rights in America. For McIntosh (1989), exploring the different forms of privilege that exist in the U.S. (male privilege, white privilege, etc.) has had a different effect. She noted that the study of privilege has turned out to be an elusive and fugitive subject. The pressure to avoid it is great, for in facing it I must give up believing in democracy. If these things are true, this is not such a free country; one's life is not what one makes it: many doors open for certain people through no virtues of their own.

While I would not go so far as to say that Americans "must give up believing in democracy," I think McIntosh's point does suggest the need to question the meaning of such words as "democracy," "equality," and "freedom."

Identity Shift I: The Self as Cultural Product

According to Hyacinth, her intercultural travels during and after the Peace Corps made her much more aware of how "American" she was. In one example, while travelling through Guatemala she remembered seeing a number of starving dogs in the streets. She thought of this as animal cruelty until she realized that as an American, she had both the time and money to lavish on the care of her pets, unlike Guatemalans. This, along with her other intercultural experiences, got her to thinking about how culturally defined her perceptions were. She explained at length:

> We think of ourselves as being unique, we're not. We are a representation of our culture. There are parts of our culture we can reject. I don't have a huge pickup truck. I can choose what political party I want to vote with, for example. I can pick and choose, but I'm still picking and choosing from the smorgasbord that's laid in front of me and it's not the same as the buffet table that a Kenyan encounters or someone from Guatemala encounters. I still am very, very, very much a product of my own culture in ways that I just really would not have accepted. I thought I was much more individually formed, or somehow I was more in charge of who I was, or the values that I have. My values are very American. I feel like everyone should have a free education. I feel men and women have equal rights. I feel the freedom of speech thing.

She also noted how "scary" it was to come to this realization that she was more culturally than individually defined.

In this story, Hyacinth suggests that people are embedded in their culture (or conversely that their culture has been embedded in them), which has implications for the ways in which people define themselves, their values, their beliefs, and their actions. In essence, she felt that she was a "product" of American culture rather than being "individually formed." In making her case, Hyacinth implies that there are two ways of defining oneself—culturally or individually—even though she indicates that culture has a stronger influence on forming the so-called individual. In making this division, she also appears to cast culture in the role of social structure and individuality in that of human agency. Both notions—structure and agency—are discussed further below.

According to Hays (1994), social structure is often framed as "systematic and patterned," as a form of "constraint," as "static," and as "collective" (p. 58). Social structures are also portrayed as "primary, hard, and immutable, like the girders of a building...impervious to human agency, to exist apart from, but nevertheless to determine the essential shape of, the strivings and motivated transactions that constitute the experienced surface of social life" (Sewell, 1992, p. 2).

That social structures are reproduced by individual actors is evident in the observable patterns of social relations individuals engage in, whether or not those individuals are aware of or wish to participate in this reproduction (Sewell, 1992, p. 2). One of the ways cultures work to reproduce social structure is through the values they emphasize. Schwartz (n.d.) noted,

> These value emphases express shared conceptions of what is good and desirable in the culture, the cultural ideals. Cultural value emphases shape and justify individual and group beliefs, actions, and goals. Institutional arrangements and policies, norms, and everyday practices express underlying cultural value emphases in societies. (p. 2)

These perspectives highlight the rigid, patterned, and somewhat hidden nature of social structures, as well as the power of structures to shape—either consciously or unconsciously—the relationships in which individuals and groups participate. This is achieved through the reproduction of value emphases and supported by "policies, norms, and everyday practices." Some of the American value emphases—or structural girders—that Hyacinth began to recognize through encountering different cultures included her beliefs about the proper treatment of animals, her beliefs about certain freedoms (speech, education), and her belief in female and male equality.

In contrast to social structure, human agency implies "freedom," and is "contingent and random," "active," and "individual" (Hays, 1994, p. 57). It has also been linked with "selfhood, motivation, will, purposiveness, intentionality, choice, initiative, freedom, and creativity" (Emirbayer & Mische, 1998, p. 2). While Hays (1994) pointed out the "privileged status" that "*individual* freedom" holds in American culture, she also noted the "long history of social order" in the U.S.—an expression of which is the "modern privileging of science" (p. 59) as the search for structure in the life-worlds of people. Others question whether or not individual freedom is even possible. Sommers (2007), for example, argued that in order to think of ourselves as individuals with "free will...we would have to be *causa sui*, or "causes of oneself," which she argued would be "*logically* impossible" (p. 61, emphasis in original). She explained,

> We are aware of our desires and our volitions and that they cause our behavior. But in most cases we are ignorant of the causes or motives behind the desires and the volitions themselves. Thus, as reflective and self-conscious creatures, we have developed this view of free will, this idea that certain volitions have no causes or hidden motives—that they derive from us, from the self, and only there. We believe we are *causa sui* because we don't know what else could have caused our volitions. (p. 64)

In addition to suggesting that one cannot be the source of one's own making, Sommers also observed that it is the "phenomenology of decision-making" within the "immediate moment" that creates the feeling of freedom (p. 62). In other words, society provides choices and the "hidden" motivation behind making those choices in order to create a sense of freedom in the individual. Therefore, in some ways, no matter what one chooses, one is still supporting the structure. As an example of this concept, Hays (1994) pointed to Willis' research with a group of working-class school boys who used their "agency" to reject school norms by misbehaving in class. On the surface, the boys seemed to be resisting the social order, and yet their behavior served to "reproduce and further solidify both their working-class culture and their own position as members of that subordinate class" (p. 63). This suggests that even in one's attempts to escape the social structure one may actually be serving it.

The above theory and research suggests that despite the American cultural appeal of "individual freedom" as an expression of free will or human agency, Americans—as Hyacinth notes—are both culturally constructed and culturally bound. Hyacinth also challenges the notion of individuality as the practice of free choice in that despite being able to "pick and choose" it is one's culture that provides the "smorgasbord" or "buffet" from which the individual chooses. In this regard it would seem that culture not only structures what may be thought of as social "reality," it also structures individual responses to that reality. A "scary" realization, as Hyacinth argues, indeed.

Re-reading Identity Shift I: The Self as Cultural Process

In re-reading Hyacinth's story, I look at ways in which agency and structure are constructed, relational, and indicative of identity as a *process* related to culture(s) and not entirely a *product* of culture. Arguing from a clinical psychological perspective, Lefcourt (1973) posited that "freedom" (agency) and "control" (structure) are "both illusions" and "inventions of man [people] to make sense of his [their] experience" (p. 417). He also pointed out that "Whether people perceive themselves as free or controlled in their actions is a constructive process and not a 'given'" (p. 417). At the same time, he noted that both "illusions" have consequences and that both illusions can be de/constructed and challenged. He wrote that one

> could easily counter the individual's vision of free choice by referring to the effects of public relations, mass media, and man's susceptibility to influence others....On the other hand, clinical psychologists often encounter individuals who believe they are helpless pawns of fate or other persons...[which] is often judged to be inappropriate or obstructive. (p. 417)

This suggests that the boundaries of individual experience are drawn in relation to the interplay of freedom and control and may be constructed differently even among people within the same culture. It also seems that freedom is contingent on the existence of control. Echoing and expanding this view, Sewell (1992) made the case that "human agency and structure, far from being *opposed*, in fact *presuppose* each other" (p. 4). Using Gidden's notion of the "duality of structure," he called attention to how structures have changed throughout history and "how historical agents' thoughts, motives, and intentions are constituted by the cultures and social institutions into which they are born" and yet how these same agents "improvise or innovate in structurally shaped ways that significantly reconfigure the very structures that constituted them" (p. 5). In other words, cultures have the potential to shape people and people have the potential to shape cultures.

Just as Sewell (1992) encouraged the rethinking of structure as more dual and relational, Emirbayer and Mische (1998) argued for a vision of agency as contextual, relational, and situated in time. They "reconceptualize" human agency as,

> a temporally embedded process of social engagement, informed by the past (in its habitual aspect), but also oriented toward the future (as a capacity to imagine alternative possibilities) and toward the present (as a capacity to contextualize past habits and future projects within the contingencies of the moment)....As actors move within and among these different unfolding contexts, they switch between (or "recompose") their temporal orientations—as constructed within and by means of those contexts—and thus are capable of changing their relationship to structure. (pp. 963–964)

This view recognizes that humans can draw upon multiple temporal modes (past, present, and future) from which to reconstruct meaning in order to shift their understanding of self in relationship to the structure. For example, during periods of stress I have found that time and distance enable me to rethink my initial reactions to situations that caused the stress in the first place. Knowing this, I try (but don't always succeed) to hold off on any definite judgment making. I also think revisiting the past can guide behavior in the present by reclaiming forgotten knowledge or by recognizing and breaking with tradition in order to move in a new direction. Likewise, envisioning the future can guide decision making in the present. One method that encourages teachers to explore this notion of temporality in their own lives and which holds possibilities for teacher agency is Pinar's (1975) method of currerre. For this method, Pinar suggested that when teachers carefully examine their biographical past, present, and (imagined) future and analyze the relationship between the three, they may take on a "new vantage point" (p. 2) from which to view their present circumstances in a manner that encourages them to "move on, more learned, more evolved than before" (p. 15). Taken together, the preceding theorists offered a messier and more complicated view of the relationship between agency and structure—a relationship shaped by human perception, human inter/action, temporality, and context. They also suggested that humans play a role in the process of building the structures that shape them and likewise that they have the power to reconfigure those structures in turn.

Hyacinth's point that we are "representations" and "products" of our culture and can only "pick and choose" from the "smorgasbord" that our culture provides us implies that as members of one culture, one cannot eat at other tables. Adler (2002) disagreed. He argued that the technologies associated with globalization now make it possible for the interconnection and blending of cultural elements. He also noted that "A new type of person whose orientation and view of the world...is developing from the complex of social, political, economic, and educational interactions of our time," which he referred to as the "international," "transcultural," "multicultural," or "intercultural" person. He explained,

> What is new about this person, and unique to our time, is a fundamental change in the structure and process of identity. The identity of the "multicultural," far from being frozen in social character, is more fluid and mobile, more susceptible to change, more open to variation. It is an identity based not on "belongingness" which implies either owning or being owned by culture, but on a style of self-consciousness that is capable of negotiating ever new formations of reality...he or she is neither totally apart from his or her culture; instead, he or she lives on the boundary. To live on the edge of one's thinking, one's culture, or one's ego...is to live with tension and movement.

Tillich (In Adler, 2002) called this place of tension and movement a "third area beyond the bounded territories, an area where one can stand for a time without being enclosed in something tightly bounded." Using Hyacinth's food metaphor, Adler's and Tillich's perspectives suggest that one can eat from a global buffet where sharing and mixing is possible—that one "negotiates" among, and draws sustenance from, different cultural elements both within and outside of those provided by one's home culture. By living at the boundaries of cultures and drawing on one or more other cultures, the concept of what one's "culture" is becomes enlarged.

In reflecting on these notions of structure and agency as relational, contextual, and temporal, and the possibility of creating a "third area" between cultures, I note an example of one "third area" that Hyacinth and her husband Richard seemed to create and recreate every evening at their dining table. Hyacinth explained to me that practically every night for the past 25 years since returning from the Peace Corps, she and Richard eat their dinner by candlelight just as they ate by firelight during their time in Kenya. This simple habitual act connected them with Kenya across distance and time, through past, present, and future, and created a space that was neither wholly Kenyan nor wholly American. This suggests that beneath the placid waters of cultural conformity, currents of uniqueness and individuality are at play.

Identity Shift II: "Interweaving" as Cultural Practice

Something profound that Hyacinth said she "learned" from her "international" experiences was how to integrate others into her life. In this regard, she viewed American culture as more "formal" whereas Kenyan and Mexican cultures offered more "openness." In explaining the cultural differences in relating to people, Hyacinth talked about her Mexican neighbor in the border town where she and Richard lived after their Peace Corps service ended. Hyacinth began,

> she'd be making enchiladas, putting them on my plate, mopping, sweeping, taking care of children, people coming, people going, but I was welcome there and she wanted me to eat with her, and she wanted to talk with me, but not just me, anyone, anyone who was there; her family, her friends, her neighbors. There was an openness there. It was the same in Kenya. It's like sit at my table in my kitchen and I'm going to mop, okay. Life goes on. I felt so comfortable with that. It's like you're not stopping your life because I'm here. Your life continues and I'm just woven into the fabric of your life, but I'm not an inconvenience....There was something really affirming about that. I didn't stand out, nobody necessarily spoke to me in English...they didn't speak English anyway, but nobody made any grand effort on my behalf....It wasn't about language, it was just being woven into the fabric of somebody else's life.

In contrast, she said that in the U.S.,

> we're so formal. We're busy. You call for invitations. American culture is different. I would never think I could say hey I'm lonely, I don't want to eat by myself tonight, I'll go see what my neighbors are having. That would be the farthest thing from my mind. You call a week in advance. It just would never happen. That's not an American thing that we do. It's different, we're busy. I'm not even home. Nobody could come to my house at dinner time and expect to find me here, I'm probably somewhere else. I'm at yoga. I'm here, I'm there.

For Hyacinth, her Mexican neighbor's and her Kenyan friends' openness and ability to integrate others into their everyday existence without "interfering" with the work that needed to be done was so surprising because it was "radically different" from the way she was raised. Hyacinth noted that when she was growing up, her family's "home really wasn't open to other people, it just was not. It was very formal and very nicely done, and very graciously done, but mainly for ourselves." Despite her more formal upbringing, Hyacinth "appreciated" how good she felt in the intercultural contexts she experienced and therefore organized her own life with a certain sense of openness and informality when possible.

I also noticed this sense of openness and interconnectedness in the Cameroonian village where I lived during the Peace Corps. It seemed that no invitation was ever needed and people were not only welcomed to visit and/or receive others, this was an expectation. I also recall getting scolded during my first year by my principal for not attending a party at his house held in honor of his wife who had won some type of government education award. I had heard that she had received an award, but I hadn't received an invitation to any party and I barely knew her. How was I supposed to know I was required to attend a party? I was also politely scolded a few times when there would be impromptu meetings held after school that I missed. Nobody invited me to the meetings so I didn't show up. I often asked my Cameroonian teacher counterparts, "How did you know there was going to be an unscheduled meeting?" Their reply, "We just knew." They were certainly interwoven in each other's lives, but I, on the other hand, felt like a stray thread.

Hyacinth's use of the metaphor of "interweaving" gives the sense that Mexican and Kenyan social networks were "joint, interactive" (Wilce, 2004, p. 3) "unified complex system[s]" (McDaniel, 2010, p. 7), and "relational" in the way that "each individual strand interacts with others to form an integrated whole" (Meltzoff, 1994, p. 15). On the other hand, she described American culture in terms of formality, busy-ness, and being self-occupied. These descriptions seem to mirror the ways in which the "self" is understood from different cultural perspectives. While Western self-construal has been described as "individualist, independent, autonomous, agentic, and separate," the self in other cultures has been described as "collectivist, interdependent, ensemble, communal, and relational" (Kashima et al., 1995, p. 925). Triandis (1989) used the terms "ideocentric" (self-centered) and "allocentric" (other-related) to characterize the people in those cultures respectively. He also referred to an earlier study he helped conduct in which "ideocentrics" reported that "they are concerned with achievement, but are lonely, whereas the allocentrics report low alienation and receiving much social support" (p. 509). In the U.S., Hyacinth indicated that if she were "lonely" or "hungry," visiting her neighbors "would be the farthest thing from [her] mind" and that she would likely be occupied with other pursuits such as yoga during mealtimes anyway. On the other hand, she expressed appreciation for the system of interweaving employed in Mexican and Kenyan homes in that she felt "welcome," "so comfortable," "not an inconvenience," and the experience was "really affirming." These reflections seemed to point to a difference in social interaction, with Mexican and Kenyan cultures highlighting "allocentric" values and the U.S. as more "ideocentric."

Re-reading Identity Shift II: "Interweaving" as Gendered Practice

As I re-read Hyacinth's story, I began to notice how the person who was doing the mopping up, the sweeping, the cooking, the taking care of children and entertaining a seemingly steady stream of visitors was ostensibly a woman. In addition, I began to recognize the similar roles that women in my village performed in Cameroon, as well as the women in my own family spread across Arkansas and Oklahoma. I also recalled that it was Hyacinth who took care of and connected various individuals and groups throughout our time together. In their study comparing cultural and gender differences regarding dimensions of individualism, relatedness, and collectivism, Kashima et al. (1995) found that gender was a better predictor of "relatedness" than the collectivism/individualism construct used to label various cultures, with women across five cultures largely reporting greater degrees of relatedness than the men across those same cultures. This suggests that gender and not necessarily national culture is the basis for the notion of the relational self. Building on the writings of Gilligan and Miller, Surrey (1985) asserted that

> Our conception of the self-in-relation involves the recognition that, for women, the primary experience of self is relational; that is, the self is organized and developed in the context of important relationships…[which] makes an important shift in emphasis from separation to relationship as the basis for self-experience and development. (p. 2)

Hyacinth seemed to appreciate the relatedness that the women in the other cultures displayed and she expressed feeling comfortable and connected though not the center of attention. She also didn't try to claim her individuality and was happy that she "didn't stand out." In addition, she tried to implement the other women's practices and approaches to social relationships whenever possible in her own home in the United States.

Returning to Hyacinth's metaphor, the practice of "interweaving" appears to rest squarely on the shoulders of women. For Hyacinth, the role of weaver seemed to be an empowering one. According to Shoichet (2007), the classical writers Homer and Ovid used the weaving metaphor to "challenge the conventional idea of womanly virtue in the classical world" and "recast women in a role that emphasizes their social influence rather than their deference to authority" (p. 23). She wrote, "both poets…invert the weaving metaphor, using an activity traditionally emblematic of feminine virtues (such as modesty, chastity, and obedience) to symbolize female resistance to the mores of a social patriarchy" (p. 24).

For example, Homer told the story of the wealthy and newly widowed woman, Penelope, who was socially expected to remarry soon after her husband's death. Instead, Penelope used the excuse of weaving her husband's death shroud as a respectable way of staving off remarriage. Penelope's technique was to unravel everything at night that she had woven during the day so that the shroud would never be completed. In other examples, "The weaver records events *as she wishes to record them,* wielding power not only over which information is told, but how it is told" (Shoichet, 2007, p. 25). This implies that the act of interweaving, the ability to connect with and care for others out of choice, can be an expression of women's power.

Reverse Culture Shock I: Sameness as Competition and the U.S. as Un/Real

For Hyacinth, returning to the United States involved "so many aspects of life" such as meeting Richard's family and vice versa, deciding on where to live, and finding jobs, that "there wasn't really a lot of time to reflect deeply on reverse culture shock." She explained that noticing cultural differences and reflecting on them "lasted a long time…really in the years." One thing that she did notice immediately, much like other volunteers, was the "overwhelming" variety of goods at the grocery store, especially with regard to cereal, which had its own dedicated aisle with what seemed like hundreds of choices, whereas in Kenya there was only one choice of cereal. But it was another topic that Hyacinth discussed—"banter," or "small-talk," and its relationship to the notions of sameness and difference that I found most interesting.

Hyacinth felt that sometimes she wanted to have conversations with a little more substance but that in the U.S. "with people you don't know very much, the kind of conversations that people have can be draining" and she didn't like the "tension that it required." She explained that most conversations were "superficial" or "banal" and tended to leave her feeling "intimidated" or "inferior" because she didn't play some of the social "games" as well as others or they might make her feel "redundant" or bored if the person was too similar to herself. She added,

> That kind of banter, that kind of detail doesn't seem interesting to me and maybe if you talk to an international person, their details may be equally as banal and mundane, but they're different from mine, so they seem more interesting.

She also noted that "ultimately it has something to do with not feeling completely at ease with your own culture" or finding your own culture "boring."

When I pointed out to Hyacinth that there must have been boring conversations in Kenya, she recalled going to parties in Kenya where much of the talk centered on farming, which tended to be "mundane," repetitive, and lacking in "variation." But she also pointed out a difference. She argued that the seemingly routine discussions about farming in Kenya "are significant conversations to have because it means my family is living, my animals will live, my children will live, or they won't. It's right there. It's what life is about.... It's important."

Conversely, she believed that in the U.S., "So much of our world really is directly related to nothing" and it was difficult to be interested in anything for very long that didn't seem "important."

For Hyacinth, the experience of being different in other cultures was also a means for feeling "special." She first experienced this when she was an exchange student in Australia just after she completed high school and also later in Kenya with the Peace Corps. She explained,

> When I was in Australia...I didn't feel awkward where I had in the South growing up...because I was special, because I was an international student. So, people had something to talk to me about, so there was kind of this specialness. So that kind of helped me not feel quite so shy, not so awkward. Then I had the Kenyan experience, again similar, you're special because you're from the United States, you have something to talk to people about....So there's this thing about being special, but also there's an awkwardness....You know, you're vulnerable, so people help you. It's like, I don't know how to get around in the market, so people help you get around in the market.

Accordingly, it seemed that for Hyacinth, difference could stimulate intercultural interest and connection in ways that sameness could not.

As a shy and awkward child growing up in a small, nearly all-white town in Oklahoma, I could certainly relate to Hyacinth's story. The social system I grew up in appeared to work to insure that everybody did the same things, liked the same things, and thought about things in the same way. It seemed boring and limiting to me because once one mastered life in a small town (which didn't take too long), there really wasn't much left to learn. It was also painful to the extent that I was different in ways that the system couldn't seem to tolerate. Yet travelling among other cultures seemed interesting and thought provoking and I found acceptance and sometimes appreciation for my differences. I did find it odd though that living in rural Cameroon seemed more tolerable than living in rural Oklahoma. People talked about basically the same issues—religion, politics, each other's daily happenings, sports (in Cameroon, mainly during World Cup season), food, etc., and, like Hyacinth, some of those conversations that I likely would have found boring back home seemed more interesting by comparison. Hyacinth's story made me reflect on why some people find sameness comforting while others draw strength from difference and diversity.

In the beginning of the story, Hyacinth related sameness with conversation that could be "draining," required "tension," and left Hyacinth feeling "inferior." She also said she didn't play social "games" as well as other Americans. In looking more closely at the game metaphor, on one level, playing games can be fun and exciting, but on another level, they can be tense and draining, especially if one doesn't appreciate competition. Most games have winners and losers and losing may give one feelings of inferiority. Although Hyacinth suggested that vulnerability in other cultures could provide openings for connection, vulnerability under competitive conditions might feel threatening instead of bonding. Games also have rules that must be understood and followed by all the players. When all the players look and sound alike, it is easier to lose the sense of individuality that is otherwise highlighted through the contrast of differences. Differences, in a sense, open a door to uniqueness, and because the rules of the game are not shared between culturally dissimilar players, there exists the possibility of reshaping the rules to fit the needs of players. To me it seems that the feelings of competition and not being able to play the game as well as others made Hyacinth feel like an outsider in American culture and enabled her to seek connections with others outside American culture.

On the subject of difference, one difference that Hyacinth pointed out was that in the U.S., "So much of our world really is directly related to nothing," whereas the Kenyan world was directly tied to nature, life, death, and reality (a similar sentiment was expressed by Ryder, who also taught in Kenya, though at a different time). Her view seems to equate survival and closeness to nature with reality, whereas distance from nature and social construction seemed tied to the unreal. Yet, while Hyacinth lived among Kenyan farmers who worked closely with nature and their survival was greatly affected by climactic change, illness, etc., the Kenyan social practices Hyacinth described in other sections in relation to male privilege, pedagogy, religious beliefs, political beliefs, and interpersonal interactions were all social constructions that weren't tied to a "natural" reality. Hyacinth also talked about the Kenyan shift away from farming toward a more Western-style economy. To this extent, Kenyan culture seems to be a mix of both the "real" and "unreal" (as described by Hyacinth) and in a process of change.

Expressing a Buddhist "middle way" perspective of reality and non-reality, Cheng (2001) wrote of the fallacy of "subscribing to the appearance of things in change as real" as well as "holding things as absolutely unreal or empty" and offered that "We simply have to stay unattached and non-clinging" (p. 449). This suggests a view of the world as constantly changing, the impossibility of making a firm distinction between the real and unreal, and the need to let go of such distinctions altogether. I think this may be challenging from a Western perspective that is founded on the "notion that any given thing either is or is not. It exists or it does not exist" and by extension is real or it isn't (Olson, 2001, p. 116). Yet, one could argue that Western culture is constantly changing as well and its complete story has not yet been written.

Re-reading Reverse Culture Shock I: A Different Kind of Sameness and Reality as Floating

In re-reading Hyacinth's story, I looked more closely at sameness and difference at a conceptual level. In her story, Hyacinth constructed sameness in terms of boredom, redundancy, and discomfort. Difference, on the other hand was more interesting and made Hyacinth feel special. Speaking to the notion of sameness and difference, Olson (2001) wrote,

> The duality of sameness and difference is an underlying principle of classification as we construct and practice it in Western culture. We try to group similar things together and separate them from things that are different. This principle is taught at an early age. In children's books and television shows, we learn to identify "which of these things is not like the other"....Once we learn to view the world in this manner, classification that groups similar things together seems to be an almost natural or innate way of organizing things. Indeed, for those of us who have been acculturated to identify sameness and difference, we find classification an extremely useful arrangement. (p. 115)

Certainly, within Western cultures the same/different construct has been used to explore issues related to race, gender, sexual orientation, physical ability, pedagogical style, and various combinations of these categories (Harris, 2000; Nagel, 2002; Benjamin, 2002; Tucker, 2003; Cammissa & Reingold, 2004; Epstein, 2004; Mackie, 2001; Clarke, 2002; Woodhams & Danieli, 2000; Broady, 2004). Olson (2001) noted, though, that there is a problem in classifying things (and people) as the same or different in that they may be the same in some ways and different in others. Additionally, Young (1995) argued that as cultures begin to intermingle they take on a greater sense of "hybridity," and that this hybridity "makes difference into sameness, and sameness into difference, but in a way that makes the same no longer the same, the different no longer simply different" (p. 25). For Benjamin (2002), this calls for "straddling the space between the opposites" of sameness and difference in ways that do not value one side while deprecating the other (p. 182). This research implies that people are a mix of sameness(es) and difference(s) at both individual and cultural levels, which in turn seem to defy simple categories of different/same.

In Hyacinth's story, she seemed to associate positive experiences with difference and negative experiences with sameness, yet although Hyacinth was similar to other middle-class American white women in some respects, she was different in other ways, and it was this difference that was discomforting. Additionally, even though Hyacinth was outwardly different from the Kenyans and Mexicans she knew, it is possible she shared similar interests with them despite being from different cultures—including a desire for intercultural connection. This implies that judgments of sameness/difference may be superficial or related to associated positive or negative experiences and that one *constructs* and *chooses* (Olssen, 1996) the differences and similarities one wishes to focus on in the process of interaction and meaning making. Hyacinth even hinted at this herself when she noted that her views on sameness and difference may be related to not being completely satisfied in her own culture. In other words, different and same may be convenient categorizations for other types of associations that may have nothing to do with either category.

Pedagogy I: Teacher as "Ambassador" and "Bridge"

In describing the teacher/student relationships in Kenya, Hyacinth generally felt that there was a "formality," "coldness," and a "distancing" that "interfered with intimacy in teacher/student relationships." Conversely, she described the teacher/student relationship in the United States as more "relaxed, happy, jovial," "warm," "intimate," and more balanced with regard to teacher/student closeness and discipline. She felt teacher/student closeness "enhanced" teaching rather than distracted from it because students "want to please someone who cares about them." Of her Kenyan students, Hyacinth lamented that

> even after 2-and-a-half years I didn't feel that I knew my students well. I certainly didn't know what they were thinking. I didn't know the issues of their hearts. They respected me. We had a pleasant relationship, but not a close relationship.

She added that within such a formal relationship, the teacher couldn't "accomplish the same things" as she could in a close relationship.

Two factors that seemed to add to teacher/student distancing in Kenya were student punishment and testing. Hyacinth recalled that students who were late to school were required to lie on the ground and have their feet beaten and that at other times they would be subjected to "very brutal beatings" as a form of punishment. As a teacher, she was expected to "beat" the students as well, and this made Hyacinth "very uncomfortable." On one occasion, she remembered that her head mistress insisted she "strike a student with a stick" for either being disrespectful or not completing homework, and that if she didn't she would "never be taken seriously and all teachers do that here, and it's really essential that you do." In that instance, she gave the student a very light "tap" on the shoulder, but she preferred to use another form of punishment, having students kneel for a class period, because even though it may be humiliating it "wasn't violent." She argued, "I could use that without feeling guilty about it, but those kinds of things I felt like fostered this real extreme respect and the real extreme respect interfered with intimacy in teacher/student relationships."

Another thing that seemed to distance teachers and students was testing. Hyacinth explained that students were focused on passing their National Exams in the hopes of going to university, either in Kenya or the United States. Accordingly,

> Students did not want you to waste their time. They wanted solid, consistent, test driven instruction. They wanted to pass a test and if you can help them do that, that was good...any kind of relationship building...that was frivolous...was outside their focus....They were very focused, because their future was passing that test and in terms of being inculcated, that was part of their reality and you didn't get in the way of that.

Hyacinth also pointed out that even though the state where she was currently teaching, like most states in the U.S., was "very, very, very test driven," the focus that Kenyan students had on passing their exams was much greater by comparison. She noted too that in Kenya, even if a teacher was sick and no adult was present in the classroom "students continued with an assignment on their own without a substitute" and class would be taught by "two student leaders, a boy and a girl."

Hyacinth also talked about the different roles she performed as a teacher depending on the context. While she conceptualized her teaching role as an "ambassador" in Kenya, she saw herself as making and being a "bridge" for students in the United States. In Kenya, she noted that some of the challenges she faced in teaching were that "the subtleties and nuances of their system were unfamiliar" to her. Along these lines she wasn't sure that her teaching had made a difference in the lives of her Kenyan students. She said,

> I don't think that my teaching was somehow magic or they got something so different from me than they could have gotten from a regular Kenyan teacher. Kenyan teachers were very good, *very good*, and they understood the system so well.

Instead, she felt her role to be that of "ambassador" for the "United States" and perhaps "Western culture." She explained, "People could meet someone who was real and pleasant and living a life similar to the lives that they were living." In this role, Hyacinth did feel she made a difference. She concluded, "I think it was a good experience for us all. It was broadening for them in a way, and for the teachers to have contact with someone from someplace else in the way those things are broadening for us all."

In enacting her role as ambassador, Hyacinth felt it was important to match the Kenyan pedagogical style while she was there as closely as possible. When I asked if she ever "challenged" the system by teaching in a manner that was more comfortable for her, she said that she didn't. She reasoned,

> I was there to move along with the culture that I found there, and...I stood out so much being White and being American and being Western. I didn't want to be any weirder than I was. I tried diligently to work within their system and what they knew and what they expected and they were up against something really different, and that was passing the [national exam] and their life and their future did rest on that.

In short, even though she didn't always feel comfortable with the Kenyan teaching system, she felt it was in both her and her students' best interest to adopt Kenyan pedagogical practices as closely as possible.

In the United States, on the other hand, she saw her teaching role as that of "bridge." She wrote the following passage as a final reflection on her pedagogy, and interestingly, she wrote it in the form of a prayer with an "Amen" added at the end. She wrote,

> I probably did not do anything that changed the world while I was in Kenya with the Peace Corps. I have probably done lots of tiny things that changed the world in small ways since I have been back. I think having your teacher year after year say, "I love Africa and its people. Let me tell you why" has been eye opening for students. I have been able to share a lot of intimate details about the place and its people and animals. Also, I think I have been able to welcome Africans from all over the continent to our small [sic] community because of a connection I had a long time ago. I can make a bridge. Also, I have been a bridge for African students. I have been able to share an enthusiasm for a place that often gets a lot of sad and true press...bring another side. Of course, all PC volunteers do this. We can't help it. But it makes a difference.... Africa has so much beauty and there are so many incredible cultural aspects. It is good to instill respect and appreciation when possible. Maybe it helps break down stereotypes or maybe it will peak someone's interest in the place...here I am talking to you about an incredible experience that touched my life deeply 25 years later. So in the end, we do (as a people) at times, influence each other. So, let it be in positive ways. Amen

For me, Hyacinth's articulation of her teaching role as that of making and being a bridge, as well as her brief reflection on her Peace Corps experience overall, seemed a touching tribute to Peace Corps volunteers everywhere. She expressed so easily what I have felt about my Peace Corps service but could not put into words.

Overall, Hyacinth's discussion of her pedagogy spoke to the notion of distance and closeness in the teacher/student relationship. While she felt that the teacher/student relationship was enacted through distancing in Kenya, she indicated that teacher/student relationships in the U.S. were indicative of closeness and warmth. The metaphors she used for her teaching role in both Kenya and the U.S.—"ambassador" and "bridge" respectively—emphasized her role in connecting the two cultures.

Beginning with the "ambassador" metaphor, Murphy (n.d.) described the ambassador role as follows:

> When foreign ambassadors arrive in a new country, they do not start telling people what to do. They look, listen, and learn....Good ambassadors are eager and humble learners who approach the country's inhabitants as essential teachers of key cultural

beliefs and practices....Like good ambassadors, effective practitioners fit their approach to the people instead of trying to fit the people to their approach. (p. 211)

Hyacinth's story seems to reflect the qualities of a "good" ambassador as described above. She recognized that there were "subtleties" and "nuances" within Kenyan culture that she did not understand. She deferred to the other Kenyan teachers who were *"very good"* and "understood the system so well." She also decided she "was there to move along with the culture" and "tried diligently to work within their system and what they knew and what they expected" rather than trying to challenge or change the system. In short, she adapted to the Kenyan system rather than expect it to adapt to her.

In reflecting on the bridge metaphor, I think the notion of connection stands out most clearly. A student-teacher participant in Bullough and Stokes' (1994) research on teaching metaphors also used the bridge metaphor. She noted that,

> Although no single word can sum up what I want to be, the word "bridge" covers part of it. I want to be able to create a bridge between the content and the lives of the students. I want some aspect of the class to personally touch and engage each student.

This student-teacher's desire to bridge the content and student lives in a personally touching way reminds me of Hyacinth's comment that

> having your teacher year after year say, "I love Africa and its people. Let me tell you why" has been eye opening for students. I have been able to share a lot of intimate details about the place and its people and animals.

Hyacinth seems to be utilizing her close relationship with students to make a bridge to Africa so they may see Africa from a different yet familiar perspective. In this sense, she is connecting curriculum with both their lives and hers.

However, Aoki (1991) questioned a purely instrumental focus on the bridge metaphor. He offered that "Bridges...are not mere paths for human transit; nor are they mere routes for commerce or trade. They are dwelling places for people," which invite "educators to transcend instrumentalism to understand what it means to dwell together humanly" (p. 439). Aoki's bridge bids one not to move across but to linger and to live together in spaces between cultures. During the weekend I spent interviewing Hyacinth, I watched as she invited others to share time and space together in humanly gratifying ways. She was our connection; the bridge that brought us all together while she simultaneously created a space for us to dwell humanly and happily together.

Re-reading Pedagogy I: The Ambassador as Distance and the Bridge as Separation

I must admit, I was surprised to hear that Hyacinth did not share a close relationship with her students in Kenya. During the weekend that I spent interviewing and accompanying Hyacinth through her daily activities, she seemed to be so close and connected with everybody we encountered. In contrast to Hyacinth's experience, I often felt closest to my Cameroonian students despite the formality, the importance placed on testing, and the corporeal punishment that also punctuated the Cameroonian school system. I was so close to the students that the Cameroonian teachers would sometimes sarcastically tease me by referring to the students as my "friends." They acted as if I broke the rules by crossing the student/teacher divide. But I didn't really know the rules or what students thought or expected of me, so I asked them. In each class, the students and I discussed what they expected of me and I shared what I expected of them. Their first request was always, without fail: "Do not beat the students!" which I never did. Whenever I was asked to do something I didn't want to do (such as teach a class of 125 students in the heat of the late afternoon for a second term), I claimed my volunteer privilege and I flatly refused.

The students and I also often shared confidences and jokes. The eighth-graders had science class before mine and wanted to know ALL of the body parts in English, along with their functions, to which I obliged without batting an eye. I also assisted when the school accountant, a Cameroonian man, would come to my class to collect tuition from a student but couldn't tell one student from another in my classroom of 60-plus students, and I, knowing that the student was sitting in my class but not able to pay just yet, would tell the accountant that the student wasn't in class that day. Sometimes I even loaned students the money they needed to bribe school officials so that they could stay in school, and the students always paid me back. On the other hand, I would also return students to their classes when they tried to skip school and go to the village market on Thursdays since they had to walk along the same route I took to school. When I was leaving Cameroon, one of the eighth graders, whose English was fairly well-developed, came to me and said "We know that you love us!" and I thought, "How did they know?"—I never told them.

I think it is interesting that Hyacinth saw her role in Kenya as that of "ambassador," which may have actually added to the sense of distancing from students. In Angel's (2004) research on metaphors for educational leaders, the role of "ambassador" was described in terms of "dispassionate aloofness" (p. 14). Further, in a study of the metaphors generated by Malaysian university students regarding the roles of their language teachers, Nikitina and Furuoka (2008) noted that one student's use of the "ambassador" metaphor indicated a "greater degree of 'power distance' in the teacher-student relationship" (p. 202) in that an "ambassador is a person of an elevated position…coming from a different country and culture" (p. 198). It is not clear from Hyacinth's story if being an ambassador was a guiding metaphor for her teaching or was reflective of the distancing from students she felt as a teacher in Kenya. Either way, the term "ambassador" could also be seen as one of distancing in addition to closeness or connection.

Likewise, as I think about the metaphor of teacher as bridge, I think about how, despite connecting distant shores, bridges may also work to maintain the separation, or at the very least emphasize the separateness, of things rather than the closeness. Strack (2006) wrote that "Bridges can metaphorically link opposing ideologies…or accentuate perceived differences" (p. 1). But while Hyacinth seemed to see teacher/student distance as negative, other teachers noted the importance of distance as a form of self-preservation. For example, one teacher said,

> I put emotion into everything I do during the day. You leave kind of drained at the end.…I used to come home and sob and be so upset, and I've had to distance myself. I just had to because I had to protect myself. (Aultman, Williams-Johnson, & Schutz, 2009, p. 641)

Accordingly, Aultman, Williams-Johnson, and Schutz (2009) suggested that not having some distance "may lead to burnout or neglect of other important areas of teacher's life" (p. 642). It would seem, paradoxically, then, that the very conditions that demand closeness also require a simultaneous distancing in order to maintain a teacher's connection to self.

In addition, while Hyacinth felt her distance from her Kenyan students was limiting and that the closeness she felt with her students in the U.S. enabled her to accomplish more, Hargreaves (2001) noted that there is "no ideal or optimal closeness or distance between teachers and others that transcends all cultures" (p. 1061). For his study, Hargreaves interviewed a mixed group of 53 Canadian elementary and secondary teachers and identified five "distances" that teachers must negotiate when they and their students come from different cultural backgrounds. These included sociocultural distance (which "leads teachers to stereotype and be stereotyped"), moral distance (linked to emotional expression and goals), professional distance (related to teacher authority), physical distance (tied to interaction or the lack thereof with students' families), and political distance ("bound up with notions of power and powerlessness") (pp. 1062–1072). This work appears to suggest that the efficacy of any teaching approach is related to the social and cultural context as well as the relationships between the people within that context. Further, the same teacher beliefs and techniques may not be transferable from context to context. It also implies that the teacher must find her or his own way to connect and disconnect in generating and healing ways.

INTERPLAY 4

And a Good Time Was Had by All

> He liked parades with floats full of Miss Americas and Miss Daytona Beaches and Miss Queen Cotton Products. He didn't have any use for processions and a procession full of school teachers was about as deadly as the River Styx to his way of thinking.
> Flannery O'Connor (1995) from *A Late Encounter with the Enemy*

The best time to be in a small African village was during the celebrations and gatherings that came just in the nick of time to save us from absolute boredom. Luckily, Cameroonians know how to have a good time. They have a genuine interest in people, they love dancing to wild, throbbing music, they have an interesting sense of fashion (I saw one guy wearing pants made out of green shag carpeting), they have no earthly idea what time it is so the party may just go on forever, and they have a natural flair for the dramatic. Whether it was a religious holiday, a tribal meeting or ritual, or a school function, it was a chance for everyone to come together to break the daily monotony of small village life and give us something to talk about for the next few weeks, until something else happened to divert our attention.

Initially, going off to live in a mainly Muslim village made me have second thoughts. I figured that everyone would be very strictly religious and try to convert me to Islam or I wouldn't be welcomed into their secret goings on. I suppose I had gotten this idea from the TV, where most people who are of the Muslim persuasion were mean and terroristic. I couldn't have been more wrong. I was pleased to find out there were as many "back-sliding" Muslims in Olawati as there were back-sliding Christians in my hometown. A few older male villagers came around to welcome me one day and they said that there was a Protestant church just outside Olawati to the east and a Catholic mission just outside Olawati to the west and there were many small Muslim mosques throughout Olawati. They said they didn't care which one of these I went to as long as I believed in God in some way so that I would have something to give me spiritual comfort. This seemed a lot more fair than the Christian people that I grew up around who said it was their way or the highway and that if you didn't like it, you were going to hell!

Of course, growing up in the U.S., one gets the idea that the Muslim religion is some completely foreign idea that has no relation to Christianity. After reading part of the Koran, which is the Muslim holy book, and discussing it with one of the older men in the village, I realized that it is basically the same as the Bible except that in the Muslim version there is one more major prophet after Jesus, who was named Mohammed. They still believed Jesus was important; heck, lots of men in my village were named for the Muslim equivalent of Jesus, which was Issa. They just didn't think that Jesus was the final prophet of God.

For Muslim holidays, I dressed up in the typical garb of the area, which included loose-fitting trousers with a drawstring waistband and embroidery around the foot openings, a long tunic-like shirt over that with embroidery at the neck, and if you were wealthy, a large loose-hanging robe over that with extensive embroidery on the chest. This was what they called a "gondura" and it was all topped off with a matching little pillbox hat. It was during these times that the men of the village looked the most handsome. They would be well-scrubbed and clean-shaven. Wrapped up in so much loose-fitting fabric, they looked like enormous pastel-colored clouds dreamily floating down the street toward their appointed destination, which was the big mosque on the outskirts of town (which was less of a mosque and more of a large field). Seeing me arrive dressed as they were thrilled some people and it made other people confused. One man asked why I would wear Muslim clothes if I was a Christian. I explained it like this. Clothes don't have a religion, if they did, that would mean that he couldn't wear jeans, trousers, t-shirts, or shoes that came from the largely Christian world of the West, which most villagers did wear at some point or another. Besides, I asked, didn't I look *good* in these clothes?

Wasn't I *handsome*? That kind of logic made people smile and then walk away with a puzzled look on their faces.

Dressed in those long flowing robes, living in modest natural surroundings, and participating in ceremonies that have existed for hundreds of years made me feel as if I could almost understand what it was like to live during biblical times. Do you remember that story from the Bible about God telling Abraham to sacrifice his child as a symbol of his faith but at the last minute God provides a goat for Abraham to kill instead of the son? Well, we didn't just talk about that in Cameroon, we acted it out! Everyone would gather and a goat would be killed and the meat shared. Wow! Now that was one way to make religion seem real and alive.

Of course the big religious Muslim celebration came at the end of a month-long period of fasting known as Ramadan. It was difficult watching people who had little food give up eating all day long. They also weren't allowed to drink, no matter how hot and dry it was. My Muslim students were always weak and tired during this time so I tried to lighten the study load as much as I could. Now, I had lost about 20 pounds since coming to Cameroon, so when people asked me if I was going to fast, I said that I was raised a Baptist and that we have a tendency to eat everything in sight. I went on to say that if the good Lord saw fit to give me food of any kind, I felt obliged to eat it. Call me typically American, but that's how I felt.

For Christmas and New Year, since these were less important celebrations to Olawatians, I usually spent these with Sara or other volunteers. One Christmas I spent with Sara and her Cameroonian family, which consisted of her neighbor-lady and their children and the students who lived with her. I had just come from the more developed South where I was able to get some battery-operated toys and other goodies. Sara had bought gifts during her travels and everyone had prepared stockings full of candy and fruit. We woke up early the next morning and everyone was excitedly waiting to open their presents. With each present that we gave, the recipient would scream, "Papa Noel!" and begin to jump and writhe as if they had been electrocuted and then they would slap the wrapped package in rapid succession. Upon seeing this, Sara and I deduced that beating the gift was a signal of how excited the recipient was to receive it so we followed suit by screaming "Papa Noel!" and beating our presents too. All of this release of caged energy so early in the morning and the excitement of these children was an assault on my emotions and quite frankly nearly drove me to tears.

Sara and I also hosted a group of friends for Thanksgiving one year and that was fun even if it was a little less exciting. We spent weeks on developing the menu and finally settled on Cameroonian chicken cooked in a rich tomato gravy with mashed potatoes. My contribution was going to be the mashed potatoes. Now potatoes as we know them in the U.S. were rarely available in northern Cameroon. In the South, they referred to them simply as "Irish." Luckily I found some in the market in Sara's village, and though they were expensive, they were going to be well worth their price. There was also a place in the village where one could buy French-style butter. I was set. I had seen my mother work with potatoes all my life. Growing up, we had potatoes at every meal. They were mashed, baked, boiled, creamed, au gratin-ed, pan- and French-fried, as well as made into soup. I boiled and mashed the potatoes and added a large block of butter and stirred in some milk that I had made from instant. I added salt and pepper and I was ready to serve. Then we had a sudden twinge of panic. Would the Cameroonians eat this? They seemed to like rice and couscous a lot, would they go for this mashed mess? As the spoon scraped the bottom of the mashed potato bowl, I came to the conclusion that my taters were a big hit. Who would have thought that I had taken for granted something as simple as mashed potatoes for all these years?

Another good occasion for a celebration was a tribal reunion. Once a year, the members of a tribe would get together and talk about tribal matters. They would go through descriptions of planned developments and raise money for scholarships and supplies. This was a day-long affair and most of it was pretty boring. To break up the boredom, there was always a sort of court jester who would harass people until they gave him a tip or a donation to the tribe. Since Sunny was from the Dabba tribe, I got invited as an honored guest to the Dabba reunion both years that I was in Cameroon. Of course, the court jester was all over me. Since I was white I was automatically rich. He had a bull horn into which he would scream things in the native language like, "White man! You have money! You have chickens! You have cooking oil at your house! Give me money!" You have to know that richness was determined by things such as having chickens, or cows, or cooking oil at your house. I watched people buy cooking oil by the spoonful in the market and cigarettes by the cigarette. Even down South, where store-bought liquor was preferred to homemade, you could get whiskey in a small plastic baggy. These were called "whiskey condoms." How convenient!

Anyway, after all of the business of the day had been conducted, it was time for the traditional dancing. Large groups would come forward and dance or play music in front of the bigwigs and the bigwigs would eventually stand and tip the musician by sauntering up to the main performer, waving a bill in front of him like trying to mesmerize a cobra, and then pressing the bill to his sweaty forehead and pretending to get an electric jolt; the performer would pull away and the bill would stick to the man's forehead.

I even got into the act as the various village chiefs pushed me forward into the dancing and drumming masses. Evidently, tipping wasn't enough. They wanted me to dance as well. I didn't have to be pushed too hard. I grew up with Soul Train during the 1970s, therefore, I was born to boogie. Besides, it made people happy to think that a white person could and would dance with them. I'm really glad that I danced with them too as I was informed later that I have the distinction of being the first white person to dance with the Dabba tribe. Coolio! Or as they say in the Dabba language, "Nineck!" which is the only Dabba word I knew because it involved two parts of the body—knee and neck.

In between the religious holidays and the tribal gatherings were the school functions, which could also be entertaining and enlightening. The most fascinating school event by far that I ever attended was the school talent show. This was truly a remarkable event. Somehow, one of our classrooms was to be wired for electricity. There would be lights, a microphone, and a stereo sound system—unbelievable. The classroom would serve as the dressing room and staging area and the long porch outside the classroom was to be the stage. A curtain would be strung along the stage to enable transitions between entertainers.

In the U.S., you practically had to bribe students to be in a talent show, but in Olawati, everyone wanted to participate! Once the acts had been chosen, they were expected to rehearse on a daily basis after school. I can't tell you how many people tried to crowd into the small classroom designated as a rehearsal hall just to watch the performers practice. Some of the teachers literally used sticks to drive the non-performers away from rehearsals. In my hometown in the States, we seemed to have the reverse problem. Our teachers begged us to show up!

The big night finally arrived. Invitations had been sent out to all the major dignitaries and chiefs. I was going to take a bucket bath and wear a tie. This was the big time! The show was to begin at 8:00 p.m. and finish around 10:00 p.m., after all, the next day was a school day. Of course, when I showed up at 7:30 p.m., absolutely nothing, and I mean nothing, had been done to prepare for this thing. Around 8:00 p.m. or so, someone showed up and said,

"Chairs, we'll need some chairs. What else?" What? No chairs? No stereo? No electricity? I was sure this was a plot to drive me, the ever-eager American, completely and totally insane!

Ironically though, everything came together, piece by piece, and when the show finally started around 11:00 p.m. I looked out into the courtyard and saw every seat full, every tree limb occupied, and every inch of space in the school courtyard filled by an excited Cameroonian. Evidently, any lights in the middle of the night draw everyone in the tri-county district out for a bit of theater.

I was inside the classroom and my task was to prepare the students for going out on stage. This was no easy task. Students and other visitors were jumping in and out of the classroom windows on the other side of the classroom. While I was trying to prevent this from happening, the large group of students who were waiting to go on stage were actually crowding out onto the stage because they wanted to see what was going on outside. They weren't having much luck outside either. The excited throng outside was pushing forward into the stereo system stand where the stereo had been precariously pieced together, which of course kept making the sound go out. The teacher who was emceeing was outside hollering at the audience to stay back and I was inside hollering at the students to get back. Even the students who were normally shy and well-behaved were going totally wild! From where I stood, the entire place resembled a madhouse, and I thought to myself, if these people wanted to, they could kill me by sheer force of numbers stampeding over me.

Just then, I remember staring at the one light bulb lighting up a small corner of the pale blue classroom where I was supposed to be watching over the students. I felt as if I were having an out-of-body experience and I was looking at myself looking at the light bulb. I remember thinking that this was so wild and disorderly and this wasn't how we did things, and...ah, ah, ah! I had forgotten that I promised to accept the system here as it was, and here I was making comparisons. This would not do. I began to laugh the laugh of a deranged person and thought to myself, let them burn the place down, I'm going to find a seat outside and have a good time!

And I did, eventually, have a good time once I realized that I didn't have to be responsible for everything being perfect in my eyes. It was perfect and wonderful and exciting to everyone else and I began to see it that way myself. My 11th graders were to sing the Cameroonian national anthem in English. We had practiced a lot, mind you, but when they sang, the words came out not as English, or French, or Fulfulde, or any identifiable language, but it was beautiful and funny nonetheless and the audience clapped for them exuberantly as if they figured since they hadn't understood a word that it probably was English they were singing in anyway.

The other acts included a girl lip-syncing to Celine Dion, various traditional dances, one of which earned a reproach from the politician's wife the next day for involving, "trop du movement du fesse" which meant "too much butt movement." There was a trio of my male students who did a sort of break dance to the song "O.P.P.," except when they put it in the program, they understood the song to be "Pippy, Pippy." One group of students did a play in which a young Cameroonian man returns from Europe with a flashlight and convinces the old men of the village that it is magic. This caused everyone to laugh hysterically.

But my favorite performer was a student by the name of Idrissou. Larger than the other students, Idrissou was big, bulky, and mean-looking. He had red eyes with a yellow undercoating. From the very first day, he scared me. You see, I just did to him what everyone else had, I felt, done to me. I underestimated him based on his looks. When I finally got to know him, he was one of the gentlist, kindest, smartest students I knew. For the show, he recited a poem called, "Africa, My Africa" in pretty good English. To this day he writes poems about friendship and other subjects and mails them to me from time to time. Remember that I had set out to accept people for what they were and not what they appeared to be. I had failed and I realized that I had failed with other students as well. When the quiet, odd students came up to me in class wanting my attention, I could feel my brow furrowing and a sour feeling come over me. When the cute, funny, outgoing students came up to me, I felt light and happy. After reexamining my own ignorant behavior, I realized that the cute, out-going students were always the easiest to be around because they were so attractive, which gave them a bit of a manipulative power over me. But when I gave the shy, perhaps less-attractive students a chance, gave them my most nurturing love and attention, they almost always came through with work that far surpassed the others, and their true beauty began to shine through.

By the time the talent show ended sometime around 2:00 a.m., I was tired and bewildered. "What just happened?" I thought. But by the time my head hit the pillow that night, I was resolved to stop feeling responsible for everything, stop judging others by their looks, and to never on any account ever be on time for anything ever again. It was time to stop being a control freak and time to start letting go.

· 6 ·

SIMILARITIES, CONTRASTS, AND SHADES

> The most tranquil house, with the most serene inhabitants, living upon the utmost regularity of system, is yet exemplifying infinite diversities.
> (Henry Ward Beecher, 1869)

In this chapter, I discuss some of the themes that emerged in the process of bringing the "infinite diversities" within participants' stories to light. I am concerned, though, that the concept of "theme" might imply a sense of unified wholeness, therefore, in the following sections I look at each of the themes while simultaneously pointing out some of the similarities, contrasts, and shades of meaning that occurred within and between participants' stories. I also suggest other areas within those themes that require further study in intra- and inter-cultural contexts.

Drawing Gender Lines

All of the participants made references to gender and alluded to gender-based inequalities. According to Cole (2009), "In almost every culture, 'being' 'male' or 'female,' however that might be interpreted, is used to 'define' people… [in ways that] inevitably involve inequalities" (p. 563). Likewise, each of the participants spoke of gender inequalities that affected themselves or others, both overseas and in the United States. For instance, in his struggles to become a more caring teacher in the U.S., Joe argued that although female teachers could demonstrate closeness with students, male teachers had to be careful and "watch that line." For her part, Harley's sense of gender was also connected to her racial identity in the sense that she believed she had to work harder than others because she was an Asian woman. This was a powerful belief that was shared and passed down from Harley's mother. Ryder also suggested that "despite what people say, men and women are treated differently" and he hinted that women gained unfair protection from the social system, which required men to demonstrate restraint or politeness when discussing certain topics with women. And lastly, Hyacinth pointed out the ways in which male privilege was constructed in Kenyan culture and I re-read her story by thinking about the ways in which male privilege was structured in American culture.

On the topic of gender, Chodorow (1974) proposed that "in any given society, feminine personality comes to define itself in relation and connection to other people more than the masculine personality does" (p. 44). She felt that these differences were related to the socializing processes involving gender identity development through which boys develop a masculine identity as a "denial of attachment or relationship" and the "devaluation of femininity on both psychological and cultural levels" (p. 51), whereas girls were expected to accept a caring and nurturing role. The image Chodorow created was that men's identity was marked by rejection of emotional attachment, which was seen as an expression of the maternal or feminine role. Women's identity, on the other hand, was defined more by acceptance of the maternal role and relation to others. There was some evidence of these gendered differences not only in the stories that participants told, but also in the way that I, as researcher, was hosted by each of the participants in their town or city. With the male participants, who were both single at the time, the interview experience was centered upon them somewhat exclusively. On the other hand, both of the female participants planned gatherings in my "honor" and introduced me to other connections (students, educators, friends, church members, significant others, etc.) that were important in their lives.

Additionally, both men talked about growing up within largely male households with brothers—in Ryder's case, his mother left the home when he was a young child and Joe said that he grew up with a "hardcore" group of guys and that caring was not a part of his early life. Harley and Hyacinth, on the other hand, shared stories about their mothers or talked about the ways in which their mothers influenced their perspectives. I also noted gendered differences in Hyacinth's and Joe's perspectives on vulnerability related to their intercultural experiences. Miller wrote that in Western cultures, "men are encouraged to dread, abhor or deny feeling weak or helpless, whereas women are encouraged to cultivate this state of being" (In Jordan, 2008, p. 193). For Hyacinth, being vulnerable was a way to enlist help from others, but for Joe, being vulnerable was described as a horrible state of helplessness.

The male RPCV educators' envy of women's social position and their feelings of anger, powerlessness, and/or vulnerability, could be considered, as Johnson (2005) pointed out, a paradox of patriarchal power and tied to issues of control. Johnson noted especially that within patriarchal societies, maintaining self-control and controlling others as objects is considered a hallmark of a "real man" and signifies male privilege (p. 201). Consequently, when men are not in control they can begin to feel powerless, vulnerable, and emotionally disconnected from others and themselves (p. 202). Since intercultural engagement, culture shock, and reverse culture shock can heighten the feelings of being out of control and challenge socially constructed masculinity, intercultural interaction may lead men to greater attempts at self-control, attempts to control others, emotional and social withdrawal, expressing feelings of powerlessness and anger, and focusing on women's perceived social power. It may also give men a new awareness and enable them to rethink issues regarding their interpersonal, pedagogical, and social relationships. In Joe's case for example, although he struggled with the notion of caring, he looked for ways to infuse his pedagogy with a sense of caring for his students in ways that would be considered appropriate for male teachers. Further, that showing caring was a way for eliciting it from others.

Women also play a role in maintaining this socially engineered gender boundary and are expected "go along with male privilege, to prop up men's egos, and to compensate men for what male privilege costs them as human beings" (Johnson, 2005, p. 200). In other words, women are expected to take on the role of emotional support and serve as emotional gatekeepers. Yet, they may or may not conform to societal expectations. Since both men and women may be disenfranchised in the process and both must navigate systems of control, I would argue that addressing gender issues both intra- and interculturally requires women and men who offer a variety of cultural perspectives to work together if any challenge to the patriarchal system(s) of control is to be meaningful. This does not mean that these challenges will take the same form, only that there needs to be broad input from people with differing points of view for deeper and more complex understanding.

Resistance, Negotiation, and Shift

Foucault (1990) famously observed that wherever there are power relations, there are "resistances," including those that are "possible, necessary, improbable…spontaneous, savage, solitary, concerted, rampant, or violent…quick to compromise, interested, or sacrificial" (pp. 95–96). Yet, some suggest that scholarship in the area of resistance—especially non-violent resistance—is lacking, due to a more prominent focus on violence and oppression, the difficulty in measuring resistance empirically, and the association of the term "non-violence" with weakness (Haslam & Reicher, 2012; Chenoweth & Cunningham, 2013). Further, Ewick and Silbey (2003) argued that everyday individual acts of resistance, which they describe as the "ways in which relatively powerless persons accommodate to power while simultaneously protecting their interests and identities," are often overlooked in the literature in favor of those that represent "more organized challenges to power," such as lawsuits, strikes, marches, boycotts, revolutions, protests, etc. (p. 1329).

Additionally, I would argue that current definitions of resistance are incomplete in covering the wide range of "resistances" available to social actors. For example, resistance has variously been described as a "type of nonconformist behavior that questions the legitimacy of the current social order" (McFarland, 2004, p. 1251); a "conscious attempt to shift the dynamics or openly challenge the given-ness of situational power relations" (Ewick & Silbey, 2003, p. 1331); and, as the "*process and action of challenging one's subordinated position in a given social system*" (Haslam & Reicher, 2012, p. 2). While each of these definitions is useful, they also provoke various questions. For example, what if one engages in "conformist" behavior in order to make a space for questioning the social order? What if one unconsciously or subconsciously challenges the social order in subtle, less obvious ways? And, what if one doesn't see oneself as subordinated or doesn't attempt to challenge the social system, but does so simply by their very existence? Could these also be considered forms of resistance? Certainly, these questions are not meant to detract from the original definitions, but rather to expand them.

Further, each of the above definitions of resistance appears to involve the questioning and challenging of social structures and systems. Yet, I wonder to what extent the self is implicated in this process. hooks (1989) noted, for instance, that we all have the power to oppress others and as such "it is first the potential oppressor *within* [emphasis added] that we must resist—the potential victim *within* [emphasis added] that we must rescue—otherwise we cannot hope for an end to domination, for liberation" (p. 21). hooks' insightful view shifts the site of resistance from the relationship between the self and society to the relationship between a self and "othered" selves. In so doing, she added layers of complexity regarding the way resistance may be understood, and suggested the need to explore the notion of self-resistance further.

As some have noted, individual stories of personal experience have broader social significance (Bell, 2002; Ewick & Silbey, 2003; Clandinin & Connelly, 2000). In particular, individual stories of resistance extend the "social consequences of resistance" as they interact with other stories and "become part of a stream of sociocultural knowledge about how social structures work to distribute power and disadvantage" (Ewick & Silbey, 2003, p. 1328). In examining RPCV educators' stories of resistance, I hope to create a dialogue for other educators to engage in with regard to their own experiences. I also hope to provide a means for re-thinking and broadening an understanding of resistance by drawing out the multiplicity within and among participants' stories, by examining how participants position themselves in relation to others, and by looking at the "contradictions and accommodations" (Beal, 1995) participants make as they negotiate power dynamics and shift their identities or worldviews.

Each of the participants negotiated issues of power within their stories. In one story, Joe compared the Anglo American domination of Hispanics to the Russian domination of Moldovans. As a Hispanic American growing up in the 1960s, he fought for Hispanic civil rights by directly challenging the social structure. In Moldova, he observed a more "accepting" than "confrontational" response, which he believed was "healing," and he tried to foster a sense of acceptance within himself. For Ryder, having his non-standard dialect of Ozark English mocked by other Peace Corps volunteers, as well as his observations of how perceptions of language use affected the lives of his Kenyan and Saudi students, gave him the desire to adopt a more standard English dialect, earn a doctorate in linguistics, and fight for social justice through his pedagogy and participation in various social movements. Clearly, he has used one part of the social system to gain deeper knowledge in order to challenge another part of the same system.

In Harley's case, she had to deal with issues of racial prejudice, both in Kazakhstan and the U.S., because her Asian appearance did not seem to fit with the Eurocentric image of America. Although these experiences frustrated and angered Harley, she continually worked to understand the reasons behind the prejudice and to educate others about both the racial prejudice and the racial diversity within the United States. For Hyacinth, when she was confronted with gender bias in Kenya, her response was to focus on her own purposes. Although she found the inequitable gender practices uncomfortable and ridiculous, she explained that she was there in Kenya to learn about their world, not to change it. Along these lines, Hyacinth seemed to adapt to and work around any structural barriers she faced.

Accordingly, it seemed that each of the RPCV educators negotiated power in different ways: through shifting from a confrontational to an accepting stance (Joe), through personal and professional social critique (Ryder), through constant evaluation and educating others (Harley), and through focusing on one's own goals while simultaneously fluidly adapting to the social structure (Hyacinth). Taken together, these perspectives appear to indicate that negotiating power involves elements of both acceptance and resistance. Participants' stories also suggest that negotiating power relationships in the intercultural context is more complex, as intercultural actors engage power structures from the home culture while simultaneously trying to determine their position in the power structure of the Other. Additionally, the power shifts they experience in other cultures may be more ambiguous, tenuous, and contingent as meaning is continually renegotiated.

Making Time to Get Real

Referring to time as "the silent language," Hall (1990) wrote that "Time talks" and "speaks more plainly than words" (p. 1). He also noted though that one's use of time sends unintended messages and leads to "difficulties in intercultural communication" (p. xv). Further, he argued that a key reason for exploring the use of time as a culturally related value was that "we must learn to understand the 'out-of-awareness' aspects of communication…[and] must never assume that we are fully aware of what we communicate to someone else" (p. 29). The ways in which time was culturally structured also spoke to the RPCV educators in this study. In Harley's case, the use of time spoke to the ability to nurture close social relationships. While she appreciated sharing long periods of uninterrupted time with others in Kazakhstan, she felt that the busy lifestyles and the lack of shared face-to-face time with Americans prevented the development of close relationships. I argued, though, that because of the differing contexts, in the U.S., close relationships were maintained at a distance through social media. Similarly, Joe explained that in Moldova, time was spent building social relationships or focusing on one's work, but in the U.S., he felt that time was used to focus on materialism, satisfying one's "little comforts," and watching television—causing him to decide he didn't want to play the American game. I re-read his story in terms of postmaterialism, through which material security created the conditions for non-materialistic pursuits and enabled one to "play the game differently."

For Ryder, he linked the use of time in Kenya to fatalism and a lack of control in the lives of Kenyans, which I re-read in terms of fatalism as a form of self-management. In addition, for both Hyacinth and Ryder, the time and effort spent on survival in Kenya made Kenyan culture seem more real, whereas the lack of time and effort spent on basic survival needs by Americans (specifically middle class Americans and Kenyans in Ryder's case) was suggestive of non-reality. While I re-read Ryder's story by pointing out the possibility of multiple realities and layers of existence, for Hyacinth's story I referred to a Buddhist teaching to suggest that life is neither completely real nor unreal and that one has to remain "unclinging" to either side.

In brief, the ways in which time is structured and utilized appears to be an important means of communication. Time appears to strongly influence perceptions of what is real and what is not. It also seems to highlight the relative importance placed on interpersonal relationships. That participants' stories expressed both similar and different perspectives related to the use of time suggests the potential for both misunderstanding and learning. Accordingly, the ways in which time influences intercultural understanding deserves further exploration.

Metaphorically Speaking

Each of the participants also used metaphor to describe their intercultural experiences. Lakoff and Johnson (2003) described metaphor as "principally a way of conceiving of one thing in terms of another," and its main purpose is to facilitate understanding (p. 36). In addition, they suggested that metaphors not only describe prior experience, they also help create a conceptual reference for guiding future action. Lakoff and Johnson also argued that metaphors create new meanings by highlighting and emphasizing certain experiences while masking and suppressing others (pp. 141–142). From a post-structural hermeneutic perspective, new meaning is also created by unmasking and examining the suppressed experiences in addition to those that have been highlighted.

As such, for each of the metaphors participants used to describe their experiences, I suggested other possible meanings through my re-readings. Some of the metaphors generated by the participants included Hyacinth's metaphors of "interweaving" (as a cultural practice) to describe the ways people from other cultures hosted people in their homes, and her metaphors for teaching as "ambassador" (in Kenya) and as "bridge" (in the U.S.) to describe positive and interconnected relationships with students. In my re-reading, I proposed that the notion of "interweaving" was a gendered practice. Likewise, I noted that the metaphors of "ambassador" and "bridge" could also suggest power distance and separation respectively. Hyacinth and Joe also utilized the metaphor of "playing the game" to suggest the negative, and in some ways silly or childish, aspects of social interaction, which I re-read as offering ways to "play the game differently" and viewing games as "fun."

Other metaphors included Joe's description of intercultural experience as "walking on ice" because of the danger and feelings of vulnerability. Another example included Harley's description of feeling like an "extra foreigner" in Kazakhstan because she was not perceived as a "real American" due to her Filipino heritage. Additionally, Ryder described RPCVs as "freed prisoners" owing to the fact that they have had a chance to step outside the "cave" of American culture and get a new perspective on socially constructed and mediated "reality." Further, for each of these metaphors, I have offered separate re-readings in previous chapters.

That each of the participants utilized metaphors to describe their intercultural experiences suggests the importance of understanding how metaphor is used to create intercultural meaning and likewise how metaphor can shape intercultural understanding. Lakoff and Johnson (2003) argued, for example, that metaphor can help communicate across cultures, given that one has

> enough diversity of cultural and personal experience to be aware that divergent world views exist and what they might be like…[in addition to] patience, a certain flexibility in world view, and a generous tolerance for mistakes, as well as a talent for finding the right metaphor to communicate the relevant parts of unshared experiences. (p. 231)

However, through his cross-cultural research on the use of animal metaphors, Taki (2011) cautioned that metaphorical meanings are not universal and are most often interpreted from one's own cultural paradigm. Still, understanding how one's metaphor(s) may be used and perceived differently by intercultural actors holds interesting possibilities for learning about the way meaning is generated in the intercultural relationship. Likewise, understanding how educators use metaphor to describe, guide, and modify the ways in which they conceptualize their pedagogical practices offers deep insight into their beliefs and experiences.

Home Is Where the Hurt Is

Noting the relationship between home and travel, Mallett (2004) suggested that "ideas about staying, leaving, and journeying are integrally associated with notions of home" (p. 77). This seemed to be the case for the participants in this study. Their early experiences of home not only provided an impetus for leaving home; they also shaped participants' experiences of culture shock and reverse culture shock as well. For instance, Hyacinth recalled feeling awkward growing up, and that her childhood home was rather formal and not "really open to other people." Through her travels, she found that journeying into other cultures made her feel special. She explained that cultural differences gave her and others a reason to start conversations with each other and to learn from one another. After she returned from the Peace Corps and lived for a time on the Mexican border, Hyacinth felt a sense of stifling sameness among other Americans, and rejected the formality of her upbringing in favor of the type of openness she had experienced with both Kenyan and Mexican women. She also found her conversation with other Americans boring and limited and less tolerable than some of the boring/limited conversations she had in Kenya. When I asked her why this was, she argued that even though discussions in Kenya were often limited to issues involving crops or the weather, those conversations were invariably tied to survival, unlike those in the U.S., where most conversations were "directly related to nothing." She also noted that in living in Kenya and on the Mexican border she felt that she was "constantly learning" something just by being there and that, conversely, she has "moved here [to her current city] and…learned [practically] nothing." Overall, she surmised that "maybe people who thrive in the Peace Corps, who really like it, who really are affected by it, maybe are people who in some way want to leave their own culture or don't feel completely at home in their own culture, and they want to try something else."

Similarly, before leaving for the Peace Corps, Joe described himself as a restless spirit who was never happy. He said he joined the Peace Corps because he wanted some excitement and wanted to see if he could be happier somewhere else. In discussing his childhood, Joe talked about the racial prejudice he experienced as a Hispanic teenager during the Civil Rights era. He also mentioned being raised in a largely masculine household in which "caring" was rarely displayed. Accordingly, Joe seemed to evaluate each shock experience both in the Peace Corps and after his return home in terms of caring. When he returned home, he expected Americans to be more caring than he found them to be; they were more consumed by satisfying their personal comforts than with helping one another. This made him feel that he had in some sense become Moldovan and he decided that he no longer wanted to play what he called the American "game."

Likewise, Ryder talked about his painful childhood growing up poor with a conservative father and an absent mother. One of his main reasons for joining the Peace Corps was to have an experience that few Americans (at least no one that he knew of) had ever had. Both during the Peace Corps and after, he linked each story about culture shock and reverse culture shock to negative features of American culture, especially those surrounding issues of social and material inequity. He also found it frustrating that Americans made so many "mistakes" yet were still much more prosperous than the poor, yet generous, Kenyans whom he suggested often "did things better." For Ryder, teaching abroad acted as a temporary escape from the American social structure and he described returning home as re-entering a "cave" and a "prison" where most people did not want to hear anything negative about American culture.

And, finally, Harley mentioned feeling different from her friends growing up because they didn't seem to have all of the same responsibilities that she did, which included working in the family business and taking care of a brother who was in a coma from an early age. Some of her culture shock in Kazakhstan was related to feeling "isolated." She said she didn't expect to feel as isolated as she did from the other American Peace Corps volunteers who were from different parts of the U.S. and were so culturally and personally different than she was. She felt in many ways more culturally similar to the Kazakhs that she lived with. And, yet, she felt isolated from the Kazakhs, because even though there were Kazakh friends and families she was close to, she said it was "still not my home" and "still not my family." She also found freedom travelling through other countries and learning about other cultures overseas, so much so that she was fearful about returning to the United States. She eventually returned to the States after nine years so that she could earn a doctorate degree, which she felt would be respected more than if it were from a university overseas. After she returned home, she was surprised that few people wanted to hear her stories from abroad and that they didn't have much time to share with her in general. This was a shock to Harley because she felt that home was a place where she was "supposed to be comfortable." She recreated a sense of freedom by learning to ride a Harley-Davidson motorcycle, becoming a member of biker culture, and experiencing the different cultures that make up the United States.

For these participants, leaving home seemed to offer the opportunity to find at least some of the things that they felt were lacking at home: the chance to feel special and to learn both about and from people who were culturally different; a stronger focus on personal relationships than on materialistic pursuits; insights into the nature of social structure and a voice with which to advocate for social justice; and, a greater sense of confidence and freedom through living and travelling among other cultures. Perhaps, it is the sense of personal growth and (temporary) escape from the (American) social structure that made returning home all the more disappointing. Further, it was the inherent ambiguity in the intercultural relationship (the inability to know the rules) that required the renegotiation of identity and enabled the participants to partially recreate themselves in other cultures in ways that challenged the American status quo. In other words, in a foreign culture one has to create a space for oneself whereas at home, it seems that the space is already created, and it requires significant effort to reform that space.

It is also possible that participants reserved their strongest critiques for home because the notion of home seems more permanent and far-reaching than the brief respite from it. In my experience it is often easier to tolerate something negative or find it more interesting when one's identity is not drawn from that place. Home seems to define one and stays with one wherever one goes. Further, when home fails to live up to certain expectations, e.g., as a place where one should feel comfortable or a place where things should be more equitable, error-free, and caring, in some ways, the disappointment is felt more strongly. Along these lines, some researchers argue for the need to reconsider notions of "home" that often focus only on positive attributes (warmth, comfort, security, safety, refuge, etc.) in order to create a more nuanced and complicated image of home as both negative and positive (Moore, 2000; Manzo, 2003; Mallett, 2004) . In doing so, Mallett (2004) also suggested the need to recognize that just as home may carry negative connotations, likewise "danger, fear, and insecurity are not necessarily located in the outside world" (p. 72).

With so much movement and change in the world today, perhaps this signals a need to resist relying on a notion of "home" to create the illusion of comfort and security—to take on life wherever it is found and in the manner it is found, to find ourselves at home in homelessness, and to withstand the need to have our identities bounded by space, time, and place. It may also be useful to develop what might be termed a "wildflower" mentality. How does the song go? "When a flower grows wild, it can always survive. Wildflowers don't care where they grow" (Parton, 1986).

Looking for Traces and Signs

My analysis of participants' stories revealed that the words that the RPCV educators used to describe their intercultural experiences carried "traces" of other words, concepts, and meanings. In Derridean terms, trace is the "absent part of the sign's presence," and because "all signifiers will necessarily contain traces of other (absent) signifiers, the signifier can be neither wholly present nor wholly absent" (Prasad, 2007, "Trace"). Stated another way, words (signifiers) gain partial meanings from other words that do not appear to be present in the word itself. In the introduction of this book I recalled asking students to suggest words that exemplified "Africa." The trace meanings they offered included poverty, disease, and corruption. After my own experiences in Africa, the words that conjure up "Africa" in my mind include love, health, and hospitality. Each of these words describing Africa is tied to other words as well. To the extant that words carry traces of other words and because meaning is constructed contextually and temporally and is not fixed, this implies that one can never arrive at a complete or final meaning (Sarup, 1993).

That traces point to the inability of language to convey complete meaning is, however, not necessarily a bad thing. Recognizing both the incompleteness and the multiplicity of meanings within words (even those meanings that appear to be absent) creates possibilities for reimagining the ways in which meaning and experience is communicated. For example, two of the volunteers used the word "vulnerability" in describing their intercultural experiences. Joe referred to vulnerability in terms of painful helplessness and Hyacinth suggested that vulnerability was a means to invite helpfulness from others. My analysis drew out traces of other meanings such as vulnerability as an indication of strength when not taken to the extreme. I also noted that demonstrating feelings of vulnerability in a competitive culture could lead to feelings of powerlessness and rejection. Additionally, I pointed to the ways in which the participants referred to vulnerability in a cultured and gendered manner. Other examples included finding traces of emotional self-management in "fatalism," meaningful learning in "rote learning," and commonality within "individuality," to name but a few. Recognizing that words carry traces of other words and connections to other meanings enables seeing the world in a more multiple and complex fashion. It also reminds us that when using words in a singular sense, there are other attached meanings that may not be apparent on the surface, but likewise cannot be completely erased, avoided, and hidden.

From an intercultural perspective, understanding that words do not communicate complete and shared meanings implies that meaning must be negotiated rather than taken as granted. However, the negotiation of meaning is shaped by power relationships, and often the meaning-making process serves to legitimize the meanings of those in power. Along these lines, it is important to understand in the intercultural context how "whiteness," "maleness," "heterosexual-ness," "wealthy-ness," and "American-ness" confer power to educators who are members of those dominant social groups, and likewise how power and the circulation of power shapes meaning in turn. Contemplating what is absent or missing in one's thinking and speech provides directions for learning, growth, and seeing things from a broader perspective. Yet, inviting new and different meanings into one's midst—especially those of marginalized groups—may feel threatening, empowering, healing, may inspire guilt, or all of these, in different measure. I would further argue that the ethical challenge is to remain open to the experiences and understandings of others while simultaneously resisting the temptation to force one's perspective onto the experiences of others. For educators, this means inviting sometimes painful knowledge into the classroom and working to recognize and appreciate the multiplicity in both self and others. It also suggests the need to be aware that each meaning has its own shadows or its traces.

INTERPLAY 5

Returning Home to Fantasyland

"Don't let me interfere with your pleasure in it," she said, "but this whole place is false and rotten to the core." Her voice came with a hiss of indignation. "They prostitute azaleas!"

Flannery O'Connor (1995) from *The Partridge Festival*

When it came time to leave Cameroon, I thought that I would be extremely sad. Strangely though, I wasn't in the least bit sad. I was happy that I had come to Cameroon and happy to have met the people that I did. I had worked hard and I was satisfied that I had done a good job. I had made lasting friendships and I felt that I could do more for my friends, financially, in the U.S. than I ever could have in Cameroon. Besides, waiting for me on the other side were hamburgers, pizza, tacos, and, of course, my family and friends.

Wanting to take a long last look at Olawati, I walked to the outskirts of town where I could see everything stretched out before me. It seemed to gleam like pale gold in the afternoon sun. And then, it hit me. The first pang caught me off guard, the second made me nervous, and the third one meant that if I didn't find someplace to have diarrhea soon, I would be washing out my dainties later that evening. Then I thought, "Oh, what's the big deal?" I had seen thousands of Cameroonian men pooping and peeing along the roadside hundreds of times before and nobody ever seemed to take notice, especially because in a squatting position their long robes seemed to act as a personal port-a-potty. I had barely gotten my pants down and I was leaning backward in a sort of backbend to prevent the watery feces from running into my pants. Just at that very moment a bush taxi passed by, filled to overflowing with passengers who couldn't take their eyes off of me. They had surprised looks on their faces as if they didn't believe that I was human, like them, and that I couldn't possibly have to take a dump like they did. They looked so surprised that I could imagine that if we had been in a Hollywood musical the people on the bus would have run through town singing in an operatic tone:

> He's going to poop, he's going to poop,
> He's really, really going to poop!
> He's going to poop, he's going to poop,
> He's going to leave a nasty soup!
> He's going to poop, he's going to poop,
> Just watch his ass, it's gonna droop!
> He's going to poop, he's going to poop,
> Can you believe that awful goop?
> He's going to Poooooooooooooooooooooooop!"

Luckily, I didn't have to feel humiliated too long as shame turned to fear when I looked up just in time to dive out of the way of a herd of long-horned cattle barreling toward me. It seemed I would have to hand-wash my undies that night after all. But somehow that seemed like a fitting goodbye. I had spent 2 years being perplexed, so I didn't even bother to ask "why me?" when this happened. I had given up that way of thinking a long time ago, and began to ask myself, "why not me?"

As for the good people of Olawati, they dropped by individually or in small groups to pay their final respects to me. Students gave me little drawings that they had done of flowers. The teachers from my school gave me a little going-away party at my house. Mr. Ndu-du was noticeably absent. They gave me a little fringed wall hanging that had the outline of Cameroon stenciled on it, and the outline was filled in with the three bands of color from the Cameroonian flag. In addition, one of the teachers gave the following speech, which he had written. This is the written version, which I have hung onto these past few years:

> Mr. Smythe, As president of APLYO [the acronym for our teachers' association, le association des professuers du lycee de Olawati], at the name of all teachers of Government secondary school of Olawati, I take the speech to say a small message

to you: You are about to go back to America, you're about to leave us tomorrow morning, we would like you to know that we have all been very glad to spend those two years with you. We are all grateful for the assistance you brought to Our country, and specially to Govern. Secondary school of Olawati. Despite the fact that there is many things wrong in our society, despite the fact that our culture and behaviour are very frend [different] from American way of life, We are convinced that when you get back to U.S.A., you will tell Mister Clinton that you have discovered a great country, a country call Cameroon, and example of hospitality. Never and never, don't forget us! Goodbye to you Mr. Jon.

Very touching, and I'll be sure to let Bill and Hillary know I had a good time in Cameroon when I see them over at the Piggly Wiggly.

Mr. Bonti had been transferred to a large school a couple of hours away so we had said our good-byes months earlier. The only person that I really worried about was Sunny. He had come to live with me and he had become my son. This had made some of the people in the village jealous and prone to picking on him. What would happen to him once I was gone I wondered. I let Sunny choose whatever he wanted from our life together and told him that if he knew any people that wanted to buy my assorted knick-knacks, to just let me know. The next day, I came home to find a swarm of excited Cameroonians walking away with everything but the kitchen sink, but only because I didn't have a kitchen sink. Sunny was right in the middle of the chaos collecting money from the highest bidders. I must say I was a bit surprised to see all of my stuff flying out the door tucked up under the arms of smiling Cameroonians, but I thought every franc that it brought in would help me do what I needed to get done.

On the night before I was to leave Olawati, I gave Sunny all of the money I had made from the "everything must go sale," and what little money I had managed to save. He seemed taken aback and visibly happy. He had worked very hard and he deserved every franc I gave him. He also had a gift for me. He had my tailor make a little matching shirt-and-pants set from some of the brightest fabric I have ever seen. And I realized why I really appreciated Sunny so much. He was the only person outside my family who ever reciprocated in my life. Most people, Cameroonian, American, or otherwise, worked only one way, they either gave things to me or they took things from me. But Sunny always gave as much as he took and there was always a sense of balance about him. As aggravated as I could get at most people at some point in our relationship, I don't think I ever got mad at Sunny at all, except for the time when I painstakingly transported a piece of handmade clay pottery from a high mountain village only to have Sunny break it into a hundred pieces within minutes of my arrival home. But even then I realized that he didn't do it on purpose and that sparing his feelings was worth more than even the most priceless object of art.

Did I have any regrets? Well, maybe really just one. Shortly before I was to leave Cameroon, a young boy in the village came to bring me something; what, I can't remember. It began to pour down rain so I asked him to come in. We sat and looked at my pictures from back home and talked about some of the things I was looking forward to when I got back. Then he had a story for me. He said that he and many of the other people in the village were happy to have me in Olawati. He mentioned one old man in particular who was proud because of the fact that I gave him some cold and flu tablets one day. Actually, the old man had nagged me from time to time to buy him some medicine but I just didn't feel comfortable giving people drugs because if something bad happened I was afraid I would get sued. Finally, one day while I was standing by the pill stand—who knows where that stuff came from—I relented and bought him some pills of his choice and he wandered off somewhat contented. A few weeks later, he was nagging for more pills and I told him that I wasn't a doctor and I didn't have any more pills. "Nip this habit in the bud," I was thinking to myself. But that had been many months ago and I hadn't seen him in a long time. The young boy visiting my home explained that the old man had died, but not before expressing to everyone how proud and happy he was that I had bought him some medicine when even his sons would not. I felt like dying myself thinking about the times I rebuffed him. Why was I so afraid to get involved in this man's life or worry about some imagined rules? Why didn't I just buy him some drugs if it would ease his suffering? I would have if I had known what I know now.

That last night in Olawati, I also said my goodbyes to Niko, whom I considered to be the sharpest person in Olawati and one of my best friends. "You're always thinking," he said, "and your brain is always turning too much." While I was deeply amazed at his powers of observation, I really wished he hadn't said that, because then I just began to think about how not to think. How do you not think? Even when I'm not thinking, I'm thinking something. Things like, "I like that," "I don't like that," "It's hot," " it's cold, "I'm hungry," "I'm tired," "what is the meaning of life," or "cheese, I do love cheese." What does everyone have against me and thinking?

Anyway, feeling pretty proud of myself, I asked Niko, "So, how did I do? What did people think?" He calmly replied, "Half the people liked and appreciated you and realized why you were here. The other half thought that you were here to exploit them." "Exploit them!?" I growled, "how did I exploit them by teaching their children every day in this heat without food, huh!?" He said, "You and I know why you are here, so why do you care about what other people think?" He continued with the following story.

> There was an old man who had a young son and a donkey. The old man was riding the donkey while the young boy led the donkey through town. They passed some of the townspeople who said "look at that old man making his young son walk." Feeling guilty, the old man got off the donkey and let the son ride. But when they passed some of the other villagers, they said "look at that boy riding the donkey while his poor old father has to walk." So, then neither person rode the donkey and both the father and the son began to walk. But another group of villagers passed by and said how stupid these people were for not riding the donkey. The point is, you can't please everyone.

And of course he was right. And with that, he flashed a twinkling little grin and toddled off into the darkness. Sadly, I won't get another chance to see him again. According to Sunny, Niko died a few years after I left Cameroon.

The final and biggest hurdle to cross was to say goodbye to Sara and Sunny as I got on the bus that would take me to the city where I could catch the train to get me to the city where I could catch the plane so that I could go home. I was tired just thinking about it. On the way to the bus Sunny began to whimper and then cry. I felt bad for him but I was still thrilled at the prospect of going home. I guess I just believed that I was coming back some day so why bother getting so worked up? The final photograph I took of them as my bus was leaving the station looks pathetic. In their final picture of me, I'm grinning from ear to ear and am completely shocked to think I am actually going home. HOME!

Things went remarkably smoothly and I had an all-night train trip down to Peace Corps central, during which the memories of my time in Cameroon came washing back over me. I had come to Cameroon with images of hunger, poverty, corruption, tribal warring, malaria, and a whole host of exotic diseases flashing through my head. While it is true that Cameroon was all of those things, I now knew that it was much, much more. To me, Cameroon meant groups of small children following me everywhere I went; strangers sneaking a peek at me when they thought I wasn't looking; being called white man, Chinese man, and "Banderas" all in one day; losing my privacy by being included in everything; dancing half-naked in the rain after 7 months of dry season; celebrating Ramadan and Christmas in the same year; greeting old friends on market day; eating pot cookies by mistake; learning French and Fulfulde; dreaming about America; discussing politics at the crossroads; living creatively; telling jokes and laughing out loud; going without and making do; waiting for letters from home to arrive; eating termites on purpose; teaching English; giving smiling lessons; learning how to shrink myself down to nothingness on overcrowded bush taxis; being welcomed with handfuls of corn; hats—lots of hats; keeping my camera loaded with film; students sitting up straight in sky-blue uniforms; attending births, weddings, and funerals; locating the best shade for late-afternoon naps; pooping in pit toilets and dixie cups; wearing tailor-made clothes; dissing Mr. Ndu-du; dozing under mosquito nets; dancing with the Dabba tribe; reading a Flannery O'Connor compilation someone had left behind through which I discovered parts of myself; eating mangos, guavas, and papayas fresh and ripe from the tree; getting harassed by kind-hearted old men; experiencing time-honored traditions; picking through piles of t-shirts in the market in search of the one with the fewest holes; reading cookbooks and fantasizing about ingredients; brightly colored everything; observing wild animals from a polite distance; boiling my drinking water (at first); marching for the government; traveling over mountains, deserts, grasslands, rainforests, plateaus, and beaches; having conversations with God; and hoping to make it through just one more day. But most of all, I thought about the people who watched out for me; made sure I had food, water, and clean clothes; kept me company; made me laugh; bugged me from time to time; and treated me as though I belonged with them. Even now I can see their beaming faces turning towards me underneath a brilliant blue African sky–Niko, my neighbor Fanta, Mr. Bonti, and most of all Sunny–and even now they represent for me the face of love.

 The flight back to the States was long and tiring and the last leg of my journey had been over-booked. I was informed that I might have to spend the night in Ohio. OHIO? I had traveled millions of miles just to get stuck in Ohio? I thought I had left all of this craziness back in Africa. Well, I guess they were afraid that I was going to go insane so, fortunately, I got the last seat on the plane. When I arrived in Oklahoma, my family was waiting to greet me with signs and balloons and I was very happy to be home. Everybody told me how skinny I looked and so off we went to the Mexican buffet. That's where the trouble started. Everyone took out huge portions that nobody could possibly eat and yet they still went back for more even though they hadn't finished what was on their plates. As I surveyed the room, the skinny black people who had been a part of my life for the last 2 years had been replaced by a room full of white people who filled and overflowed the seats they were sitting in. Seeing all of the food that everybody was wasting made me want to eat every leftover scrap until I saw all the overfilled seats, which made me never want to eat anything ever again.

My return to the U.S. has confirmed my belief that white Americans live in a fantasy world and need to feel like they are in control of everything or else they will have a panic attack. Before returning to the States, one of my best friends wrote to me about a great movie that he had seen and said I should see it when I returned home. Once I came back to the U.S., he tried everything to induce me to watch it. I had to remind him that considering where I had been living for the last 2 years, seeing one over-hyped movie wasn't on my big to-do list. After all, it was only a movie. ONLY A MOVIE?! This seemed to make him angry that I would refer to this so-called epic film as only a movie and it was clear that our friendship was ending. Why couldn't he let it go and why couldn't I just watch the movie? The movie that sunk my friendship was *Titanic*. Get it? Sunk?

I also wasn't a big hit with my two young nieces. They begged my Mom to let them stay the night at her house and then 15 minutes later they said, "We're bored. Take us to the mall. This is soooo boring." I had just come from a place where children were seen and not heard and under no circumstances would they have EVER told their parents that they were bored. By the time that I told them to shut up and never to speak that way to my mother again, the tears had already started streaming down their faces. Later, I found a half-finished letter that my niece wrote to one of her school friends in which she said she wished I would "just go back to Africa." That's funny, I was thinking, "beat them and they will stop."

And not long thereafter I received my first letter from Sunny. Not the happy, jovial letter I expected but one in which he described how one of my favorite students had died of malaria. This really upset me. The student was sick the last time I had seen him. Why hadn't I offered him medicine from my overflowing Peace Corps health kit? Or, at the very least, got him some kind of treatment at the local health clinic? He was a kind and intelligent kid who seemed to bother no one and no one bothered him, so why him? After consoling myself that the giving and the taking of life were far beyond my control, I received another letter from Sunny stating that there had been a mistake and that the student was alive! As proof, he tracked the kid down and asked him to write a brief note to me saying that he was still alive. I couldn't have been more thrilled! The small note, written in shaky hand-writing, could have been anybody's for all I knew, but I had faith in Sunny. Anyhow, the whole experience summed up everything that I had seen, heard, and felt in Africa: life, death, and the whole mystery of it all—in addition to the realization that what Cameroon really needed most were fact-checkers, where were the FACT-CHECKERS?

Now, several years have passed since all of these events took place, and not more than a few days ago I overheard Mama whisper to one of my relatives, "He hasn't been the same since he got back from Africa," and when Mama whispered something, she meant it. No use in disagreeing with her either, she was right; Africa had changed me. Don't you think you would be changed if you had lived for 2 years in a place where you were treated as a human being and not as a target market demographic? Not one piece of junk mail did I receive while I was in Cameroon. Not one phone call during dinner from some bothersome telemarketer. Not one request to "super-size" anything. Not hours and hours of mind-melting TV and movies. Only people. People to talk to. People to share with. People to laugh and cry with. People to discuss world politics without hating you forever. People to dream with. People to love and people to notice if you died. Of course, there are lots of people right here in the U.S., it's just that so many things go unnoticed amidst the buzz and the chaos, and that includes people. People go unnoticed.

· 7 ·

ENVISIONING A KALEIDOSCOPIC CURRICULUM

Life is like an ever-shifting kaleidoscope—a slight change and all patterns alter. (Sharon Salzberg, n.d.)

The artful curriculum theorist Dwayne Huebner (1999) wrote the following passage in 1966—the year of my birth:

> The curriculum becomes a symbol of his life; to make this curriculum stand out with beauty and truths requires artistic power. Somehow the educator must not solve educational problems. He makes his mark on the world through his artistry, by projecting himself out into the world so he can say: "This is what I am, what I believe. Here is my contribution to the truth and the beauty in the world." (p. 127)

In spite of the use of gendered language that was common in the 1960s, what I appreciate about Huebner's statement is the idea that curriculum can be a work of art. That this work of art is designed to exemplify the educator's vision—their beliefs, their feelings, and the ways in which they go about making meaning. Further, that curriculum is a way to enter into a broader more worldly dialogue that goes beyond the educational realm. This refreshing perspective brings much needed life into the discussion of curriculum and demonstrates that curriculum is an intensely personal undertaking, and as such is not prone to mass replication. The following is my simple contribution, my work of art. It is not meant to solve educational problems, but to offer reflections and refractions of the images that have shaped my perspectives on education. This is who I am (becoming).

Utilizing a post-structural hermeneutic lens to draw out the multiple facets in RPCV educators' stories involving their ongoing identity and pedagogical shifts in intercultural contexts is like looking through an "ever-shifting" kaleidoscope. Although embedded in various raced, gendered, and cultured power structures, RPCV educators' experiences moving between and among foreign cultures and American culture(s) stimulated new insights and enabled the formation of dynamic new patterns with every turn. The insights that developed from this study suggest the need for new ways of looking at and educating for an awareness of multiplicity, diversity, and difference. In the following sections, I envision a kaleidoscopic curriculum, based on my own observations and experiences in conjunction with those of the other RPCV educators in this study. The areas I focus on include: multiplicity, movement, juxtaposition, ambiguity, and surprise.

Multiplicity

Multiplicity seems like an obvious choice for curriculum. In the social world, one can easily point out a multitude of differences—different colors, shapes, sizes, languages, foods, countries, cultures, and so on. However, looking beneath the surface of participants' stories, their experiences revealed a kind of multiplicity and diversity that wasn't necessarily visible on the surface. This multiplicity was more complex, less easy to categorize, and didn't fit into dualistic categories. A kaleidoscopic curriculum takes into account both the surfaces and the depths and recognizes that with each shift of the kaleidoscope, relationships change and bring to light new combinations and different points of view. It also accepts that there is always something more that isn't shown or seen, leaving open a window of possibility for multiple interpretations.

Drawing out and appreciating this more complex vision of diversity is a timely and much needed curriculum practice. As the world becomes a much more globalized space, bringing people together from different cultural backgrounds with different life experiences, learning to look beneath the surfaces of things is a useful skill. An important first step to welcoming multiplicity into the curriculum is to recognize and question the dualistic hierarchies that form the substructure of Western culture and work to shape thought and behavior. These dualisms attempt to suppress multiplicity by placing meaning into simplistic either/or structures and by filtering out the shades, the variegations, the inner contrasts, and the possibilities of meaning. These dualisms are also produced through power relationships and are designed to support the hierarchical structure. Resisting the dualisms and shifting the power dynamics enables a messier and complicated multiplicity to reveal itself.

One way to shift the power dynamics is to learn a new language. The language of "both/and" (Aoki, 1993) is the language of multiplicity. Learning the language of "both/and" is a small but revolutionary act that holds immense potential for new ways of thinking. Further, the opportunities for teaching and learning this new language are widespread. For example, in a student-teacher essay I recently received, the student wrote that schools can either harm students or they can nourish them. Yet in my opinion, schools can BOTH harm AND nourish students and sometimes do both simultaneously in intricate ways. This is only one example, certainly there are so many others. Learning this "both/and" language, as well as other ways for speaking in "pluralisms," has been both professionally and personally satisfying—it has changed the ways I envision myself and my work as an educator. Opening up the competitive win/lose, right/wrong, this/that framework has enabled me to see the world as more subtle, complicated, and interconnected. It is also a more creative world in which I become responsible for generating my own interconnections and my own subtle shades of meaning.

Another move that shifts the power dynamics is to "decenter" (Derrida, 1978) one's self. I think of decentering the self in two ways. The first is through an inner reorganization process in which my imagined culturally approved, socially acceptable self is set aside (yet not abandoned) in order to make room for other "selves"—the delegitimized, the feminine, the strange selves that are culturally forbidden—to emerge. This is an important shift as these selves help fill in the "gaps" in my fractured understanding. Decentering also leads to a more holistic form of self-acceptance in which all of the inner pieces, the fractals, and the variations are valued. Similarly, I also think of de-centering as an outer move in which I make a space in my teaching and the other parts of my social life for otherness and difference to thrive. For me, this includes withstanding the urge to make the self the primacy against which all others are judged so that I can create a socially inviting space for those who seemingly think, act, and look differently. Sometimes, I have to remind myself,

I am not the center! In reflection, this makes me think about how many times I have wanted to discount and change those who I have perceived as different than me, and conversely, how I have wanted to discount and change the parts in myself that were different from others, especially those parts that seemed to make other people feel uncomfortable. Although I am not the center, I am still a part of the whole, and in making a space for difference, I make a space for myself.

Finding ways to coax out the diversity of thought and experience within the curriculum, sometimes occurs in unexpected ways. Once, I was teaching a humanities course as an adjunct instructor. This was a short-term 4-week course that moved very quickly. There was one student in the course from Mexico who had some difficulty following along in English due to the rapid pacing of the course. The final exam comprised essay questions and artworks to identify and comment on covering various periods of Western art and architecture. I had also spontaneously assigned a final project, as we were studying the German artist Albrecht Dürer who popularized the self-portrait. The students and I decided we would create our own self-portraits in one of the artistic styles we had studied. Well, the Mexican student didn't do very well on the final exam. Yet, for his self-portrait he painted a large portrait of himself in the style of Leonardo's *Mona Lisa*. He had researched the clothing that men wore during that time period so that his painting would be as historically accurate as possible. He also copied the landscape from the background of the *Mona Lisa*, and for artistic flourish he incorporated various symbols and images that expressed his personality, his likes, his job, his hobbies, and his Mexican heritage, all around the border. I, along with the rest of the class, was amazed by the detail and the quality of his work, in addition to the fact that it actually looked like him. I could easily have failed the student for his test score alone, but his ability to synthesize his knowledge through his art seemed infinitely more generative than the essay questions on my exam. He found a way to show me his knowledge in his own language. The other students also found various ways to express the tensions, the concerns, and the relationships in their own lives. In sharing the meanings we had woven into our art pieces, we began to see each other in a new light. How glad I was to have made that assignment, which turned into something quite beautiful, meaningful, and educational. For a kaleidoscopic curriculum, finding ways to bring out the differences in identities, experiences, and perspectives is a way of giving multiplicity a chance to play in the dancing light.

Movement

Keeping in mind that curriculum is a verb (Pinar, 2004), a kaleidoscopic curriculum shifts the emphasis from a focus on knowledge and what can be known to the process of knowing and the ways in which meaning develops through experience and interaction. In this study, depths of understanding revealed themselves through shifts and turns that were sometimes fluid and other times abrupt. Moving through various cultural landscapes and interacting with those who were culturally different enabled the participants in this study to self-reflect, question their beliefs, and shift their identities. Further, once set in motion, the questioning, the reflections, and the identity shifts continued long after participants returned home. Infusing curriculum with the questions, the reflections, the shifts, and the experiences all aid in the process of knowing. Each is discussed in turn below.

In a kaleidoscopic curriculum, movement is dialogic and conversational. Sharing one's inner dialogues through conversation with others is important for negotiating the meanings of outer actions. Applying meaning from the outside without open dialogue can lead to misperceptions and mistrust in others' intentions. For Huebner (1999), conversation is an active and engaging process. He wrote,

> Conversation is not simply talking. It is talking and listening. It demands internalization of what the other says and reworking of one's own thought and being. It requires a willingness to give of one's self and to receive from the other, and an eagerness to bring the I and the Thou together in a significant act of relationship and living. (p. 68)

In pointing out the movements that underlie conversation—the talking, the listening, the internalization, the reworking of thought and being, the giving and receiving, and the joining together in a relationship, Huebner shifted the focus away from the privileged act of talking and suggested a more meaningful purpose for engaging others in conversation. Further, I have noticed that talking seems to be the easy part. It is the listening and all the other hidden work involved that makes conversation challenging. I think one way to open up meaningful dialogue in the classroom is in asking provocative questions.

I would argue that we live in a world that focuses on giving the right or at least the culturally correct answer. In essays, homework assignments, classroom discussions, standardized tests, on discussion boards, and through grading rubrics, we teach students how to craft answers that fit the expectations of the teacher. But rarely is there a focus on asking the kinds of questions that aid in a critical analysis of our shared social world. Imagine a test or an essay in which students compose nothing but questions? I have found that a well-asked question is equally as imaginative as a well-answered one and can lead to other questions and other pathways worth exploring. Asking provocative questions also requires careful listening and looking beneath the surfaces of words for meanings that might have been overlooked. For the educator, this requires a doubled listening in the sense that "When a teacher listens, [s]he listens not only to the student that asks the question, but to the world that is the source of the answer" (Huebner, 1999, p. 145). This requires the teacher to be especially attentive and sensitive to the ways in which the world at large attempts to impose and structure meaning. Emphasizing the generative role of conversation, listening, and questioning in the exploration of a world of meanings extends curriculum by providing new directions for teaching and learning.

Self-reflection and identity shifts are other important aspects in the process of knowing. In many ways, the foreign cultures through which participants travelled acted as mirrors through which participants were able to see themselves from different vantage points, in ways that did not occur to them previously. This enabled them to compare the carefully constructed cultural images they had previously developed of themselves with these new images. In noting the differences in these images, they were able to more readily reflect on the ways in which culture helped shape how they saw themselves and the world around them. Providing opportunities for self-reflection in curriculum helps students and educators recognize that they are co-creators in the meaning-making process and not bounded solely by cultural mirrors that fix them in specific personas.

Along these lines, self-reflection also helped participants shift their identities and their pedagogical practices. They achieved these shifts by creating a space for including differences within themselves and their pedagogies. The ability to shift perspectives suggests greater dexterity and flexibility in the face of changing circumstances. It also suggests that learning is not a static process that occurs in a cultural vacuum. It involves dialogic interaction and engagement with differences. Helping students to adapt, to keep moving, to avoid being paralyzed, and to resist getting stuck in unitary visions of self, are also important so that they too may fluidly navigate change and difference.

All in all it was the lived experiences of study participants that brought them greater insights into other cultures, other ways of teaching, and other ways of seeing themselves. Finding meaningful ways for students to engage with cultural differences and share their lived experiences through curriculum is crucial. Lived experience helps shape knowing and provides a context for future learning. It also challenges disembodied and decontextualized narratives that fashion learning as a sort of coasting on cultural auto-pilot. By examining and reexamining these lived experiences in concert with others, new questions are asked, new patterns appear, and new directions for curriculum begin to develop.

Juxtaposition

Juxtaposition typically involves laying two dissimilar things side by side for purposes of comparison and contrast. By looking at the differences between the two things, it helps to consider what they are and what they are not. The categories used to describe these differences often hint at the relationship between the two entities: extravert/introvert, individualist/collectivist, developed/underdeveloped, beautiful/ugly, and so on. However in shifting the kaleidoscope, juxtaposition takes the additional step of looking at the contrasting features within the same entity/person/culture. It also works by placing the self/Other in strange and non-prescribed categories and sometimes by placing the self in the same category one uses to describe the Other, as when I described the U.S. as a collectivist culture. Further, in juxtaposing their experiences living and teaching abroad with those at home, RPCV educators let uncomfortable tensions and insights emerge that can inform curriculum.[1]

"What purpose does this serve?" one might reasonably ask. Casting light beneath the social labels reveals the hidden layers of diversity inside. That's what the labels do—they hide some aspects while highlighting others, but the layers are always there. They are culturally nominated and socially reinforced. They have the power to wound in ways that we don't always realize. By making these labels seem natural and taken-for-granted, they take on the appearance of reality and are so ingrained in the West that they can be difficult to challenge. Yet, I would argue that the need to disrupt these labels is both significant and urgent.

One of the more troubling curriculum practices I have encountered in recent years is the labelling of ESL students in schools. Some of the graduate students in my diversity course who teach English as a second language at local schools, have shared with me that newly arrived non-English-speaking students are given an English test on their first day, and if they fail the test, they are dubiously placed in the category of "delayed." One teacher in particular shared her own sadness when she had to inform the mother of an ESL student that her young son was considered "delayed" and upon hearing this, the mother began to cry. I too am saddened by any educator who is knowingly charged with inflicting such a wound on a child or a parent. How many of us would be labelled "delayed" on our first day in a language class in a foreign country and/or culture? Why wasn't the student considered "culturally advanced" for bringing with him knowledge of other worlds and being poised to learn an additional language? Who and what purpose do these labels serve? I cannot believe the term "delayed" serves the student's, the parents', or the educator's interests.

In recognizing the ways in which cultures try to silence or punish difference, we can work to reclaim those differences. In reclaiming those differences, we begin to heal the socially nominated wounds and fractures. Ironically, many of these wounds we unwittingly inflict upon ourselves in the hopes of societal inclusion and rewards, some of which never come or come at the expense of our mental, physical, or spiritual health. Once we are able to embrace the divisions, the contrasts, the inconsistencies, the fractures, and the differences within ourselves, we become better able to recognize them in others. More hopefully, this recognition of our own diversity turns into an acceptance of the diversity in others.

Resisting the impulse to judge others and ourselves by dualistic hierarchies dynamically shifts our power relationships and enables a freer and potentially more equitable reimagining of our shared world. Certainly, confronting the hierarchy of self over Other can have far-reaching ethical implications. To accept another person—especially a stranger—at face value without judging them as less than, to work toward another's success not simply one's own, to become conscious of another person's suffering as well as the ways in which that suffering is socially accepted and reproduced, requires awareness, insight, and stamina. It also suggests a new way of thinking about and speaking about ourselves and others. I have found that people often describe themselves in ways that are opposite to what they "mean." For instance, I have had students who have described themselves as "shy" and "introverted," yet they often spoke up loudly and passionately in class, revealed intensely personal information about themselves in our classroom and online discussions, sought attention in numerous ways both positive and negative, and didn't seem at all what I considered to be shy or introverted. Why do we humans sometimes do this? Perhaps it is the desire to recast oneself into the world in a new, idealized way. But can one engender a sense of completeness and wholeness by cutting out the less-desired parts? Doesn't this create more distance between one's selves and others?

I have to admit that I cringe every time I am asked to take a personality test, usually at some school-mandated function designed to help my co-workers get to know me better. I guess we can't just talk and hang out together—maybe go to a movie, do some shopping, cook a meal together. No, we need a scientific tool to tell us who we are and to fix us within our various cages. According to these tests, I am a "blue/green," "INFP," "Appraiser," and a "triangle"—oh goody! What these tests fail to take into account are the myriad ways that I do not inhabit the characteristics in the labels they project on me. What most of us test-takers fail to realize is that the test designers must carefully construct the test questions in order to force us into an either/or category so that the tests can be "statistically valid" for their own purposes. In other words, the game is rigged in favor of the house before we darken-in one single bubble.

Again, it is imperative to remember that the social labels, categories, and dichotomies do not exist in nature and we must often force ourselves and others into these categories. A bird, a fish, a cloud—they wouldn't proclaim themselves to be individualists or collectivists—they are what they are. Can we do the same and just be?

Ambiguity

One of my favorite comediennes of all time, Gilda Radner (n.d.), is quoted as saying, "Life is about not knowing, having to change, taking the moment and making the best of it, without knowing what's going to happen next. Delicious ambiguity." She made this statement as she was dealing with the cancer that would ultimately claim her life. What an interesting and perceptive thing to say at such a moment. Interesting, because she described ambiguity as "delicious," when most of the people I know categorize it as something awful to be avoided. In naming ambiguity as something delicious, Radner redirected the focus to the tasty and exciting parts of ambiguity, which reminds me of how useful ambiguity can be when woven into an understanding of curriculum.

Many of the insights that the RPCV educators in this study gained were made possible in large part due to the ambiguity of the cross-cultural situations in which they found themselves. When placed in unfamiliar territory without shared understandings, these educators improvised, changed course, and creatively modified their beliefs. They learned how to negotiate cultural differences, not by being sure what would happen next, but in "not knowing." This realization could have a profound influence on curriculum, given that current educational policies focus more rigidly on creating a sense of "sureness" by promoting standardized perspectives and singular meanings disembodied from the diverse lived experiences of students and educators. This is further reinforced through an emphasis on testing and the one right answer.

Why is there such an anti-ambiguity movement in the American educational mainstream? The freedom to decide meaning is powerful. Cultural teachings work to pre-determine the meanings of words, actions, people, and appearances. Yet, if meanings are pre-determined, how does thinking and learning take place? Ambiguity creates openness and enables multiplicity to thrive. It creates an alternative space of infinite possibilities that disrupts the either/or perspective of Western dualism and is limited only by human creativity. Further, it generates learning by necessitating new approaches in the face of the unknown.

For De Beauvoir (1976), embracing "our fundamental ambiguity" also has profound ethical implications (p. 9). In her book, *The Ethics of Ambiguity*, De Beauvoir argued that humans attempt to escape their inherent ambiguity by creating God (gods?) in order to give their lives meaning. In a way, we yield our ability to make meaning so that our lives are given meaning by an outside entity. Yet, insisting that "ethics does not furnish recipes" (p. 134), De Beauvoir rejected the notion that ethics can be mandated a priori from outside human experience and still serve the needs of people. Instead, she proposed embracing ambiguity, which requires developing an ethics in context and in relation to others. In a sense, she suggested cutting out the middleman in order for people to create and take responsibility for the ethical treatment of others more directly. I didn't read this as a rejection of God or gods per se, but as an appeal to argue that we don't need grand authorities to mandate meaning and decide what ethics is through the creation of laws. The laws cannot save us—it is recognizing the ambiguous in the situation without forcing our pre-determined interpretations on others that enables ethics to bloom.

De Beauvoir's writings remind me of a story from when I was a new international student advisor. I was at a conference, and during one session the presenters conducted a poll on the interpretation of some matter of international student policy. I recall that many institutions interpreted the policy so differently that it left me with the feeling that knowing what was "right" with regard to policy would be an impossible task. There were also sessions with government representatives to help clarify policy interpretations, but these often muddied the waters more than they clarified. Expressing my frustration to an older, more experienced and wiser colleague from a different institution, she seemed somewhat amused. She wondered why so many advisors wanted to pin down matters of policy, when the ambiguity in the policy could be used to serve the needs of the students. This was a great lesson that has served me well in many instances. It taught me that I needed to feel comfortable with the decisions I was making while working to balance the needs of the students, my school, and myself. While not always an easy task, it required me to think, to seek out other perspectives, and to stand up for my own perspectives. Especially since no policy ever written could take into account the totality of the experiences and circumstances in which students often found themselves.

In my kaleidoscopic curriculum, ambiguity is a useful teaching resource. Since there is no one single or right way to "read" situations, patterns, people, and texts, curriculum becomes a fertile ground for exploring differences. In this curriculum, part of the educators' role is helping students develop their own voices and drawing out their oftentimes marginalized, hidden, and conflicting perspectives. It is also to help them synthetically combine their understandings with those of others in order to join a broader social dialogue and inspire new ways of understanding our shared world. As a teacher, this suggests that I have to shift my expectations from what is or what should be to what is possible. I have to sometimes give up the safety and security of my carefully planned lessons and my goals for students and have faith in the interplay of our dialogue together. This means taking a chance and having faith in the course of things—that something wonderful may happen, and if not, that's okay too.

Convincing students that embracing ambiguity holds creative possibilities is another matter. In some classes I have taught, the students wanted grading rubrics, copies of PowerPoint presentations, study guides, sample test questions, and I am positive I overheard them saying "just tell me what you want me to say." They wanted a sure thing, the one right answer. So many safety nets seemed to make them afraid of or lose faith in their own ability to make their own meanings. I have found that making something out of ambiguity requires work, but it also requires play. In addition to the element of open possibility, it is the element of play that often gets lost in all the plans, goals, objectives, standards, and rubrics. If anything, shifting the kaleidoscope as a curriculum practice is an invitation to play. Inviting ambiguity and play into the curriculum carries its own risks, in that you can never be sure of the outcome. Of course, that is the "delicious" part of teaching and learning—the not knowing, but understanding that anything is possible.

Surprise

With every turn of the kaleidoscope, surprising new images and interrelationships begin to take shape. It is very often this feeling of surprise—or shock—that leaves a lasting impression. When I think about the notion of surprise, I wonder what it is about it that makes it so tantalizing. For me, two elements of surprise seem to stand out. These are tension—that inner feeling that something bad is going to happen, which makes you want to run, and paradox—when you expect one thing and another thing happens.

One of my favorite TV shows growing up that exemplified surprise, tension, and paradox was Rod Serling's *The Twilight Zone*. For example, in one episode, a woman on a routine shopping errand finds herself accidentally locked in a department store at night only to discover that she is, in actuality, a mannequin who longs to be normal like the "real" people who visit the store each day. On another episode, a woman frets as her face is slowly being unwrapped after plastic surgery, only to discover that the surgery has failed—except that she's actually beautiful, and as the cameras turn, we see that it is the doctors and nurses who have strangely deformed faces, yet they are the norm. My favorite episode, though, is about an "ugly" young girl who grows up in a culture that espouses beauty and happiness, so much so that at an appointed time each young person must choose their face and body style from a state-mandated set of blue-prints and then they undergo a scientific procedure called "the change." Apparently only a few of these body models are popular as everyone looks the same (there is one male model and two female models). To tell each other apart, people wear name tags and call each other by their first names. They also drink something called "instant smile." Everyone—her mother, an uncle, two doctors, a nurse, and her best friend—tries to convince the girl that she will be beautiful and happy when she looks like everyone else, but when the girl resists, her mother sends her for biological and psychological testing to determine what is wrong with her. Ironically, while trying to escape from the hospital, the girl steps right into an operating room where they are ready to perform "the change." When she emerges from the operating room, she falls in love with her own image while looking in a mirror and—surprise—

she is happy to discover that she looks exactly like her best friend (and presumably millions of others).

These shows were certainly dramatic and conceivably shocking in the late 1950s and early 1960s. Yet, what I really enjoyed most were the ways in which human "truths" were revealed in those surprise moments of tension and paradox in ways that made me pause to think. Especially, those truths about what it meant to be "normal," the ways in which cultures work to replicate this sense of normalcy as well as to exclude difference, and the exacting toll this could have on people. It also taught me about how people can change once they become legitimized by the mainstream. Somehow, the surprise twists, the odd paradoxes, and the unnerving tensions, all helped in making these lessons possible in a unique and indirect way.

Certainly for the participants in this study the shocks and surprises they experienced have had an enduring influence on their worldviews and their pedagogical perspectives in ways that weren't possible when everything went as planned. My wakeup call as an educator came early on after my return to the U.S. following my Peace Corps service (see Smythe, 2009). Working as an international student advisor, I was asked to speak to a faculty group on tips for working with international students. I drew my information from textbooks, international student advisement guides, and asked a few students for their perspectives. I created a nice outline with two columns—one for the U.S. and one for Other Cultures—and filled each column with various cultural traits that my research had suggested, everything nice and neat and in its place. I had also used this handout in international student orientations to demonstrate how different American culture is from other cultures. The faculty group seemed pleased with my presentation and I felt I had done a good job representing international students, until a professor friend confided that one of the international faculty members had referred to my presentation as "racist." Initially, I was stunned. I felt defensive. But once I moved past those feelings, I was even more stunned that I thought I could explain what American culture and all other cultures "were" in highly simplistic, stereotypical categories that pitted the U.S. against the rest of the world. Further, that I had failed to consider the ways in which individual lived experiences shape one's worldview and disrupt those simple categories.

It was in that moment of surprise and self-reflection that I created my own policy of "Ask, don't tell." How could I possibly be responsible for telling faculty and students what other cultures (and American culture for that matter) were like or how to predict student/faculty behavior based on cultural labels without knowing the people themselves? Now I ask both students and faculty about their experiences instead of projecting my own cultural biases on them. In asking and not telling, I am better able to tease out the diversity of perspectives that take into account their life experiences. I am also able to challenge some of their cultural biases when my experiences contradict their assumptions. This has been immensely freeing for me as an educator in that I no longer have to be a cultural expert—just an expert in my own life and the contradictions that I live among. It also makes me thankful for those uncomfortable moments and those inner pangs of awkwardness—it lets me know that there is something I need to investigate and learn from.

Learning together with students from these moments of surprise has been a deeply enriching curriculum practice. At the beginning of a recent Multicultural Diversity Issues in Curriculum course, I asked students to note the moments of surprise—especially the tensions—in their own lives as they interacted with others both inside and outside the classroom. I also asked them to linger with these moments of tension—to stay with them—to learn from them and to not run from or become paralyzed by them. There was no shortage of shocking and uncomfortable moments, some of which were generated during classroom discussions. In taking a moment to draw out the educational value within those moments of discomfort when it would have felt better to stay quiet, exclude, avoid, and even punish those seen as culturally insensitive, students often commented that what they learned most was about their own responses to people who they perceived as different. One student in particular found this whole process to be "healing." This seems to be the biggest paradox of all—that in looking past the jarring, angry, and sometimes hurtful words of another person, to work to understand the place of pain in which they dwell, and to embody compassion through our actions—we are really healing ourselves.

Note

1. Other curriculum scholars have also noted the value of juxtaposition for informing curriculum. For example, Janet Miller (2005) and her colleagues highlighted the "performative" aspects of juxtaposition "across moments of research, writing, and teaching" for the purpose of exploring "how meanings of performance that get solidified in one educational situation are set into play in another time and place" (p. 114). William F. Pinar (2009) added that the "juxtaposition of the past and the present, the subjective and the social, can produce the shock of self-engagement" (p. 41). I use both perspectives in developing my thoughts on juxtaposition in the sense that this study looked at the ways in which RPCV

educators shifted their pedagogical perspectives and made meaning at various points in time across different cultural settings. Further, that in doing so, such juxtaposition created the "shock of self-engagement" and enabled uncomfortable insights to emerge. Further, investigating these shocks enabled me to examine how RPCV educators used subjective and socially constructed labels to make meaning amidst the tensions they experienced. For an in-depth exploration of juxtaposition, see Pinar 2009.

REFERENCES

Abdallah-Pretceille, M. (2006). Interculturalism as a paradigm for thinking about diversity. *Intercultural Education*, *17*(5), 475–483.

Adelman, C., Spantchak, Y., & Marano, K. (2012, April 2). *The index of global philanthropy and remittances 2012*. Retrieved from the Hudson Institute website: http://www.hudson.org/research/8841-the-index-of-global-philanthropy-and-remittances-2012

Adler, N. J. (1981). Re-entry: Managing cross-cultural transitions. *Group & Organization Studies*, *6*(3), 341–356.

Adler, P. S. (1976). The transitional experience: An alternative view of culture shock. *The Journal of Humanistic Psychology*, *15*(4), 13–23.

Adler, P. S. (2002, November). *Beyond cultural identity: Reflections on multiculturalism*. Retrieved from http://www.mediate.com/articles/adler3.cfm

Aguiar, M., & Hurst, E. (2007, August). Measuring trends in leisure: The allocation of time over five decades. *The Quarterly Journal of Economics*, 969–1006.

Akinola, M., & Mendes, W. B. (2008). The dark side of creativity: Biological vulnerability and negative emotions lead to greater artistic creativity. *Personality and Social Psychology Bulletin*, *34*(12), 1677–1686.

Angel, R. (2004). *Educational leadership frameworks: Looking to archetypal images for twenty-first century wisdom*. Retrieved from http://ucealee.squarespace.com/storage/convention/ convention2004/proceedings/04ucea21.pdf

Anjarwalla, T. (2010, August 24). *Dealing with reverse culture shock*. Retrieved from http://articles.cnn.com/2010-08-24/travel/cultural.reentry_1_peace-corps-volunteers-culture-shock?_s=PM:TRAVEL

Aoki, T. (1991). Bridges that rim the Pacific. In W. Pinar & R. Irwin (Eds.), *Curriculum in a new key: The collected works of Ted Aoki* (pp. 437–439). Mahwah, NJ: Lawrence Erlbaum.

Aoki, T. (1993). Humiliating the Cartesian ego. In W. Pinar & R. Irwin (Eds.), *Curriculum in a new key: The collected works of Ted Aoki* (pp. 291–301). Mahwah, NJ: Lawrence Erlbaum.

Aoki, T. (2005). *Curriculum in a new key: The collected works of Ted Aoki*. W. Pinar & R. Irwin (Eds.). Mahwah, NJ: Lawrence Erlbaum.

Archer, C. M. (1986) Culture bump and beyond. In J. M. Valdes (Ed.), *Culture bound: Bridging the cultural gap in language teaching* (pp. 170–178). New York, NY: Cambridge University Press.

Armstrong, A. (1986). Peace Corps volunteer suffers reverse culture shock. *The Baton Rouge Sunday Advocate*, p. 2–J.

Ashabranner, B. (1968). From the Peace Corps, a new kind of teacher. *The National Elementary Principal*, 47(5), 38–42.

Aultman, L. P., Williams-Johnson, M. R., & Schutz, P. A. (2009). Boundary dilemmas in teacher–student relationships: Struggling with "the line." *Teaching and Teacher Education*, 25, 636–646.

Bakhtin, M. M. (1986). *Speech genres and other late essays*. C. Emerson & M. Holquist (Eds.). Austin, TX: University of Texas Press.

Balfour, L. (1998, June). "A most disagreeable mirror": Race consciousness as double consciousness. *Political Theory*, 26(3), 346–369.

Balkin, J. M. (1995–1996). Deconstruction. Retrieved from http://www.yale.edu/lawweb/jbalkin/articles/deconessay.pdf

Barbalet, J. M. (1985). Power and resistance. *The British Journal of Sociology*, 36(4), 531–548.

Bardhan, P. (1997). Corruption and development: A review of issues. *Journal of Economic Literature*, 35, 1320–1346.

Barnett, C. (2005). Ways of relating: Hospitality and the acknowledgement of otherness. *Progress in Human Geography*, 29(1), 5–21.

Bazerman, C. (1992). From cultural criticism to disciplinary participation. In A. Herrington & C. Moran (Eds.), *Writing, teaching, and learning in the disciplines* (pp. 61–68). New York, NY: Modern Language Association of America.

Beal, B. (1995). Disqualifying the official: An exploration of social resistance through the subculture of skateboarding. *Sociology of Sport Journal*, 12(3), 252–267.

Beecher, H. W. (1869). *The sermons of Henry Ward Beecher in Plymouth Church*. Brooklyn, NY: Harper and Brothers.

Belk, R. (1984). Three scales to measure constructs related to materialism: Reliability, validity, and relationships to measures of happiness. *Advances in Consumer Research*, 11, 291–297.

Belk, R. (1985, Dec). Materialism: Trait aspects of living in the material world. *Journal of Consumer Research*, 12(3), 265–280.

Belk, R. (2001). Materialism and you. *Journal of Research for Consumers*, (1). Retrieved from http://jrconsumers.com/academic_articles/issue_1/Belk_.pdf

Bell, J. S. (2002). Narrative inquiry: More than just telling stories. *TESOL Quarterly*, 36(2), 207–213.

Bell, N. J., & Das, A. (2011). Emergent organization in the dialogical self: Evolution of a "both" ethnic identity position. *Culture Psychology, 17*(2), 241–262.

Benet-Martínez, V., & Haritatos, J. (2005). Bicultural identity integration (BII): Components and socio-personality antecedents. *Journal of Personality, 73,* 1015–1049.

Benjamin, J. (2002). Sameness and difference: An "overinclusive" view of gender constitution. In M. Dimen & V. Goldner (Eds.), *Gender in psychoanalytic space: Between clinic and culture* (pp. 181–236). New York, NY: Other Press.

Bennett, J. (1977). Transition shock: Putting culture shock in perspective. *International and Intercultural Communication Annual, 4,* 45–52.

Bennett, W. J. (2011, December 15). America the generous. Retrieved from http://www.cnn.com/2011/12/15/opinion/bennett-generosity/index.html

Benton, D. (2009, December 19). How giving are Americans. Retrieved from http://www.helium.com/items/1687369-how-giving-are-americans

Bhala, R. (2005). The limits of American generosity. *Fordham International Law Journal, 29*(2), 299–385.

Brindley, R., Quinn, S., & Morton, M. L. (2009). Consonance and dissonance in a study abroad program as a catalyst for personal and professional development. *Teaching and Teacher Education, 25,* 525–532.

Brislin, R. W., & Kim, E. S. (2003). Cultural diversity in people's understanding and uses of time. *Applied Psychology: An International Review, 52*(3), 363–382.

Broady, E. (2004). Sameness and difference: The challenge of culture in language teaching. *The Language Learning Journal, 29*(1), 68–72.

Brooks, A. (2009, December 18). Are Americans generous? Retrieved from http://www.patheos.com/Resources/Additional-Resources/Are-Americans-Generous.html

Brotto, F. (n.d.). Momo summary. Retrieved from http://www.crtlinguebergamo.it/media/Momo_Summary.pdf

Brown, C. (2005). Illuminated by African light. *Arts & Activities, 137*(2), 23.

Bullough, R. V., & Stokes, D. K. (1994, Spring). Analyzing personal teaching metaphors in pre-service teacher education as a means for encouraging professional development. *American Educational Research Journal, 31*(1), 197–224.

Burroughs, J. E., & Rindfleisch, A. (2002). Materialism and well-being: A conflicting values perspective. *Journal of Consumer Research, 29*(3), 48–370.

Butin, D. W. (2001). If this is resistance I would hate to see domination: Retrieving Michel Foucault's notion of resistance in educational research. *Educational Studies, 32*(2), 157–176.

Buttaro, L. (2004). Second-language acquisition, culture shock, and language stress of adult female latina students in New York. *Journal of Hispanic Higher Education, 3*(1), 21–49.

Caldwell, C. D., & Cunningham, T. J. (2010). Internet addiction and students: Implications for school counselors. Retrieved from http://counselingoutfitters.com/vistas/vistas10/Article_61.pdf

Cammissa, A. M., & Reingold, B. (2004). Women in state legislatures and state legislative research: Beyond sameness and difference. *State Politics & Policy Quarterly, 4*(2), 181–210.

Carnegie Mellon University. (n.d.). *Recognizing and addressing cultural variations in the classroom*. Retrieved from Carnegie Mellon University website: http://www.cmu.edu/teaching/resources/PublicationsArchives/InternalReports/culturalvariations.pdf

Chao, E. (2012, January 5). Americans are more generous than we think. Retrieved from http://ideas.time.com/2012/01/05/americans-are-more-generous-than-we-think/

Charities Aid Foundation. (2011). *World Giving Index 2011: A global view of giving trends*. Retrieved from http://www.cafonline.org/pdf/World_Giving_Index_2011_191211.pdf

Cheng, C.-Y. (2001). "Unity of the three truths" and three forms of creativity: Lotus sutra and process philosophy. *Journal of Chinese Philosophy, 28*, 449–456.

Chenoweth, E., & Cunningham, K. G. (2013). Understanding nonviolent resistance: An introduction. *Journal of Peace Research, 50*(3), 271–276.

Chodorow, N. (1974). Family structure and feminine personality. Retrieved from http://seminariolecturasfeministas.files.wordpress.com/2012/01/nancy-chodorow-family-structure-and-femenine-personality.pdf

Chronic, D. (2011). How generous are we Americans? [Blog post comment]. Retrieved from http://davidchronic.com/2011/05/12/how-generous-are-we-americans/

Clandinin, D. J., & Connelly, F. M. (2000). *Narrative inquiry: Experience and story in qualitative research*. San Francisco, CA: Jossey-Bass.

Clark, B. (2008, January 9). Letter to the Editor. *The New York Times*. Retrieved from http://www.nytimes.com/2008/01/13/opinion/l13corps.html

Clarke, V. (2002, May-June). Sameness and difference in research on lesbian parenting. *Journal of Community & Applied Social Psychology, 12*(3), 210–222.

Cohen, E. (2007). Push to achieve tied to suicide in Asian-American women. Retrieved from http://www.sfwar.org/pdf/Suicide/SUI_CNN_05_07.pdf

Cohen, B. (2012, April 26). Uncovering America's generous side. *The Huffington Post*. Retrieved from http://www.huffingtonpost.com/ben-cohen/uncovering-americas-gener_b_1453709.html

Cole, B. A. (2009). Gender, narratives and intersectionality: Can personal experience approaches to research contribute to "undoing gender"? *International Review of Education, 55*(5–6), 561–578.

Congress told of volunteer problems, too. (1963, June). *Peace Corps Volunteer, 1*(8), 1–24.

Cross, M. C. (1998). *Self-efficacy and cultural awareness: A study of returned Peace Corps Teachers* (Doctoral dissertation). Retrieved from ProQuest Digital Dissertations. (AAT 9829288)

Cushman, K. (2007, April). Facing the culture shock of college. *Educational Leadership, 64*(7), 44–47.

Cushner, K., & Mahon, J. (2002). Overseas student teaching: Affecting personal, professional, and global competencies in an age of globalization. *Journal of Studies in International Education, 6*(1), 44–58.

Daly, M. E. (1975). The teacher as innovator: (A report on urban teacher corps, D.C. public schools). *Journal of Negro Education, 44*(3), 385–390.

David, K. (1971). Culture shock and the development of self-awareness. *Journal of Contemporary Psychotherapy, 4*(1), 44–48.

Dean, L. R., Carroll, J. S., & Yang, C. (2007). Materialism, perceived financial problems, and marital satisfaction. *Family and Consumer Sciences Research Journal, 35*, 260–281.

De Beauvoir, S. (1976). *The ethics of ambiguity* (B. Frechtman, Trans.). New York, NY: Citadel Press.

DeKorne, H., Byrum, M., & Fleming, M. (2007). Familiarising the stranger: Immigrant perceptions of cross-cultural interaction and bicultural identity. *Journal of Multilingual and Multicultural Development, 28*(4), 290–307.

DeLamater, J. (1981). The social control of sexuality. *Annual Review of Sociology, 7*, 263–290.

De Marzio, D. (2009). The teacher's gift of sacrifice as the art of the self. *Philosophy of Education Yearbook*, 166–173.

Derrida, J. (1978). *Writing and difference*. Chicago, IL: The University of Chicago Press.

Desai, S. (2010, November 30). Materialism is not all bad! *The Huffington Post*. Retrieved from http://www.huffingtonpost.com/swati-desai/materialism-is-not-bad_b_784415.html

De Zengotita, T. (2005). *Mediated: How the media shapes your world and the way you live in it*. New York, NY: Bloomsbury.

Diener, E., & Oishi, S. (2000). Money and happiness: Income and subjective well-being across nations. In E. Diener & E. M. Suh (Eds.), *Culture and subjective well-being* (pp. 185–218). Cambridge, MA: MIT Press.

Dissertations relating to Peace Corps. (2010). Retrieved from the Peace Corps Wiki: http://www.peacecorpswiki.org/Dissertations_relating_to_Peace_Corps

Dunn, E. W., Aknin, L. B., Norton, M. I. (2008). Spending money on others promotes happiness. *Science, 319*, 1687–1688.

Eckert, P. (n.d.). Hedging the English standard bet. Retrieved from http://comppile.org/archives/fforum/fforum3(1)files/fforum3(1)Eckert.pdf

Efron, S. (2004, December 31). U.S. aid generous and stingy. *Los Angeles Times*. Retrieved from http://articles.latimes.com/2004/dec/31/world/fg-generous31

Eggenberger, N. (2011, September 6). Lady Gaga reveals her new black & white "Harper's Bazaar" cover. *OK!* Retrieved from http://www.okmagazine.com/news/lady-gaga-reveals-her-new-black-white-harpers-bazaar-cover

Eisenberg, P. (2008, January 24). Americans generous? Not really. *The Chronicle of Philanthropy*. Retrieved from http://philanthropy.com/article/Americans-Generous-Not-Really/60673/

Emirbayer, M., & Mische, A. (1998). What is agency? *American Journal of Sociology, 103*(4), 962–1023.

Ende, M. (1985). *Momo*. New York, NY: Doubleday.

Englehart, J. K. (2001). The marriage between theory and practice. *Public Administration Review, 61*(3), 371–374.

English, T., & Chen, S. (2011). Self-concept consistency and culture: The differential impact of two forms of consistency. *Personality and Social Psychology Bulletin, 37*(6), 838–849.

Environmental Protection Agency. (2011). *Municipal solid waste generation, recycling, and disposal in the United States: Facts and figures for 2010*. Retrieved from http://www.epa.gov/osw/nonhaz/municipal/pubs/msw_2010_rev_factsheet.pdf

Epstein, S. (2004). Bodily differences and collective identities. *Body & Society, 10*(2–3), 183–203.

Escamilla, K., Aragon, L., & Fránquiz, M. (2009). The transformative potential of a study in Mexico program for U.S. teachers. *Journal of Latinos and Education*, 8(4), 270–289.

European Commission. (2009). *The impact of culture on creativity*. Retrieved from http://www.keanet.eu/studies-and-contributions/the-impact-of-culture-on-creativity/

Ewick, P., & Silbey, S. (2003). Narrating social structure: Stories of resistance to legal authority. *American Journal of Sociology*, 108(6), 1328–1372.

Fasko, D. (2000–2001). Education and creativity. *Creativity Research Journal*, 13(3 & 4), 317–327.

Fatal. (n.d.). In *Merriam-Webster.com*. Retrieved from http://www.merriam-webster.com/dictionary/fatal?show=0&t=1332647785

Fatalism. (n.d.). In *Merriam-Webster.com*. Retrieved from http://www.merriam-webster.com/dictionary/fatalism

Fernandez, L. (1999). Former Peace Corps teacher experiences culture shock. *San Jose Mercury News*.

Ferrari, A., Cachia, R., & Punie, Y. (2009). *Innovation and creativity in education and training in the EU member states: Fostering creative learning and supporting innovative teaching. Literature review on innovation and creativity in E&T in the EU member states (ICEAC)*. Retrieved from Joint Research Centre website: http://ipts.jrc.ec.europa.eu/publications/pub.cfm?id=2700

Fischer, F. (1998). *Making them like us: Peace Corps volunteers in the 1960s*. Washington DC: Smithsonian Institution Press.

Fischer, K. (2008, October). Professors get their own study-abroad programs. *The Chronicle of Higher Education*, 55(10), 1–4.

Fischer, R., Ferreira, M. C., Assmar, E., Redford, P., Harb, C., Glazer, S.,... Achoui, M. (2009). Individualism-collectivism as descriptive norms: Development of a subjective norm approach to culture measurement. *Journal of Cross-Cultural Psychology*, 40(2), 187–213.

Foucault, M. (1965). *Madness and civilization: A history of insanity in the age of reason*. New York, NY: Random House.

Foucault, M. (1990). *History of sexuality volume 1: An Introduction*. New York, NY: Pantheon Books.

Fought, J. G. (2005). *Correct American: Gatekeeping*. Retrieved from http://www.pbs.org/speak/speech/correct/gatekeeping/

Fox, R. W., & Kloppenburg, J. T. (1998). *A companion to American thought*. Malden, MA: Blackwell.

Fretwell, D. H., & Wheeler, A. (2001, Aug). *Russia: Secondary education and training*. Retrieved from The World Bank website: http://siteresources.worldbank.org/EDUCATION/Resources/278200-1099079877269/547664-1099079967208/Russia_Secondary_education_and_training_En01.pdf

Friedman, R., & Liu, W. (2009). Biculturalism in management: Leveraging the benefits of intrapersonal diversity. In R. S. Wyer, Chi-yue Chiu, & Ying-yi Hong (Eds.), *Understanding culture: Theory, research, and application* (pp. 343–360). New York, NY: Psychology Press.

Fuchs, E. (1969). *Teachers talk: Views from inside city schools*. New York, NY: Doubleday.

REFERENCES

Fuertes, J. N., Potere, J. C., & Ramirez, K. Y. (2002). Effects of speech accents on interpersonal evaluations: Implications for counseling practice and research. *Cultural Diversity and Ethnic Minority Psychology, 8*(4), 346–356.

Furnham, A. (2004). Education and culture shock. *The Psychologist, 17*(1), 16–19.

Gallant, S. (2008, Jan–Feb). Beware of "others." *The Fountain, 61.* Retrieved from http://www.fountainmagazine.com/Issue/detail/Beware-of-Others

Gannon, M. J., & Pillai, R. (2010). *Understanding global cultures: Metaphorical journeys through 29 nations.* Thousand Oaks, CA: Sage.

Garii, B. (2009). Interpreting the unfamiliar: Early career international teaching experiences and the creation of the professional self. *Journal of Curriculum Theorizing, 25*(3), 84–103.

Garza-Guerrero, A. C. (1974). Culture shock: Its mourning and vicissitudes of identity. *Journal of the American Psychoanalytic Association, 22*(20), 408–429.

Gibson, H. (2005). What creativity isn't: The presumptions of instrumental and individual justifications for creativity. *British Journal of Educational Studies, 53*(2), 148–167.

Gilton, D. (2005). Culture shock in the library: Implications for information literacy instruction. *Research Strategies, 20*(4), 424–432.

Gino, F., & Ariely, D. (2011, November 28). The dark side of creativity: Original thinkers can be more dishonest. *Journal of Personality and Social Psychology,* 1–15.

Glaeser, E. L., & Saks, R. E. (2006). Corruption in America. *Journal of Public Economics, 90,* 1053–1072.

Glennie, J. (2011). Giving aid to poor countries is hardly a great act of generosity. *The Guardian.* Retrieved from http://www.guardian.co.uk/global-development/poverty-matters/2011/jun/14/aid-is-hardly-an-act-of-great-generosity-effectiveness

Godley, A., Sweetland, J., Wheeler, R., Minnici, A., & Carpenter, B. D. (2006). Preparing teachers for dialectally diverse classrooms. *Educational Researcher, 35,* 30–37.

Godwin, K. (2009). Academic culture shock. *New England Journal of Higher Education, 23*(5), 30.

Good, J. (2007). Shop 'til we drop? Television, materialism and attitudes about the natural environment. *Mass Communication and Society, 10*(3), 365–383.

Gorski, P. C. (2013). *Reaching and teaching students in poverty.* New York, NY: Teachers College Press.

Gough, N. (2003). Thinking globally in environmental education: Implications for internationalizing curriculum inquiry. In W. F. Pinar (Ed.), *International handbook of curriculum research* (pp. 53–71). Mahwah, NJ: Lawrence Erlbaum.

Gross, D. R. (1984). Time allocation: A tool for the study of cultural behavior. *Annual Review of Anthropology, 13*(5), 519–558.

Guatney, H. (2011, October 10). *What is Occupy Wall Street? The history of leaderless movements.* Retrieved from http://www.washingtonpost.com/national/on-leadership/what-is-occupy-wall-street-the-history-of-leaderless-movements/2011/10/10/gIQAwkFjaL_story.html

Gullahorn, J. T., & Gullahorn, J. E. (1963). An extension of the u-curve hypothesis. *Journal of Social Issues, 19*(3), 33–47.

Gupta, S., Davoodi, H., & Alonso-Terme, R. (2002). Does corruption affect income inequality and poverty? *Economics of Governance, 3*(1), 23–45.

Hall, E. T. (1990). *The silent language.* New York, NY: Random House.

Hammerschlag, J. R. (1996). *Returned Peace Corps volunteers who teach: A profile of teachers who serve their country and their students* (Doctoral dissertation). Retrieved from ProQuest Digital Dissertations. (AAT 9703839)

Hargreaves, A. (2001). Emotional geographies of teaching. *Teachers College Record, 103*(6), 1056–1080.

Harris, A.P. (2000). Equality trouble: Sameness and difference in twentieth-century race law. *California Law Review, 88*(6), 1923–2016.

Hart, W. B. (2005). *The intercultural sojourn as the hero's journey.* Retrieved from http://www.mythsdreamssymbols.com/heroadventure.html

Haslam, S. A., & Reicher, S. D. (2012). When prisoners take over the prison: A social psychology of resistance. *Personality and Social Psychology Review, 16*(2), 154–179.

Hays, S. (1994). Structure and agency and the sticky problem of culture. *Sociological Theory, 12*(1), 57–72.

Heathwood, C. (2011). Preferentism and self-sacrifice. *Pacific Philosophical Quarterly, 92*(1), 18–38.

Hernández Flores, G., & Lankshear, C. (2000). Facing NAFTA: Literacy and work in México. *Journal of Adolescent & Adult Literacy, 44*(3), 240–243.

Hervey, E. (2009). Cultural transitions during childhood and adjustment to college. *Journal of Psychology & Christianity, 28*(1), 3–12.

hooks, b. (1989). *Talking back: Talking feminist, thinking black.* Cambridge, MA: South End Press.

How important is cultural diversity at your school? (n.d.) Retrieved from http://www.greatschools.org/find-a-school/defining-your-ideal/284-cultural-diversity-at-school.gs?page=all

Huebner, D. E. (1999). In V. Hillis (Ed.), *The lure of the transcendent: Collected essays by Dwayne E. Huebner.* Mahwah, NJ: Lawrence Erlbaum.

Huff, J. (2001). Parental attachment, reverse culture shock, perceived social support, and college adjustment of missionary children. *Journal of Psychology & Theology, 29*(3), 246.

Illich, I. (1968). *To hell with good intentions.* Retrieved from http://masoncblfaculty.pbworks.com/w/file/fetch/46705791/Ilich_To%20hell%20with %20good%20intentions.pdf

Inglehart, R. (1971). The silent revolution in Europe: Intergenerational change in post-industrial societies. *The American Political Science Review, 65*(4), 991–1017.

Inglehart, R. (2008). Changing values among western publics from 1970 to 2006. *West European Politics, 31*(1–2), 130–146.

Inglehart, R., & Abramson, P. R. (1994). Economic security and value change. *The American Political Science Review, 88*(2), 336–354.

Institute of International Education. (2012). *Fast facts.* Retrieved from the Institute of International Education website: http://www.iie.org

International Council on Human Rights Policy (2010). *Integrating human rights in the anti-corruption agenda: Challenges, possibilities and opportunities.* Retrieved from the International Council on Human Rights website: http://www.ichrp.org/files/reports/58/131b_report.pdf

Jain, A. K. (2001). Corruption: A review. *Journal of Economic Surveys, 15*(1), 71–121.

Jansson, D. P. (1975). Return to society: Problematic features of the reentry process. *Perspectives in Psychiatric Care, 13*(3), 136–42.

Javidan, M., Dorfman, P. W., de Luque, M. S., & House, R. (2006, February). In the eye of the beholder: Cross cultural lessons in leadership from Project GLOBE. *Academy of Management Perspectives, 67*–90.

Johnson, A. G. (2005). *The gender knot: Unraveling our patriarchal legacy. Revised and updated edition*. Philadelphia, PA: Temple University Press.

Jordan, J. (2008). Learning at the margin: New models of strength. *Women & Therapy, 31*(2–4), 189–208.

Kachru, B. (1992). Teaching world Englishes. In B. B. Kachru (Ed.), *The other tongue: English across cultures* (2nd ed., pp. 355–366). Champaign, IL: University of Illinois Press.

Kashima, Y., Kim, U., Gelfand, M., Yamaguchi, S., Choi, S., & Yuki, M. (1995). Culture, gender, and self: A perspective from individualism-collectivism research. *Journal of Personality and Social Psychology, 69*(5), 925–937.

Kember, D. (1996). The intention to both memorise and understand: Another approach to learning? *Higher Education, 31,* 341–351.

Kilickaya, F. (2009). World Englishes, English as an international language and applied linguistics. *English Language Teaching, 2*(3), 35–38.

Kim, K. H. (2005). Learning from each other: Creativity in East Asian and American education. *Creativity Research Journal, 17*(4), 337–347.

Kim, Y.-H., Peng, S., & Chiu, C.-Y. (2008). Explaining self-esteem differences between Chinese and North Americans: Dialectical self (vs. self-consistency) or lack of positive self-regard. *Self and Identity, 7,* 113–128.

Kittay, E. F. (2007). Searching for an overlapping consensus: A secular care ethics feminist responds to religious feminists. *University of St. Thomas Law Journal, 4*(3), 468–488.

Klotz, S. S. (2012, February 14). American generosity improving women's health in Ethiopia. Retrieved from http://www.usglc.org/2012/02/14/american-generosity-improving-womens-health-in-ethiopia/

Knight, J. (2003). *Internationalization of higher education practices and priorities: 2003 IAU survey report.* Retrieved from http://archive.www.iau-aiu.net/internationalization/pdf/Internationalisation-en.pdf

Korf, B. (2007). Antinomies of generosity: Moral geographies and post-tsunami aid in Southeast Asia. *Geoforum, 28,* 366–378.

Koro-Ljungberg, M. (2004). Displacing metaphorical analysis: Reading with and against metaphors. *Qualitative Research, 4*(3), 339–360.

Kron, K. (1972). Culture shock and the transfer teacher. *Bureau of School Service Bulletin, 45*(2), 1–73.

Kron, K., & Faber, C. (1973). How does the teacher cope with the culture shock? *Clearing House, 47*(8), 506–508.

Kubey, R., & Csikszentmihalyi, M. (2002). Television addiction is no mere metaphor. *Scientific American, 86,* 74–77.

Kulkarni, S. P., Hudson, T., Ramamoorthy, N., Marchev, A., Georgieva-Kondakova, P., & Gorskov, V. (2010). Dimensions of individualism-collectivism: A comparative study of five cultures. *Current Issues of Business and Law, 5,* 93–109.

La Brack, B. (n.d.). *Theory reflections: Cultural adaptations, culture shock and the "curves of adjustment."* Retrieved from the National Association of Foreign Student Advisors website: http://www.nafsa.org/_/File/_/theory_connections_adjustment.pdf

La Brack, B. (1985, March 5–9). *State of the art research on re-entry: An essay on directions for the future.* Paper presented at the 26th Annual Convention of the International Studies Association, Washington, DC.

Lakoff, G., & Johnson, M. (2003). *Metaphors we live by.* Chicago, IL: University of Chicago.

Laozi (2009). *Tao te ching* (C. Hansen, Trans.). New York, NY: Metro Books. (Original work published in the third century B.C.)

Leask, B. (2004, July). *Transnational education and intercultural learning: Reconstructing the offshore teaching team to enhance internationalisation.* Paper presented at the Australian Universities Quality Forum: Quality in a Time of Change, Adelaide, South Australia.

Lee, M. S. (2007). International education research in globalization era. Retrieved from https://www.hyogo-u.ac.jp/files/wj_article_20060302.pdf

Lefcourt, H. M. (1973, May). The function of the illusions of control and freedom. *American Psychology, 417*–425.

Leff, N. H. (1964, November). Economic development through bureaucratic corruption. *American Behavioral Scientist, 8*(3), 8–14.

Leiken, R. S. (1996-97). Controlling the global corruption epidemic. *Foreign Policy, 105,* 55–73.

Levy, D. (2007). Price adjustment under the table: Evidence on efficiency-enhancing corruption. *European Journal of Political Economy, 23,* 423–447.

Longsworth, S. (1971). The returned volunteer: A perspective. *Transition, 1,* 11–17.

Lorber, J. (1994). "Night to his day": The social construction of gender. Retrieved from http://www.old.li.suu.edu/library/circulation/Gurung/soc2370sgNightToHisDaySocialConstGenderFall10.pdf

Louis, W. R., & Taylor, D. M. (1999). From passive acceptance to social disruption: Towards an understanding of behavioural responses to discrimination. *Canadian Journal of Behavioural Science, 31*(1), 19–28.

Mackie, V. (2001). The trans-sexual citizen: Queering sameness and difference. *Australian Feminist Studies, 16*(35), 185–192.

Maertz, C., Hassan, A., & Magnusson, P. (2009). When learning is not enough: A process model of expatriate adjustment as cultural cognitive dissonance reduction. *Organizational Behavior and Human Decision Processes, 108*(1), 66–78.

Malewski, E., & Phillion, J. (2009a). Curriculum-in-the-making. *Journal of Curriculum Theorizing, 25*(3), 1–6.

Malewski, E., & Phillion, J. (2009b). Making room in the curriculum: The raced, classed, and gendered nature of preservice teachers' experiences studying abroad. *Journal of Curriculum Theorizing, 25*(3), 48–67.

Mallett, S. (2004). Understanding home: A critical review of the literature. *The Sociological Review, 52*(1), 62–89.

Malterud, K., & Hollnagel, H. (2005, July/August). The doctor who cried: A qualitative study about the doctor's vulnerability. *Annals of Family Medicine, 3*(4), 348–352.

Manzo, L. C. (2003). Beyond house and haven: Toward a revisioning of emotional relationships with places. *Journal of Environmental Psychology, 23*, 47–61.

Martin, P. (2005). *NAFTA and Mexico-US migration*. Retrieved from the Giannini Foundation website: http://giannini.ucop.edu/Mex_USMigration.pdf

Matus, C., & McCarthy, C. (2003). The triumph of multiplicity and the carnival of difference: Curriculum dilemmas in the age of postcolonialism and globalization. In W. F. Pinar (Ed.), *International handbook of curriculum research* (pp. 73–82). Mahwah, NJ: Erlbaum.

Mauro, P. (1997). *The effects of corruption on growth, investment, and government expenditure: A cross-country analysis*. Retrieved from http://www.adelino torres.com/economia/Os%20 efeitos%20da%20corrup%C3%A7%C3%A3o%20no%20mundo.pdf

Mayer, R. E. (2002). Rote versus meaningful learning. *Theory Into Practice, 41*(4), 226–232.

Maynard, D. W., & Zimmerman, D. H. (1984). Topical talk, ritual and the social organization of relationships. *Social Psychology Quarterly, 47*(4), 301–316.

McDaniel, S.V. (2010, February). *The philology of the idea: An essay in eidophonetics*. Retrieved from http://www.stanmcdaniel.org/pubs/development/eidophon.pdf

McFarland, D. A. (2004). Resistance as social drama: A study of change-oriented encounters. American journal of sociology. *American Journal of Sociology, 109*(6), 1249–1318.

McIlwraith, R. D. (1998). "I'm addicted to television": The personality, imagination and TV watching pattern of self-identified TV addicts. *Journal of Broadcasting and Electronic Media, 42*, 371–386.

McIntosh, M. (1968). The homosexual role. *Social Problems, 16*(2), 182–192.

McIntosh, P. (1989, July/August). White privilege: Unpacking the invisible knapsack. *Peace and Freedom*. Retrieved from http://www.library.wisc.edu/edvrc/docs/public/pdfs/LIReadings/InvisibleKnapsack.pdf

McLaren, R. B. (1993). The dark side of creativity. *Creativity Research Journal, 6*(1–2), 137–144.

Meltzoff, N. (1994). Relationship, the fourth "r": The development of a classroom community. *The School Community Journal, 4*(2), 13–26.

Merryfield, M. M. (2000). Why aren't teachers being prepared to teach for diversity, equity, and global interconnectedness? A study of lived experiences in the making of multicultural and global educators. *Teaching and Teacher Education, 16*, 429–443.

Meyers, B. (1999, May). A lie. *Commonweal*, 31.

Miller, J. (2005). *Sounds of silence breaking: Women, autobiography, curriculum*. New York, NY: Peter Lang.

Miller, M. (1988). Reflections on reentry after teaching in China. *Occasional Papers in Intercultural Learning, 14*, 3–25.

Minnicks, M. (2011). "Don't let your left hand know what your right hand is doing." Retrieved from http://www.examiner.com/article/don-t-let-your-left-hand-know-what-your-right-hand-is-doing

Moeller, P. (2012). Why seeking more money hurts happiness. Retrieved from http://money.us-news.com/money/personal-finance/articles/2012/04/09/why-seeking-more-money-hurts-happiness

Moore, J. (2000). Placing home in context. *Journal of Environmental Psychology, 20*, 207–218.

Morgan, J. (2009, January 13). Passive resistance or passive acceptance? [Blog post comment]. Retrieved from http://jacobscafe.blogspot.com/2009/01/passive-resistance-or-passive.html

Moylan, B. (2010, September 9). Americans are not the most generous people in the world. Retrieved from http://gawker.com/5634060/americans-are-not-the-most-generous-people-in-the-world

Muncy, J. A., & Eastman, J. K. (1998). Materialism and consumer ethics: An exploratory study. *Journal of Business Ethics, 17,* 137–145.

Murphy, J. (n.d.). Brief solution-focused counseling with young people and school problems. Retrieved from http://counselingoutfitters.com/vistas/vistas04/22.pdf

Murphy, L. B., & Moriarity, A. E. (1976). *Vulnerability, coping and growth from infancy to adolescence.* Oxford, England: Yale University Press.

Myers, B. H. (2001). *The impact of international experience on teaching with a global perspective: Reflections of returned Peace Corps volunteer teachers* (Doctoral dissertation). Retrieved from ProQuest Digital Dissertations. (AAT 3022545.)

Nacelewicz, T. (2002). Teacher is Portland High's keeper of cultural diversity. *Portland Press Herald,* 1B.

Nagel, C. (2002). Constructing difference and sameness: the politics of assimilation in London's Arab communities. *Ethnic and racial studies, 25*(2), 258–287.

National Council of Teachers of English. (n.d.). *Students' right to their own language: Conference on college composition and communication.* Retrieved from http://www.ncte.org/library/NCTEFiles/Groups/CCCC/NewSRTOL.pdf

Neild, B. (2012, January 5). How generous are Americans? Retrieved from http://www.globalpost.com/dispatch/news/politics/aid/120104/how-generous-are-americans

Nguyen, A. M., & Benet-Martínez, V. (2007). Biculturalism unpacked: Components, individual differences, measurement, and outcomes. *Social and Personality Psychology Compass, 1,* 101–114.

Nikitina, L., & Furuoka, F. (2008). "A language teacher is like…": Examining Malaysian students' perceptions of language teachers through metaphor analysis. *Electronic Journal of Foreign Language Teaching, 5*(2), 192–205. Retrieved from http://e-flt.nus.edu.sg/v5n22008/nikitina.pdf

Noddings, N. (2010). Moral education in an age of globalization. *Educational Philosophy and Theory, 42*(4), 390–396.

Novak, J. D., & Cañas, A. J. (2008). *The theory underlying concept maps and how to construct and use them.* Retrieved from http://cmap.ihmc.us/publications/researchpapers/theorycmaps/theoryunderlyingconceptmaps.htm

Oberg, K. (1954). *Culture shock.* Retrieved from http://www.youblisher.com/p/53062-Ejemplo/

Occupy Wall Street. (n.d.). Retrieved from http://occupywallst.org/

O'Connor, F. (1995). *The complete stories.* New York, NY: Noonday.

Oehlberg, L., Ducheneaut, N., Thornton, J. D., Moore, R. J., & Nickell, E. (2008). *Social TV: Designated for distributed, sociable television viewing.* Retrieved from http://www2.parc.com/csl/members/nicolas/documents/EuroITV06-SocialTV.pdf

Olson, H. A. (2001). Sameness and difference: A cultural foundation of classification. *Library Resources and Technical Services, 45*(3), 115–122.

REFERENCES

Olssen, M. (1996). Radical constructivism and its failings: Anti-realism and individualism. *British Journal of Educational Studies, 44*(3), 275–295.

Park, R. E. (1928). Human migration and the marginal man. *American Journal of Sociology, 33*(6), 881–893.

Parton, D. (1986). Wildflowers. On *Trio* [CD]. Los Angeles, CA: Warner Brothers.

Peace Corps. (n.d.). Retrieved from http://www.jfklibrary.org/JFK/JFK-in-History/Peace-Corps.aspx

Peace Corps. (2008). The Peace Corps'mission. Retrieved from http://www.peacecorps.gov/about/

Peace Corps. (2010a). Education. Retrieved from http://www.peacecorps.gov/volunteer/learn/whatvol/edu_youth/

Peace Corps. (2010b). Fast facts. Retrieved from http://www.peacecorps.gov/index.cfm?shell=about.fastfacts

Peace Corps. (2010c). Paul D Coverdell Fellows Program. Retrieved from http://www.peacecorps.gov/index.cfm?shell=learn.whyvol.eduben.fellows

Peace Corps is good preparation for teaching at inner-city schools. (1993, September). *Curriculum Review, 33*(1), 20.

Pence, H. M., & Macgillivray, I. K. (2008). The impact of international field experience on preservice teachers. *Teaching and Teacher Education, 24,* 14–25.

Phillips, M. (2010). Peace Corps builds cultural bridges. *USA Today.* Retrieved from http://usatoday30.usatoday.com/news/opinion/letters/2010-10-21-letters21_ST1_N.htm

Pinar, W. F. (1975, Apr). *The method of "currerre."* Paper presented at the Annual Meeting of the American Research Association. Retrieved from http://eric.ed.gov/PDFS/ED104766.pdf

Pinar, W. F. (2000). Introduction: Toward the internationalization of curriculum studies. In D. Trueit, W. E. Doll, H. Wang, & W. F. Pinar (Eds.), *The internationalization of curriculum studies* (pp. 1–13). New York, NY: Peter Lang.

Pinar, W. F. (2004). *What is curriculum theory?* Mahwah, NJ: Erlbaum.

Pinar, W. F. (2009). *The worldliness of a cosmopolitan education: Passionate lives in public service.* New York, NY: Routledge.

Pinar, W. F. (n.d.). The internationalization of curriculum studies. Retrieved from http://www.riic.unam.mx/01/02_Biblio/doc/Internationalizaton_Curriculum_W_PINAR_(MEXICO).pdf

Planty, M., Hussar, W., Snyder, T., Kena, G., KewalRamani, A., Kemp, J.,...Dinkes, R. (2009). *The condition of education 2009* (NCES 2009–081). Retrieved from the National Center for Education Statistics website: http://nces.ed.gov/pubs2009/2009081.pdf

Prasad, J. (2007). Derrida: The father of deconstruction. Retrieved from http://newderrida.wordpress.com/category/some-key-terms/

Putnam, R. D. (1995). Tuning in, tuning out: The strange disappearance of social capital in America. *PS: Political Science and Politics, 28*(4), 664–683.

Quigley, T. (2009). Structuralism and poststructuralism. Retrieved from http://timothyquigley.net/vcs/structuralism.pdf

Radner, G. (n.d.). Ambiguity. Retrieved from https://www.goodreads.com/author/quotes/145047.Gilda_Radner

Reynolds, J. (2010). Jacques Derrida (1930–2004). Retrieved from http://www.iep.utm.edu/derrida/

Riley, J. (2005, January 6). U.S. generosity level is open to debate. *The Daily*. Retrieved from http://dailyuw.com/news/2005/jan/06/us-generosity-level-is-open-to-debate/

Rochkind, J., Ott, A., Immerwahr, J., Doble, J., & Johnson, J. (2008). *Lessons learned: New teachers talk about their jobs, challenges and long-range plans*. Retrieved from http://www.publicagenda.org/files/lessons_learned_3.pdf

Rosenwald, G. C., & Ochberg, R. L. (1992). Introduction: Life stories, cultural politics, and self-understanding. In G. C. Rosenwald & R. L. Ochberg (Eds.), *Storied lives: The cultural politics of self-understanding* (pp. 1–18). New Haven, CT: Yale University Press.

Rote. (2012). In *Merriam-Webster.com*. Retrieved from http://www.merriam-webster.com/dictionary/rote?show=1&t=1332311380

Rothstein-Fisch, C., & Trumbull, E. (2008). *Managing diverse classrooms: How to build on students' cultural strengths*. Alexandria, VA: Association for Supervision and Curriculum Development.

Sahlberg, P. (2004). Teaching and globalization. *Managing Global Transitions, 2*(1), 65–83.

Salzberg, S. (n.d.). Quote. Retrieved from https://www.goodreads.com/author/quotes/17208.Sharon_Salzberg

Samples, B. (1993). *The metaphoric mind: A celebration of creative consciousness* (2nd ed.). Torrance, CA: Jalmar Press.

Sandgren, D., Elig, N., Hovde, P., Krejci, M., & Rice, M. (1999). How international experience affects teaching: Understanding the impact of faculty study abroad. *Journal of Studies in International Education, 3*(1), 33–56.

Sarup, M. (1993). *An introduction guide to post-structuralism and postmodernism* (2nd ed.). Athens, GA: The University of Georgia Press.

Schlein, C. (2009). Exploring novice teachers' experiences with intercultural curriculum. *Journal of Curriculum Theorizing, 25*(3), 22–33.

Schneider, A. I. (2003). *Internationalizing teacher education: What can be done? A research report on the undergraduate training of secondary school teachers* (ERIC Document Reproduction Service No. 480869). Retrieved from http://www.internationaledadvice.org/pdfs/What_Can_Be_Done.pdf

Schur, J. B. (2000). Founding documents of the Peace Corps. *National Archives and Records Administration*, 1–16.

Schutz, A. (1945). On multiple realities. Retrieved from https://www.marxists.org/reference/subject/philosophy/works/ge/schuetz.htm

Schwartz, S. (n.d.). *Causes of culture: National differences in cultural embeddedness*. Retrieved from http://iaccp.org/drupal/sites/default/files/spetses_pdf/3_Schwartz.pdf

Seay, A. F., & Kraut, R. E. (2007). Project Massive: Self-regulation and problematic use of online gaming. *Proceedings of the SIGCHI Conference on Human Factors in Computing Systems, USA*. Retrieved from http://repository.cmu.edu/cgi/viewcontent.cgi?article=1106&context=hcii

Sewell, W. H. (1992). A theory of structure: Duality, agency, and transformation. *American Journal of Sociology, 98*(1), 1–29.

Shoichet, J. G. (2007). Warp, weft, and womanly wiles: Weaving as an expression of female power. *Illumine: The Journal of the Centre for Studies in Religion and Society, 6*(1), 23–33.

Simmel, G. (2007). Individualism. *Theory, Culture & Society, 24*(7–8), 66–71.

Sitton, T. (1976). The pedagogy of culture shock. *The Social Studies, 67*(5), 206–212.

Smith, D. (2003). Curriculum and teaching face globalization. In W. F. Pinar (Ed.), *International handbook of curriculum research* (pp. 35–51). Mahwah, NJ: Erlbaum.

Smythe, J. (2009). Conversation and globalization: An international student advisor's intercultural path. In H. Wang & N. Olson (Eds.), *A journey to unlearn and learn in multicultural education* (pp. 117–124). New York, NY: Peter Lang.

Somberg, B. (2005, October 1). The world's most generous misers. *FAIR*. Retrieved from http://fair.org/extra-online-articles/the-world8217s-most-generous-misers/

Sommers, T. (2007). The illusion of freedom evolves. In D. Ross, D. Spurrett, H. Kincaid, & G. L. Stephens (Eds.), *Distributed cognition and the will* (pp. 61–76). Cambridge, MA: Massachusetts Institute of Technology.

Sonu, D., & Moon, S. (2009). Re-visioning into third space: Autobiographies on losing home and homeland. *Journal of Curriculum and Pedagogy, 6*(2), 142–162.

Stam, A. J. (2008). *The church in relation to the world*. Delft, The Netherlands: Eburon.

Stillar, S. (2007). Shocking the cultureless: The crucial role of culture shock in racial identity formation. *Electronic Journal of Sociology*, 1–16.

Stone, D. N., Wier, B., & Bryant, S. M. (2008, Feb). Reducing materialism through financial literacy. *The CPA Journal*. Retrieved from http://www.nysscpa.org/cpajournal/2008/208/perspectives/p12.htm

Stonequist, E.V. (1935). The problem of the marginal man. *American Journal of Sociology, 41*(1), 1–12.

Strack, D. C. (2006, October). When the path of life crosses the river of time: Multivalent bridge metaphor in literary contexts. *University of Kitakyushu Faculty of Humanities Journal, 72*. Retrieved from http://www.dcstrack.com/

Straub, J. (2009). Intercultural competence: A humanistic perspective. In J. Rusen & H. Laass (Eds.), *Humanism in intercultural perspective: Experiences and expectations* (pp. 199–224). Bielefeld, Germany: Verlag.

Strauss, R. (2008, January 9). Too many innocents abroad. *The New York Times*. Retrieved from http://www.nytimes.com/2008/01/09/opinion/09strauss.html?_r=1

Suh, E. M. (2002). Culture, identity consistency, and subjective well-being. *Journal of Personality and Social Psychology, 83*, 1378–1391.

Surrey, J. L. (1985). *Self-in-relation: A theory of women's development*. Retrieved from http://www.wcwonline.org/pdf/previews/preview_13sc.pdf

Sussman, N. (1986). Re-entry research and training: Methods and implications. *International Journal of Intercultural Relations, 10*, 235–254.

Szkudlarek, B. (2009). Reentry—A review of the literature. *International Journal of Intercultural Relations, 34*, 1–21.

Takano, Y., & Sogon, S. (2008, May). Are Japanese more collectivistic than Americans? Examining conformity in in-groups and the reference-group effect. *Journal of Cross-Cultural Psychology, 39*(3), 237–250.

Taki, S. (2011). Cross-cultural communication and metaphorical competence. *International Journal of Language Studies (IJLS), 5*(1), 47–62.

Tan, P. (2011). Towards a culturally sensitive and deeper understanding of "rote learning" and memorisation of adult learners. *Journal of Studies in International Education, 15*(2), 124–145.

Tang, S. Y. F., & Choi, P. L. (2004). The development of personal, intercultural, and professional competence in international field experience in initial teacher education. *Asia Pacific Education Review, 5*(1), 50–63.

Todd, S. (2003). *Learning from the other: Levinas, psychoanalysis, and ethical possibilities in education*. Albany, NY: State University of New York Press.

Tong, E. M. W., & Yang, Z. (2011). Moral Hypocrisy: Of proud and grateful people. *Social Psychological and Personality Science, 2*(2), 159–165.

Torghabeh, R. A. (2007). EIL, variations and the native speaker's model. *Asian EFL Journal, 9*(4), 67–76.

Torres, K. (2009, June). "Culture shock": Black students account for their distinctiveness at an elite college. *Ethnic & Racial Studies, 32*(5), 883–905.

Triandis, H. C. (1989). The self and social behavior in differing cultural contexts. *Psychological Review, 96*(3), 506-520.

Tripathi, S. (2006, April 19). America's aid iceberg. *The Guardian.* Retrieved from http://www.guardian.co.uk/business/2006/apr/19/businesscomment.indianoceantsunamidecember2004

Trudgill, P. (2011, November). Standard English: What it isn't. Retrieved from http://www.phon.ucl.ac.uk/home/dick/SEtrudgill2011.pdf

Tuan, Y. (1998). *Escapism*. Baltimore, MD: The Johns Hopkins University Press.

Tucker, F. (2003). Sameness or difference? Exploring girls' use of recreational spaces. *Children's Geographies, 1*(1), 111–124.

Uchitelle, L. (2007, February 18). Nafta should have stopped illegal immigration, right? *The New York Times*. Retrieved from http://www.nytimes.com/2007/02/18/weekinreview/18uchitelle.html

Updegraff, J. A., & Taylor, S. E. (2000). From vulnerability to growth: Positive and negative effects of stressful life events. In J. Harvey & E. Miller (Eds.), *Loss and trauma: General and close relationship perspectives* (pp. 3–28). Philadelphia, PA: Brunner-Routledge.

U.S. Census Bureau. (2011). *Table 1130. Media usage and consumer spending: 2003 to 2009*. Retrieved from http://www.census.gov/prod/2011pubs/11statab/infocomm.pdf

Valdesolo, P., & DeSteno, D. (2007). Moral hypocrisy: Social groups and the flexibility of virtue. *Association for Psychological Science, 18*(8), 689–690.

Voigts, J. (2008, June 27). Culture shock and intercultural development. *Wandering Educators*. Retrieved from http://www.wanderingeducators.com/special-interest/misc/culture-shock-and-intercultural-development.html

Vulnerable. (2012). In *Merriam-Webster.com*. Retrieved from http://www.merriam-webster.com/dictionary/vulnerable

Wang, H. (2004). *The call from the stranger on a journey home: Curriculum in a third space*. New York, NY: Peter Lang.

Warren, C. A. B., & Karner, T. X. (2010). *Discovering qualitative methods: Field research, interviews, and analysis* (2nd ed.). New York, NY: Oxford University Press.

Weaver, G. (n.d.). *The process of reentry*. Retrieved from http://www.berry.edu/academics/study/documents/Weaver_article.pdf

Westby, E. L., & Dawson, V. L. (1995). Creativity: Asset or burden in the classroom? *Creativity Research Journal*, 8(1), 1–10.

Wilce, J. M. (2004). Passionate scholarship: Recent anthropologies of emotion. *Reviews in Anthropology*, 33, 1–17.

Willard-Holt, C. (2001). The impact of a short-term international experience for preservice teachers. *Teaching and Teacher Education*, 17, 505–517.

Williams, D., Ursu, M. F., Cesar, P., Bergstrom, K., Kegel, I., & Meenowa, J. (2009). *An emergent role for TV in social communication*. Retrieved from http://nim.goldsmiths.ac.uk/papers/as-published-in-proceedings-p19.pdf

Wilson, P. (2011, December 24). America the generous? Not according to the media. *The Wall Street Journal*. Retrieved from http://online.wsj.com/news/articles/SB10001424052970204464404577116562361487888

Wong, A. (2005, April). *Hermeneutic theory*. Retrieved from http://istheory.byu.edu/wiki/Hermeneutics

Woodhams, C., & Danieli, A. (2000). Disability and diversity—a difference too far? *Personnel Review*, 29(3), 402–417.

Wright, R. (2005, March). Going to teach in prisons: Culture shock. *Journal of Correctional Education*, 56(1), 19–38.

Young, K. (2009). Internet addiction: Diagnosis and treatment considerations. *Journal of Contemporary Psychotherapy*, 39, 242–246.

Young, R. (1995). *Colonial desire: Hybridity in theory, culture, and race*. New York, NY: Routledge.

Youth Pride Inc. (2010). *Gay-straight alliance (GSA) coalition*. Retrieved from Youth Pride Inc. website: http://www.youthprideri.org/Programs/GSACoalition/tabid/166/Default.aspx

Zaharna, R.S. (1989). Self-shock: The double-binding challenge to identity. *International Journal of Intercultural Relations*, 13, 501–525.

Zapf, M. K. (1991). Cross-cultural transitions and wellness: Dealing with culture shock. *International Journal for the Advancement of Counseling*, 14, 105–119.

Zhao, Y., Meyers, L., & Meyers, B. (2009). Cross-cultural immersion in China: Preparing pre-service elementary teachers to work with diverse student populations in the United States. *Asia-Pacific Journal of Teacher Education*, 37(3), 295–317.

Zhou, Y., Jindal-Snape, D., Topping, K., & Todman, J. (2008). Theoretical models of culture shock and adaptation in international students in higher education. *Studies in Higher Education*, 33(1), 63–75.

Zorn, J. (2010). "Students' right to their own language": A counter-argument. *Academic Questions*, 23, 311–326.

INDEX

A

Acceptance
   Complacent, 37
   Expectations of, 40
   Of contradictions, 106
   Of life circumstances, 18, 44–45, 51–54, 195–196
   Of maternal role, 192
   Of social differences, 27, 133, 143, 154, 173, 220
   Passive, 152
   Self-, 215
Ambiguity, 26, 40, 99, 116, 201, 221–224
Anxiety, 4–7, 15–17, 35–36, 50, 61, 104–106

B

Bi-cultural, 79–80, 102–103

C

Caring, 18, 43–49, 60–64, 85, 192–193, 200–201
   Uncaring, 44–46, 49, 51, 62
Collectivism/collectivist, 79–84, 169–170, 219, 221
Conversation
   As part of a kaleidoscopic curriculum, 217–218
   Cultural differences as a means to, 199
   Internationalization of curriculum studies, 22–27
   Lack of substance/boring, 171–173, 199
   Television viewing, 95–96
   With God, 210
Corruption, 1–3, 59, 80, 86–91, 202, 209
Creativity, 3, 32, 35, 45, 64–68, 143–144, 163, 222
Cultural adjustment, 80, 103–107

Culture shock
    Analytical approach, 36, 38
    As experiential learning, 37
    As learning experience, 34, 79
    As malady/illness, 34
    As transitional experience, 36–37
    Causes of, 34–35
    Critique of stage models, 35
    Definition, 5
    Emotional reactions to, 35
    Metaphorical/spiritual approach, 38–39
    Peace Corps, 29
    Practical approach, 37–38
    Stage models, 35
    Teaching/education, 5–7, 24, 36, 37
    Theoretical approach, 36–37

D

Danger, 17–18, 44–45, 48–50, 87–89, 198, 202
Decentering, 14–17, 22, 215
Derrida, Jacques, 19, 121, 128, 215
Difference(s)
    Cultural, 3, 5, 7, 32, 36–38, 56, 82, 92, 94, 105, 108, 152, 168, 171, 199, 219, 222
    Individual 4, 63
    Theoretical, 16–18, 156, 171–175, 214–216, 218, 220, 225

E

Ethics, 14–17, 22–23, 63, 222

F

Fatalism, 18, 121–125, 197, 203
Foucault, Michel, 15–16, 49, 60, 194

G

Generosity, 18, 121, 125–130
    Non-generosity, 58, 121

H

Healing, 45, 51–54, 64, 85, 182, 195, 203, 226
Hypocrisy, 121, 130–132

I

Identity shock, 97, 100–101
Individualism/individualist, 18, 79–84, 169–170, 219–121
Internationalization of curriculum studies
    Critiques of perceptions after teaching abroad, 26–27
    Description of, 21–24
    Teaching abroad as a form of, 24–26
"Interweaving," 156, 167, 169–171, 198

J

Juxtaposition, 226
    As part of a kaleidoscopic curriculum, 219–221

M

Male privilege, 18, 156–161, 174, 192–193
Materialism, 42, 55–61, 197

N

Non-standard dialect, 122, 141–145, 195

O

O'Connor, Flannery, 69, 109, 147, 183, 205, 210

P

Paradox
  As part of a kaleidoscopic curriculum, 224–226
  Of creativity, 65
  Of patriarchal power, 193
  Of Peace Corps, 29
Peace Corps
  As teach abroad program, 25
  Country/volunteer statistics, 28
  Critiques of, 29–31
  History of, 28–29
Pinar, William F., 22–24, 166, 217, 226–227
"Play the game," 45, 55–56, 60, 173, 197–198
Postmaterialism, 45, 58–60, 197
Post-structural hermeneutics, 14–19

R

Reality
  As lived, 27, 31, 173, 176
  As multiple, 122, 137–138
  As source of control, 132, 164
  Buddhist "middle way," 174
  "low wage," 91
  Mediated, 136–138, 198
  Natural, 174
  Non-reality, 122, 134, 137, 174, 197
  Poverty equated with, 122, 135, 137
  Social, 25, 137, 139, 198
  Structuralist/dualistic view, 14–15
  Theoretical, 135–137, 167, 219

Shows, 57
Uniform, 3
Resistance, 17, 45, 51–54, 59, 171, 194–196
Returned Peace Corps Volunteers (RPCVs)
  Cardozo Project, 31–32
  Characteristics of, 31
  Dissertations pertaining to, 33
  In the media, 6
  Peace Corps Fellows USA, 31–32
Reverse Culture Shock
  As learning experience, 41–42, 79
  Causes, 40–41
  Description of, 39–40
  Emotional responses to, 41
Rote learning, 45, 64, 66–68, 203

S

Sameness, 5, 17–18, 156, 171–175, 199
Standard dialect, 140–141, 144

T

Tension(s), 25, 26–27, 30–31, 37, 50, 53, 84, 102, 167, 171, 173, 216, 219, 224–227
Time
  Clock, 92–96
  Cyclic, 123
  Event, 94–95
  Linear, 122–123
The Twilight Zone, 224

V

Vulnerability, 18, 44–45, 47–50, 173, 193, 198, 203

COMPLICATED
CONVERSATION

A BOOK SERIES OF CURRICULUM STUDIES

Reframing the curricular challenge educators face after a decade of school deform, the books published in Peter Lang's Complicated Conversation Series testify to the ethical demands of our time, our place, our profession. What does it mean for us to teach now, in an era structured by political polarization, economic destabilization, and the prospect of climate catastrophe? Each of the books in the Complicated Conversation Series provides provocative paths, theoretical and practical, to a very different future. In this resounding series of scholarly and pedagogical interventions into the nightmare that is the present, we hear once again the sound of silence breaking, supporting us to rearticulate our pedagogical convictions in this time of terrorism, reframing curriculum as committed to the complicated conversation that is intercultural communication, self-understanding, and global justice.

The series editor is

Dr. William F. Pinar
Department of Curriculum Studies
2125 Main Mall
Faculty of Education
University of British Columbia
Vancouver, British Columbia V6T 1Z4
CANADA

To order other books in this series, please contact our Customer Service Department:

(800) 770-LANG (within the U.S.)
(212) 647-7706 (outside the U.S.)
(212) 647-7707 FAX

Or browse online by series:

www.peterlang.com